ALPHA

CLASSICS IN RELIGIOUS STUDIES

SCHOLARS PRESS

and

THE AMERICAN ACADEMY OF RELIGION

Number Four

ALPHA
The Myths of Creation

by
Charles H. Long

ALPHA
The Myths of Creation

by
Charles H. Long

Scholars Press
Chico, California

ALPHA
The Myths of Creation

by
Charles H. Long

Reprinted with the permission of George Braziller, Inc.

Scholars Press
American Academy of Religion

Library of Congress Cataloging in Publication Data
Long, Charles H.
  Alpha : the myths of creation.

  (Classics in religious studies / Scholars
Press and the American Academy of Religion ; no. 4)
  Reprint. Originally published: New York :
G. Braziller, 1963. (Patterns of myth)
  Bibliography: p.
  Includes index.
  1. Creation—Comparative studies. I. Title. II. Series:
Classics in religious studies of Scholars Press and the
American Academy of Religion ; no. 4. III. Series: Patterns
of myth.
[BL325.C7L6 1983]   291.2'4   82–21532
ISBN 0–89130–604–8

Printed in the United States of America

ACKNOWLEDGMENTS

The very idea of an anthology presupposes the work of others. I should like most gratefully to acknowledge the work of that community of scholarship which has produced the major body of this text. I list the members of this community, which includes the past and present, below. I must also express my appreciation to my teachers in the history of religions, Joachim Wach and Mircea Eliade. Their conviction that religion could be studied in non-reductionistic terms buttressed my own vague intimation of such a possibility. Professor Eliade discussed some of the materials with me and encouraged me to undertake this work. Hans Penner, one of my students, acted as my research assistant in this project. Finally, I must acknowledge my gratitude to the Divinity School secretaries, Mrs. Minerva Bell, Mrs. Rehova Arthur, and Miss Gloria Valentine. They were all involved in typing of the manuscript, and Miss Valentine performed the arduous task of seeking the publishers' permissions for the texts which we have used.

In spite of such gracious aid and counsel, it is possible that certain errors of judgment and scholarship appear in the text. For these errors I must take the full responsibility. I should be grateful if my fellow-workers would point these out to me.

For permission to reprint excerpts from source materials in this volume, the author is indebted to the following publishers and authors:

George Allen and Unwin Ltd.—for selection from *Religion in Essence and Manifestation* by G. van der Leeuw (trans. J. E. Turner).

The American Folklore Society, Inc.—for "Huron Folk-Lore" by H. Hale, in *Journal of American Folklore,* Vol. I;—for selection from *Navaho Legends* by Washington Matthews;—and for "Hopi Tales" by A. M. Stephen, in *Journal of American Folklore,* Vol. XLII.

The American Museum of Natural History—for selection from *Bulletin of the American Museum of Natural History,* Vol. XVII;—and for selection from *Memoir of the American Museum of Natural History,* Vol. VIII, Part II.

The American Scandinavian Foundation—for selection from *The Prose Edda* by Snorri Sturluson (trans. A. G. Brodeur).

The Bishop Museum Press—Honolulu—for selections from *Polynesian Religion* by E. S. Craighill Handy;—for selections from *Ancient Tahiti* by Miss Teuira Henry;—and for selection from *Tuamotuan Religion* by Frank J. Stimson.

The Bollingen Foundation and Routledge and Kegan Paul Ltd. —for selection from *Essays on a Science of Methodology* by C. G. Jung and C. Kerenyi;—for selection from "Primordial Time and Final Time" by G. van der Leeuw in *Man and Time;*—for selection from *The Origins and History of Consciousness* by Erich Neumann;—for selection from Vol. I of *Navaho Religion. A Study in Symbolism* by Gladys A. Reichard;—and for selections from "The Orphic Mysteries and the Greek Spirit" by Walter Wili, in *The Mysteries.*

Branner Org Korch—for selection from Vol. II of *Israel* by J. Pedersen.

Cambridge University Press—for selection from *The Negritos of Malaya* by Ivor H. N. Evans;—and for selection from *Prole-*

gomena to the Study of Greek Religion by Jane Harrison. The Clarendon Press, Oxford—for selections from Vol. XXV and Vol. XLIV of *The Sacred Books of the East*.

Walter De Gruyter and Co.—for selection from *Die Religion der Ägypter* by Adolph Erman.

J. M. Dent and Sons Ltd. and E. P. Dutton and Co., Inc.—for selection from *Kalevala: The Land of Heroes* (trans. W. F. Kirby).

The Division of Christian Education, National Council of Churches and Thomas Nelson and Sons, New York—for selection from *The Holy Bible*, Revised Standard Version.

The Dominion Museum—for selections from *Maori Religion and Mythology* by Eldson Best.

Fretz and Wasmuth Verlag—for selection from *Chinesische Mythen und Legenden* by Claus W. Krieg.

Gallimard Publishers, The Harvill Press Ltd., and Sheed and Ward Inc.—for selection from *Images and Symbols* by Mircea Eliade.

Professor Theodor Gaster—for selection from his *Thespis: Ritual, Myth, and Drama in the Ancient Near East*.

Harper and Brothers—for selection from *The Upanishads* by Swami Nikhilananda.

The International African Institute—for selection from "The Mande Creation Myth" by Germaine Dieterlen, in *Africa*, Vol. XVII.

The Liberal Arts Press Division of the Bobbs-Merrill Co., Inc.—for selection from Hesiod's *Theogony* (trans. Norman O. Brown).

Longmans, Green and Co., Ltd.—for selections from *Shinto (The Way of the Gods)* by W. G. Aston.

The Macmillan Company and Sidgwick and Jackson Ltd.—for selection from *The Wonder That Was India* by A. L. Basham.

The Macmillan Company, Macmillan and Co. Ltd., and Trinity College, Cambridge—for selection from *The Golden Bough* by Sir James Frazer.

Melbourne University Press and T. G. H. Strehlow—for selection from *Aranda Traditions* by T. G. H. Strehlow.

Methuen and Co., Ltd.—for selections from Vol. I and Vol. II of *The Gods of the Egyptians* by E. A. Wallis Budge;—and for selections from *Orpheus and Greek Religion* by W. K. C. Guthrie.

Museum of Navajo Ceremonial Art—for selection from *The Emergence Myth According to the Hanelthnaye or Upward-Reaching Rite* by Berard Haile, O.F.M.

The North-East Frontier Agency—for selections from *Myths of the North-East Frontier of India* by Verrier Elwin.

Kegan Paul, Trench, Trubner and Co.—for selection from Vol. I of *The Vishnu Purana* by H. H. Wilson.

The Philosophical Library—for selection from *Djanggawul* by Ronald M. Berndt.

The Polynesian Society Inc.—for "Tahitian Folk-Lore" by Miss Teuira Henry, in *Journal of the Polynesian Society*, Vol. X;—and for "A Maori Cosmogony" by Hare Hongi (trans.), in *Journal of the Polynesian Society*, Vol. XVI.

Princeton University Press—for selections from *Ancient Near Eastern Texts* by James B. Pritchard (ed.);—and for selection from *A Source Book in Indian Philosophy* by S. Radhakrishnan and C. A. Moore (eds.).

Routledge and Kegan Paul—for selection from *The Myth of The Eternal Return* by Mircea Eliade.

The Smithsonian Institution (Bureau of American Ethnology)—for selections from *Outlines of Zuni Creation Myths* by Frank Hamilton Cushing.

B. G. Teubner Verlag—for selection from *Natursagen* by Oskar Dähnhardt.

University of California Press—for selections from Volume IV of *University of California Publications in American Archaeology and Ethnology*.

The University of Chicago Press—for selection from *The Kumulipo* by Martha W. Beckwith;—for selection from "Methodological Remarks on the Study of Religious Symbolism" by Mircea Eliade, in *The History of Religions: Essays in Methodology;*—for selection from "Structures and Changes in the History of Religion" by Mircea Eliade, in *City Invincible;*—

for selection from *Art in Arnhem Land* by A. P. Elkin and C. and R. Berndt;—for selection from *Before Philosophy, the Intellectual Adventure of Ancient Man* by H. Frankfort, J. Wilson and T. Jacobsen;—for selection from *Kingship and The Gods* by H. Frankfort;—for selection from *The Babylonian Genesis* by Alexander Heidel;—for selection from Vol I of *Pueblo Indian Religion* by Elsie C. Parsons; and for selection from "Style" by Meyer Schapiro in *Anthropology Today*.

The University of Nebraska Press—for selections from *The World's Rim* by Hartley B. Alexander.

The University of Oklahoma Press—for selection from *Popol Vuh: The Sacred Book of the Ancient Quiché Maya* by Adrián Recinos (trans. D. Goetz and S. G. Morley).

The Viking Press Inc.—for selection from *The Masks of God: Primitive Mythology* by Joseph Campbell.

For
Alice, John, Carolyn,
Christopher, and David

EDITOR'S FOREWORD

IT HAS LONG SEEMED to me that men are always asking four basic questions, which, colloquially expressed, are these: (1) Who started it? (2) Are we going to make it? (3) Where are we going to put it? (4) Who's going to clean up? Myths are not only the earliest ways of answering these questions; they are also the most stimulating, because the image, unlike the dry proposition, evokes the endless depths of man's thought and imagination. Charles H. Long has here assembled a collection of fascinating, and rather unfamiliar, answers to the first of these questions, gathered in particular from a rich knowledge of African and Polynesian cultures. A subsidiary question to "Who started it?" is obviously "How was it done?" for it always seems somewhat magical and improbable that there is something rather than nothing. Many of the ancient answers to this problem may seem fantastic— though, when one comes to think of it, hardly more so than the strange products of reality itself.

Surveys of the world's mythologies have usually classified their materials by regions, describing the myths of the Greeks and Romans, of the Norsemen, the Egyptians, or the Hindus—as if these racial, nationalistic, and geographical categories were the really significant divisions of the subject. But what would be the significant divisions in a survey of the world's birds? Would it be of major importance to stress the difference between American and European sparrows, or between sparrows and thrushes? Birds, plants, minerals, and other natural phenomena seem to be discussed more usefully by divisions of form or behavior than of locality.

To the extent, however, that a specific region is the

cradle of a particular culture, and to the extent that myths are phenomena of cultures, the regional classification has its merits. But it should be supplemented by some other method, by a horizontal classification superimposed upon a perpendicular, and for this reason it has seemed important to discuss world mythology in terms of its themes or, to use C. G. Jung's word, its archetypes. Such an approach is therefore naturally indebted to Jung, to his provocative idea that myths are natural phenomena which grow out of the mind more or less uniformly in all places, just as the human body is of one essential pattern in China and Peru.

Yet in inviting authors to contribute to this series I have not restricted myself to those who are formally Jungian. I have tried to get as wide a variety of opinion as the thematic approach to mythology will permit.

The plan of the series is to publish, first, three volumes under the general title of *Myth and Experience* and having to do with mythological themes which treat of the ultimate structure and dynamics of the cosmos—the myths of creation, the myths of death and resurrection, and the myths of polarity. These will be followed by three volumes with the general title of *The Human Image* and dealing with myths in which the universe is understood in terms of anthropomorphic images, so that the themes here will be the father god, the goddess, and the hero.

Each volume is primarily an anthology of texts and images—*i.e.*, photographs of works of art, ritual objects, and the like—presented with an introduction and running commentary. It is not, however, the intention of the series to serve as a sort of reference encyclopedia with each volume a compendium of all the principal myths of the given type. What was desired here was a more imaginative treatment of the materials, and thus the contributing authors were selected accordingly.

ALAN W. WATTS

TABLE OF CONTENTS

LIST OF PLATES

LIST OF LINE DRAWINGS

ALPHA

The Myths of Creation

INTRODUCTION

T HE STUDY OF MYTH and mythical thinking may form a part of several disciplines, covering the areas of theology, philosophy, psychology, ethnology,
and anthropology. It is, however, in the area of the history
of religion that the interpretation of myth poses the most
crucial problem. While many in the modern world claim
that both myth and religion are vestiges of an untutored
past, no informed person will deny the importance of
these expressions for the study of cultural history. Furthermore, the contemporary discussion centering around the
adequacy of myth as a meaningful form of expression for
religious experience should be informed by the interpretations which this form of human expression has had in the
greater part of history.

Our approach to the problem of myth is that of a
historian of religion. It is for this reason that we have
thought it wise to begin this introductory chapter with a
discussion of the interpretation of the history of religion
in the modern period. The other parts of this introduction
will treat myth and mythical thinking and myths of crea-

tion. The remainder of the book will consist of various forms of creation myths.

I. *Religion*

The study of the religion of early man and contemporary primitives was considered important because the nature of religion was understood to be identical with its origin. This idea was put forth most explicitly by Sir Edward B. Tylor. This notion was combined with a historical evolutionism which interpreted the movement of human culture as a passage through various mental stages Religion was understood to be an appropriate interpretation for only the earliest stages of mankind; the subsequent stages of human history, the metaphysical and the scientific, reveal a diminution of the religious element in history and culture. The moral values of religion should not, in the thinking of these historians, be confused with their expressions in magic, myth, and superstition; rather, these values should be stripped of the religious accretions through the employment of rational scientific methods. This attitude is reflected in the publisher's promotional copy for the one-volume edition of *The Golden Bough:*

> You will find savage man enmeshed in a nightmare of magic, wizardry, taboos, and superstitions . . . a creature of such fears and terrors that you will wonder that he kept his sanity. You will see bit-by-bit modification of his weird and often bloodthirsty customs. You will watch the halting entry of religion, as opposed to magic. You will trace from their primitive sources many of the beliefs of our ancestors which still warp our lives today. In a word, *The Golden Bough* will spread before you the whole panorama of man's bitter struggle-not-yet-won—to emerge from the tragic welter of superstitious fears and hates, into a clearer understanding of the world we live in.[1]

Tylor,[2] Frazer's compatriot, who made popular the term "animism" as a description of primitive religion, thought that animism (the belief in Spiritual Beings) among primitives was based on a mistaken logical inference between that which was living and the inanimate. Max Müller, whose pioneering efforts in the area of Vedic and Indian religions opened up these religions to the Western world, explained mythology as a "disease of language."[3]

Westerners owe a great debt to these "giants" of historical cultural studies. They brought to the attention of the Western world traditions, thought forms, behaviors, and literary texts which had not previously been taken seriously by the Western historian. It is also to their credit that, in approaching exotic cultures, they tried to pick out patterns and motifs familiar to the West as a bridge for mutual understanding.

Though we appreciate the work of these men we cannot be satisfied with their conclusions. Each of them fell victim to a peculiar form of the rationalistic bias. In the case of Tylor and Frazer, the model of human experience and action was that of a narrowly conceived rationalistic form of thinking. The problems which Müller confronted in his study of myth and language stem from the same bias. Because of his limited conception of the reality which language purported to express, he was unable to understand the buoyant language of myth and religion in terms other than pathological.

But it is not just the internal methodological problems which cause us to reject the conclusions of these men; there' are other factors of a more general character which make their conclusions ineffectual. We have reference to a new hermeneutical situation. By hermeneutical we mean that attempt to understand the human reality in history. This situation has been caused by the researches of depth psychology, existential philosophy, literary and art criticism, and historical study itself.

On the philosophical level, the work of Wilhelm Dilthey[4] represents the watershed of a new approach to the human reality in culture and history. Dilthey's insistence on the uniqueness and individuality of historical forms is a criticism of rationalistic evolutionary* method in historical studies. While Dilthey's approach left many questions unanswered and led to a type of historicism and relativism, it served to highlight the peculiar problem posed when one attempted a historical study of man. Historical study should be a study of man by man. In such a study neither the interpreter nor the subject matter should be reduced to deterministic categories. In the last analysis, the value of Dilthey's method lies in his delineation of history as that area in which man expresses his most characteristic and profound being. The impact of this type of thinking has had far-reaching consequences for the study of human history.

In all of the disciplines mentioned above, approaches to the forms of human experience and expressions have taken a new turn. The self-sufficiency of the rationalistic-evolutionary mode of explanation has been challenged not simply because new methods are *en vogue,* but primarily because the older method of explanation is not adequate to its subject matter. Meyer Schapiro, in an illuminating article on style in art, shows how the new understanding of style in art enables the art historian to understand forms of art which have not been produced in his own culture, and also enables the art critic to form a more substantial basis for constructing the history of art. We quote one of his lucid statements:

In the past, a great deal of primitive work, especially representation, was regarded as artless even by sensitive people; what was valued were

* By evolutionary, we refer to that form of historical thinking which is called "positivism." In this interpretation, human culture develops in a linear manner from religion to metaphysics to science.

mainly the ornamentation and the skills of primitive industry. It was believed that primitive arts were childlike attempts to represent nature —attempts distorted by an irrational content of the monstrous and grotesque. True art was admitted only in the high cultures, where knowledge of natural forms was combined with a rational ideal which brought beauty and decorum to the image of man. Greek art and the art of the Italian High Renaissance were the norms for judging all art, although in time the classic phase of Gothic art was accepted.[5]

Schapiro shows later in his article how inadequate the norms really were, for the naturalistic forms in the Paleolithic caves of France approach the rational norms of the Italian High Renaissance to a much greater degree than the art of the sophisticated moderns in New York, London, or Paris. Furthermore, some of the art of the great modern Westerners, in terms of its style, is closer to the art of contemporary primitive cultures. This is an example of the new hermeneutical situation which we spoke of above. Evaluation of significant human expressions purely on the basis of a simplistic-evolutionary historical approach with its narrowly defined rational categories cannot give us the results we require in our task of understanding. Examples of this same problem could be cited in the area of literature.

In the case of depth psychology we have come to admit, on the most learned and also on the most popular levels, that there is a structure which is the unconscious—a psychic reality which, though not conscious, does exert a great influence upon our experiences and expression. It is difficult to overestimate the radicality of this notion in contrast to the thinking about actions and experiences which pervaded the thought of the nineteenth century. When one adds to these factors the existence of the new national states in the world—states which are not primarily heirs of the Western tradition, but in many cases, heirs of a traditional culture in either its civilizational or archaic form which seems opposed to the characteristic Western mode of thinking and acting—some idea of the new hermeneutical situation—the new problem of understanding—may be grasped.

This new hermeneutical situation has forced us to understand the profound expressions of human existence as symbols. By symbolic expression we are referring to that quality of expression which renders human experience objectively significant and at the same time allows for an intense degree of subjective participation. The interpretation of these symbols constitutes one of the major tasks of historians of religion and culture.

This is one of the best possible non-reductionist approaches to religion. The *sui generis* nature of religion must be maintained if the concreteness of man's history is to be understood and appreciated.

Rudolf Otto's classic work, *Das Heilige (The Idea of the Holy)*, published in 1917, may be seen as one of the important texts in this new attempt to understand the meaning of religious life. Otto's delineation of the structure of the religious experience in symbolic terms broke through the former sociological, psychological, and rational categories. By giving the qualitative designation of "numinous" to the religious experience and by carefully separating the elements of awe and fascination as *mysterium tremendum* and *mysterium fascinosum,* he made clear what others had only hinted. One-dimensional theory regarding the origin and nature of religion was eliminated in Otto's synthetic symbolical approach. For example, he recognized that there was an element of fear in the religious experience, but this element became something more than ordinary fear when it was seen within the context of religious experience. It is, as a part of the religious experience, combined with the desire to participate in and identify with the reality which is experienced. From the historical point of view, Otto's great value lies in his creation of structures through which the forms of religious experience could be analyzed and in his elimination of the idea of a prereligious man or age.

The work of Rudolf Otto established a methodological principle but it was not comprehensive enough to cover the entire range of historical religious phenomena. His student Joachim Wach devoted his attention to a comprehensive or integral theory of religious experience and its expression.[6] Basing his method on Otto's principle, Wach analyzed the forms of culture and society as derivatives of the religious experience.

But in spite of the works of Otto and his followers, there are critics who claim that a *sui generis* approach to the nature of religion is impossible. Religious experience and expression must be reduced to the level of biology, psychology, economics, or social structures before they can be understood. To buttress their position they point to the obvious fact that nowhere do we find religion in its pristine purity, unrelated to the biological, social, and psychological dimensions of life. Religion thus functions as a sanction and an ideology for these more essential and primary human relations. What is real or ultimate is not the religious experience but the economic, social, or psychological equilibrium which religion helps to maintain.

We must admit that we know of no religion which is unrelated to the various important dimensions of human life. Such an idea of religion is completely abstract, and even if it were discovered, could not aid us in our investigations. Religion is above all practical and this means that the important concerns of man are religious. To be sure, the consequences of the religious experience manifest themselves in culture but not by simply serving as a catalyst. Ofttimes the religious factor is disruptive of societal and cultural harmony.

One should take care not to identify the form of the religious manifestation with the totality of religious experience. If we find a case in which worshipers venerate stones, we should not presume that, because of ignorance, fear, prelogical mentality, etc., the worshipers are confusing their god who is animate, powerful, and dynamic with the inert and immobile stone. On the other hand, we should not assume that the worshipers are simply using the stone to represent a deity who has no intrinsic relationship with his mode of manifestation.

The stone is not understood to be the deity, but it is through the stone that the deity makes himself known. The "natural" structure of the stone gives qualitative specificity to the deity and the stone becomes a sacred reality because it is a mode of revelation. The complexity and subtlety of these relations are expressed in religious traditions through the use of symbols. What is revealed in the stone is a reality which is other than man. In religious communities that which is other than man (that otherness which permits the individual to have concreteness and specificity) is not spoken of in abstract terms, but in symbols which render the reality of the other accessible and open to participation and communion. Robert Redfield, the anthropologist, in discussing world-view distinguishes the three basic elements in this notion as the I, the We-They distinction, and the Not-Man.[7] The Not-Man, according to Redfield, defines the animals, invisible beings, trees, and sky phenomena. This notion of the "Not-Man" suggests what we imply by the use of the term, "other." However, this qualification and difference in meaning in our usage of the term should be stated. For the greater part of human history, the worlds of animals, plants, and sky phenomena were revealed to man and thus their otherness was a manifestation of power and sacredness. If the "Not-Man" or "otherness" defines a generic aspect of human life, then it is easy to understand that the manifestation of the sacred is at the same time a manifestation of ultimate reality-as-being. The religious revelation of being is not a revealing "in general" (this phrasing already contradicts itself), but is rather a revelation of being in a specific situation. Thus religion is related to crisis situations. These are the generic situations of birth, puberty, and death; and, in addition, there are those crisis situations which are peculiar to the culture and history of a people. From this point of view, we may define a crisis situation as a situation in which a person or a culture is in transition from one mode of being to another and therefore is threatened by nonbeing. As such, a person's response to this situation carries with it more intensity than his normal living habits. His experience of himself and of the otherness in life is heightened.

Malinowski's analysis of the relation of myth to the actual situations of the Trobriand Islanders shows how myths are related to the existential situations of birth, puberty, and death. The myths are not irrational unless one understands these situations to be irrational. They are human responses to the mysterious dimension of human existence and, according to Malinowski, should be distinguished from magic and science, which co-exist alongside of myth and serve different functions in the cultural life.

In other words, there seems to be a specific manner by which man responds to the profound and mysterious in life. This response is religion and the religious response expresses itself in symbols. Mircea Eliade has distinguished six characteristics of religious symbols. In his discussion, Eliade makes the following point: "Religious symbols are capable of revealing a modality of the real or a structure of the world that is not evident on the level of immediate experience."[8] Religious symbols are multivalent; that is, they have the capacity to express a number of meanings whose continuity is not obvious on the level of ordinary experience. In consequence of this fact, the religious symbol has the capacity to systematize or integrate a number of diverse meanings into a totality, thus expressing in a profound and intense manner the paradoxical structure of that which is ultimately real.

We have insisted on the primacy of symbols in the religious life. We must add that it is through religious expression that man gives form to his most intense experience —the experience of his totality in relationship to that which he experiences as ultimately real. The religious symbol because of its specificity takes into itself those realities which are a part of the religious man's local environment, but in the symbolic ordering the local ingredients take on meanings which are more than natural. The religious symbol expresses, in the words of G. van der Leeuw, simultaneously, *"What is given or Possibility."* In this connection van der Leeuw continues,

> But this by no means implies that man has ever accepted life simply as sacred. . . . For apart from some kind of criticism no religion is conceivable. Religion means precisely that we not simply accept life; it is directed always to the "Other," and although it has sprung from human life, religion cannot orient itself to this life as such. But it can bring into prominence specific aspects of this existence as being "sacred," and give emphasis to certain phenomena in life as being potent.[9]

Religion is not natural because man is not simply natural. The world of man exists as a limitation or qualification of his environment, and this qualification or limitation is at the same time a criticism. Man's world is an ordered world of meaning, but the organizing principle is interpreted as a revelation which comes from a source outside of his ordinary life. It is this source which is given (revealed) and (it) defines any future possibility of man's existence. The thirst for a plenitude of being and life is always a religious craving. The symbols of religion make clear the given and actual manifestation of the source of life and at the same time indicate the possibilities for the continuation of life.

The crisis periods in cultural history are those periods when new discoveries are made. These new discoveries are given, but they are always understood to be of a religious and magical character. We are thinking here of the discovery of certain tools or agriculture. These advances, which are usually spoken of as technical advances, are in the cultures where they were discovered spoken of in religious language and have about them a religious aura.

II. *The Myth and Mythical Thinking*

Because of the widespread popularity of evolutionistic and rationalistic thinking in our culture, the term "myth" usually refers to the fanciful imagination of the human mind. As such it is the opposite of the world of reality. In a similar vein, one can see that those peoples and cultures who live in terms of an explicit myth have been treated politically by the West as if they were not real, e.g., the American Indians, Africans, Indians, etc. Certain contemporary theologians in the West abhor the use of myth precisely because they think that it refers to the fanciful and unreal, and therefore is not a proper vehicle for the profound and serious "Word of God." But for any person who has studied the cultures of peoples who live in terms of an explicit myth, an opposite judgment must be made. The myth is a true story— the myth is a story about reality. It is impossible to understand the reality and being of these people, unless one understands their reality in relationship to the myth. When we speak of understanding their reality, we are speaking of their reality in the precise sense of their human presence,

their specificity and qualitative meaning in time and space.
We are not denying the possibility of understanding them
on other levels, e.g., as biological beings, but such an understanding tells us little, if anything, about their humanness.

If the myths are true stories, we must ask in what sense
are they true. They are not obviously true in the literal sense,
for they are filled with actions and characters which on the
level of literal meaning are impossible to comprehend. The
myths do not, however, purport to be discourses in the literal
form, but there is no reason for us to equate literalness of
presentation with truth.

Mythical thinking is not concerned primarily with logic.
On the other hand, it is not illogical or prelogical. As Raffaele Pettazzoni has pointed out, mythical thinking is at once
logical and illogical, logical and magical, rational and irrational.[10] It is a type of thinking which represents man's initial
confrontation with the power in life. The content of the myth
must be understood within this context. The beings referred to in the myth—gods, animals, plants—are forms of
power grasped existentially. The myths should not be understood as attempts to work out a rational explanation of deity.
Historians of religion, beginning with Rudolf Otto, have
given up this approach in the study of religious forms. Otto
himself refers to the object of religion as the Holy.[11]

G. van der Leeuw says that religious experience is concerned with a "Somewhat" which forces itself upon man as a
Something *Other*.[12] Mircea Eliade begins his work by ac-
cepting the distinction between the sacred and the profane.[13]
R. R. Marett, the anthropologist, speaks of the confrontation
of life as dynamic rhythm which leads to ritual.[14] Marett
believes that the gods themselves evolve from the ritual ap-
paratus. A similar position can be seen in the work of Ananda
Coomaraswamy.[15]

All of the above approaches emphasize the fact that in

myth expression is being given to man's reaction to life as a source of power and being. The myth expresses that qualification of life which van der Leeuw referred to above and points to the definite manner in which the world is available for man. The word and content of myth are revelations of power.

The veneration of the earth, totemic animals, and ancestors among archaic people makes it clear that the apprehension of life as potency is the overwhelming concern of the mythic consciousness. Furthermore, the sexual symbolism which appears in many myths points to the importance and recognition of this dimension of life as a resource of reality and power. It is from this level of mythic thought that the definite and precise images of deities arise.

Eric Dardel, in his discussion of Maurice Leenhardt's understanding of the mythic, emphasizes the fact that the mythic does not exclude the rational, but precedes it.[16] The coming of the rational does not, however, mean the end of the mythic. The mythic and the rational co-exist. This is an important point, for the mythic apprehension of reality is not a victim of human evolution. Alongside of the rational is remains a mode through which we have access to the real.

A great deal of our modern cultural life presupposes the equation of literalness = truth. To some degree this is dictated by the scientific-technological character of our culture, but we would find it difficult to believe that anyone in our culture lives entirely in a world of literal meanings. There are human experiences on the personal and cultural levels which can only be expressed in symbolic forms. These meanings are in many cases the most profound meanings in our personal and cultural lives. They are profound because they symbolize the specificity of our human situation—they make clear to us how the world exists for us and point up the resources and tensions which are present in our situation.

It is from this point of view that we must approach

myth. The myth is a symbolic ordering which makes clear how the world is present for man.

This fact is demonstrated by the researchers in depth psychology. The most necessary and therefore the most profound relationships of human existence cannot be rendered adequately on the level of consciousness as rational discourses or finally reduced to the forms of literal communication. These relationships are understood and participated in on the symbolic level. This is done so often that symbolic systems are often believed to be generic aspects of the common-sense literal world. A very good example of this is our kinship system, which is based on certain biological and social phenomena. One has only to compare this kinship system with others in the world to realize how highly symbolic it is. It is based upon a nonliteral understanding of man and his world. The fact that the biological father is also the social father in our system does not lessen the symbolic meaning of the system.

We see the recognition of this fact in Emile Durkheim's *The Elementary Forms of the Religious Life*. In this work Durkheim puts forth the idea that the object of religious worship is the social group. The social group is symbolized as a totem (animal or plant) and worshiped. Durkheim considered this to be the earliest form of the religious sentiment. Subsequent research has made clear that totemism is not the earliest form of religion. While we must accept Durkheim's discovery of the symbolization on the level of society, it would be incorrect to base all of religious symbolism on this theory. Man is a social being, but this means only that he has his life within the context of a social group—his life, however, is more than the social group. One must either overlook a great deal of the data of human history or bludgeon it into narrow molds if Durkheim's theory is to be accepted as a general theory of religious symbolism.

While speaking about kinship systems, we should be reminded that Freud fashions his psychological theories in the form of the Oedipus myth, in part because of the intimacy, profundity, and necessity of this type of kinship system in Western culture. The meanings which emerge from psychoanalysis are not in the conscious literal form, but are symbols expressing the apprehension of the world of the patient in terms of the tensions and resources present therein. This fact is true of both major psychoanalytical schools. It is also interesting to note that both Freud and Jung found it necessary to express their theories in terms of mythological motifs.

In philosophy and theology the use of analogy may be an attempt to deal discursively with the more profound symbolic forms of human expression. The adequacy of analogy as a theological and philosophical tool lies at the heart of the "de-mythologizing" problem in theology today.

III. *Myths of Creation*

We have considered some of the general problems of myth; let us now turn to a discussion of creation myths. A popular understanding of creation myths must be dealt with before we proceed. There is a rather widespread notion that creation myths are prescientific attempts to give an explanation of the world; in other words, they are primitive science without the proper method. We must admit that most myths are products of a prescientific age and that they came into being before the strict functional separation of forms of thought and society were predominant. We must further admit that creation myths do perform an explanatory role in the life of the society which believes in them. This follows usually from the organic character of the myth and society. But even within organic societies, if we are to believe Malinowski, myths exist alongside of what we would call scientific knowledge.[17] Specific myths or mythological structures may be superseded, but it is our position that mythic thinking as a specific mode of apprehending the world is present in man in spite of the particular world-view of his time. The advent of modern science is not the only important (and some would say, not the most important) change which has taken place in human history. Myths and mythological structures have been discarded by man throughout human history whenever new revelations of being and sacredness have been manifested, but it is precisely the mode of apprehension which we have called mythic which allows man to respond to the new and novel manifestation. We are not insisting here on a dichotomy of the mythic and the scientific. The presence of the type of thought which we call scientific is too pervasive in our contemporary life to justify such an alternative. We do not, however, interpret this to mean that the mythic as a structure of human awareness is no longer operative in our age. Rather, it presents to us the problem of dealing with the fundamental relatedness of the mythic and the scientific.* One mode cannot replace the other; the generalizing method of scientific thought cannot do justice to the life of man as he experiences it, and the mythic mode of apprehension cannot remain so specific and concrete that it becomes esoteric or subjective.

The understanding of myth primarily as a form of causal thinking is not limited to those who follow an evolutionary method in their interpretations. Father Wilhelm Schmidt, in developing his notion of "urmonotheism," attributes the idea of creator deities among archaic people to the basic need of man for a causal explanation of his world. This intellectual explanation does not account for the nonintellectual factors in human experience and fails to do justice to the complexity of the myths themselves.

---

* Certain philosophical methods are reassuring in this connection. We refer to the radical empiricist philosophies of Henri Bergson, William James, A. N. Whitehead, and to the existentialist school of Heidegger.

Pettazzoni emphasizes the role of myth in insuring the existence and permanence of the world.[18] This aspect of myth is closely related to ritual. Such relationship between myth and ritual cannot be denied, but if one examines the cosmogonic myth closely, he finds elements in the myth which cannot simply be ritually enacted. The explanatory elements in cosmogonic myths are not simply examples of causal thinking, but of existential knowledge as well.

If human life represents a particular mode of being—a mode of being which is continuous with nature on one level and discontinuous on another level—then the manner in which man understands his ordering of the world is as important as the specific form of order.

We have attempted in the two sections above to provide the reader with a context for understanding the meaning of religious expression in the form of myth in the history of religion. Before proceeding let us summarize our position. 1) From the point of view of hermeneutics, there has been a movement away from the employment of purely conceptual and evolutionistic categories in the interpretation of the history of religion. The new type of methodology may be seen in the works of Rudolf Otto, Joachim Wach, G. van der Leeuw, and Mircea Eliade. We might add here that the methods of many ethnologists and anthropologists reflect a similar approach.[19] 2) Religious experience and mythic apprehension represent an existential mode of grasping the world. In the myth, the world is understood as it exists in a particular manner for man. This type of apprehension reflects man's qualification and evaluation of the world. The sacred is therefore to be understood as that which is real. This is the import of Eliade's equation, sacredness = being, and Joachim Wach's definition of religion as the experience of ultimate reality.[20] The theologian Paul Tillich implies the same meaning when on one level he defines religion as "ultimate concern."[21] 3) The expression of this type of apprehension is through symbols. Symbolic expressions are multivalent and reveal how complex meanings are held together. Such expressions are not devoid of a rational element but the symbolic expression should not be reduced to this dimension. The rational and the a-rational co-inhere in the symbol. Symbols are expressions of man's historical concreteness. One could say that man's true history is the history of his religion. The symbolic expressions of man's historical situation include an evaluation of his "natural environment," but in terms which make this environment accessible for human participation and communion. The symbols, however, while reflecting an evaluation and qualification of the environment, at the same time refer to a dimension of the real which is other than the environmental factors. This is the transcendent pole of the symbol. In this sense, the most profound symbols of human reality seem to include as a necessary ingredient a dimension of reality which is more than human and more than natural. Part of the job of the historian of religion is to interpret the human reality in relation to this type of symbolic expression.

The symbols which express the above meanings in the highest degree are those found in cosmogonic myths. These myths are symbolic expressions of the creation of the world. They are found in almost every culture of the world, both in the religions of archaic peoples and in the great civilizational religions. The creation myth expresses in symbolic manner what is most essential to human life and society by relating it to a primordial act of foundation recorded in the myth.[22] In the most general sense we could say that the creation myth is an expression of man's cosmic orientation. This orientation involves his apprehension of time and space, his participation in the world of animals and plants, his judgment concerning other men and the phenomena of the sky, the interrelationship of these dimensions, and finally the powers which have established and continue to maintain his being in the world.

One has only to look at the table of contents of two current handbooks in the history of religions, G. van der Leeuw's *Religion in Essence and Manifestation*[23] and Mircea Eliade's *Patterns in Comparative Religion*,[24] to appreciate the complex modes of cosmic orientation found in the religious life of mankind. Van der Leeuw begins his table by listing those data of human existence which become the locus of the sacred. Thus in his section entitled the "Object of Religion," he includes such topics as "The Sacred Environment, Sacred Stones and Trees," "The Sacred World Above," "The Form of the Mother." In his second section entitled "The Subject of Religion," he points to the parallel responses of man to these loci of sacrality. Typical topics under this heading include, "The Sacred Life," "The Given and the Possible," and he then spells out these responses in terms of religious sociological types. Eliade operates in much the same manner, excluding from his analysis, however, the sociological types of van der Leeuw. Such books acquaint us with the subtleties and preciseness of religious orientation.

Obviously, we have no records of the myths of the first human beings. We have reason to believe that Peking Man (Sinanthropus) possessed fire and stone implements and observed certain burial rites. After Sinanthropus, there is the very long age of the Neanderthals, extending up to late Paleolithic times. Modern man (Homo sapiens) appears somewhere in the late Paleolithic period. It is definitely men like us whom we find in the late Paleolithic and early Neolithic ages. All myths thus presuppose a history, the existence of previous human communities. Creation myths are expressions of new beginnings, new *cosmoi*. The novelty may appear on the historical level in connection with the discovery of a new plant, animal, or technique. We know of some religious symbols and myths which give a certain evaluation to agricultural life, others in which the dominant emphases are those of the nomadic pastoralists. We also know of several instances in which the discovery of metal, of fire, or of maize is related in mythical symbolic forms. These historical situations do not produce the religious sentiment, but serve as its mode of expression. The plant, animal, or technique is the structure through which the actuality and possibility of man's being and the world's power are made known. The experience of the world in this concrete manner leads to the generalizing of reality in terms of the structure or structures through which it was apprehended. The cosmogonic myths express the power, spontaneity, absoluteness, plenitude, and mystery of reality in symbolic forms.

In the myths animals talk, superlatives abound, and easy transformations between levels of phenomena are possible. The "paradise element" in cosmogonic myths can be understood in this manner. These elements have reference to a time in which men and animals lived together; the gods and men are related in terms of mutual affection and no sexual, social, or economic tensions are present. In another form these meanings are expressed as a primordial completeness in the sense of a completeness in relationship to sexuality, the abundance of food supply, and an integrated social life. The World-Parent motif in the myth is usually spoken of as the primordial togetherness of earth mother and sky father, and in some instances the male element in the form of a Great Father gives birth to the first living creatures. In other instances, the earth, conceived of as a repository of all forms and powers, gives birth to all creatures and living things, as in the emergence myths. The emphasis on one level is the plenitude of reality as a reservoir of forms and energy. On another level the absoluteness and perfection of the cosmos is made clear through this symbolism.

Let us reiterate a point we have already made several times: the historical conditions provide the means through which the religious sentiment expresses itself but do not create by themselves the religious sentiment. For example, the symbol of completeness in high agricultural communities is often expressed by the union of earth mother and sky father. Such symbolism has a specific meaning for man in agricultural societies, but among nonagricultural peoples, the pastoral nomads, this meaning is expressed in terms of an all-powerful sky deity or by a Lord of the Animals. The meaning of plenitude and wholeness is therefore not totally dependent on the historical situation.

Historical conditions thus provide the means through which expression is given to that dimension of human experience which is more than history. We should be careful here to avoid a dichotomy between the historical and the non-historical, the material and the spiritual. Man is a spiritual being by virtue of his historical conditioning (biological form, temporal-spatial situation), and he is a historical being by virtue of his spiritual life. The research over the past one hundred fifty years into the history of man's life on earth has made it both necessary and possible for us to make this last statement. The study of man as the development of a natural form through time cannot be denied, but this development was not a matter of the sheer working out of deterministic laws. The ability of man to grasp realities deeper than his historical conditioning is equally important in this development.

We have pointed to the fact that historical conditions influence the form of symbols. On another level, we must mention the role of the human psyche in the creation of symbols. The psychic structure and the historical conditions under which it expresses itself cannot be separated. We shall speak of this structure independently only for the sake of analysis. We do not know the extent of the quantity or quality of impressions which inhere in the psychic structure as a result of its embryonic existence as a foetus. It would be safe to say that some impressions remain and influence the psychic orientation after birth. A great deal more is known about the influence of pregenital and genital sexuality on the psyche. We are all familiar with the theories of Freud regarding castration anxiety and the Oedipus complex as a total theory of man and religious symbolism. A number of scholars have protested the dogmatic use of Freudian theory as a tool of research in this area. One of the most lucid critiques is Bruno Bettelheim's *Symbolic Wounds*.[25] Though Bettelheim emphasizes the important role which pregenital sexual experience plays in the structure of religious symbolism, he finds Freud's theory of castration anxiety culture-bound and irrelevant to cultural situations which are not as sexually repressive as Western civilization at the time of Freud. Bettelheim's analysis uses as data the initiation rites and the mutilations in the form of circumcision, subincision, and superincision which usually take place during these rites in primitive societies. The great value of this work is that it presents the universality of the problem of sexual tension and refuses to reduce this problem to the late Western formulation of it in Freudian terms. Jung and his followers have pointed out the historical dimensions of consciousness.[26] The history of mankind, not simply the history of the individual, is the potentiality of the psychic structure. The symbolic images which have emerged as a result of man's experience (conscious and unconscious) in history may find their expression through the psyche. We shall not go into an analysis of the difficult problem of Jungian archetypes. Suffice it to say that his interpretation of the psychic structure enables us to envisage symbolic expressions which are more than expressions of the individual's historical conditioning.

Thus the range of symbolic expression is not limited by the type of historical conditioning under which man undergoes his experience. The myth, however, does give expression to man's situation—but man's situation as human —which for us means something more than the impingement of the material world upon him.

Cosmogonic myths refer to that power or force which centers and gives definiteness to the life of a human community. It is through a creative event that a new world, a definite order, is given to the stuff of history, the environment, and the psyche. In the cosmogonic myth these elements are centered and personalized—which is to say, they are re-presented in a new form. Creation means the modification of reality in terms of a particular structure. In the cosmogonic myths a particular form is enunciated and generalized. In this manner the dominant note of the creative order pervading the entire order opens up new possibilities for the emergence of new patterns.

This pervasive characteristic of the cosmogonic myth can be seen in the relationship of myth and ritual and in the correspondences which exist between the myth and other dimensions of the world. The dramatization of the central themes of the myth is performed to emphasize the permanence of the powerful structure which undergirds and integrates the order. This is equally a demonstration of the ontological dimension of the order and a sign of its acceptance. In other words, ritual is a sign of joy and celebration.

The orientation of time and space in relationship to the myth has been explored by many scholars. Insofar as the structures of the myth are equated with reality, the reenactment of the myth establishes time. Time in this sense is not abstract, but a lived experience. The participants in the ritual actually take on the reality of the agents in the myth. The person has reality through his participation and re-enactment of the event which brought the world into being.

Theodor Gaster[27] clarifies the relationship between myth and ritual. According to Gaster, certain activities are carried on in primitive communities which have as their function the replenishment of life and vitality. These rites are of two kinds, the Rites of Kenosis, or Emptying, and the Rites of Plerosis, or Filling. The rites of emptying

> symbolize the eclipse of life and vitality at the end of each leave, and are exemplified by lenten periods, fast, austerities and other expressions of mortification and suspended animation. The rites of filling symbolize the revitalization which is ushered in at the beginning of the new leave, and are exemplified by rites of mass-mating, ceremonial purgations of evil and magical procedures designated to promote fertility, produce corn, relieve the sun, and so forth.[28]

As a consequence of these rites, Gaster coins the term "topocosm."

> Basic to the entire procedure is the conception that what is in turn eclipsed and neutralized is not merely the human community of a given area and locality but the total corporate unit of all elements, animate and inanimate alike, which together constitute its distinctive character and "atmosphere." To this wider entity we may assign the name *topocosm*, formed (on the analogy of *microcosm* and *macrocosm*) from the Greek *topos*, "place," and *cosmos*, "world order." The seasonal ceremonies are the economic regimen of this topocosm. . . . The essence of the topocosm is that it possesses a twofold character, at once real and punctual, and ideal and durative, the former aspect being necessarily immerged in the latter, as a moment is immerged in time. If it is bodied forth as a real and concrete organism in the present, it exists also as an ideal, timeless entity, embracing but transcending the here and now. . . .[29]

Gaster's notion of the topocosm as "the total corporate unit of all elements" illustrates how the basic structure of the myth is generalized to include the dimensions of time and space. In this manner the dramatization of the elements of the myth enables us to speak of periodic creations and the cyclical regeneration of time. A thorough discussion of this aspect of the cosmogonic myth may be seen in the work of Mircea Eliade.[30]

The generalizing and integrative function of the cosmogonic myth may also be seen in the manner in which the basic structure of the myth provides a model for architectural forms and social organization. Mircea Eliade discusses this aspect of myth in *The Myth of the Eternal Return*.[31] Under the heading of "Celestial Archetypes of Territories, Temples, and Cities," he gives us many examples from the history of religion which demonstrate the fact that reality is conferred upon territories, temples, and cities, by virtue of their participation in the "symbolism of the Center." The center marks the place at which heaven, earth, and hell meet; it is, furthermore, the sacred mountain where heaven and earth meet. The center is the zone of absolute reality and thus every creation must imitate and homologize itself to this model.

Claude Levi Strauss refers to this same phenomenon among American Indians.[32] Cuzco, the capital of the ancient Inca empire, was divided into four quarters, each symbolizing a region of the world and a province of the empire. Similar cosmological symbolism can be seen among the Aztecs. Among the Zuñi the village is understood to be at the center of the world—the place from which the first men emerged from the underworld (see emergence myths in Chapter One. The *kivas* or temples of the Pueblos, simple holes dug in the ground, carry through this symbolism in which the structures of the myth are represented in the physical structures of the *kivas*. Among the Navahos, who have no religious architecture, the symbolism is assimilated in the form of a system of correspondences which relate directions, colors, mountains, plants, parts of the body, types of winds, aspects of the universe, and, finally, tutelary deities. These correspondences are depicted in the sand paintings of the Navaho.

Among the Pawnee Indians the cosmic dimension is depicted in the ceremony of the sacrifice to the morning star. Similar correlations of myth and social order are to be found among the Winnebago and Omaha Indians of North America and the tribes of central Brazil in South America.

Marcel Griaule and Germaine Dieterlen show how the geographical layout of the Dogon of the West Sudan corresponds to a divine structure of the myth.[33] H. Frankfort[34] arrives at the same conclusion regarding the relationship between myth and social structures in Egypt and Mesopotamia. Among the Australian aborigines the wanderings of the ancestors in "alcheringa times," (the time before creation) is the divine model which governs the life of society.[35]

In a similar vein, man is understood as a microcosm, a representative of the cosmos in miniature. Not only do specific types of human beings receive their sanction from the myth, but the general physiological and psychological make-up of each individual is based on a divine model contained in the cosmogonic myth.

In the Dogon myth referred to above, it is stated that the egg from which all things proceed was created through the vibrations of the seed Digitaris. This is the smallest seed known to the Dogon. The vibrations of the seed break through the enveloping sheath and the vibrations now extend to the uttermost limits of the universe. It is said that the vibrations within the seed are the model for the creative effort which produced man. The first and sixth vibrations produced his legs, the second and fifth his arms, and the third and fourth his head. The seventh movement produced his sexual organs. The correspondences between these vibrations, the organs of man, and other aspects of the Dogon social structure are very complex. We are able, however, to see how it is possible for man to mirror the cosmic order in his biological structure. The elaboration of this cosmo-biological ordering reaches its peak in the Indian discipline of Yoga. In this discipline the biological organs become symbols of the universe and the practice of the yogin is a homologue of the sacrifice.[36] The old zodiac, which still exerts great influence in our times, is an example of this form of symbolism which continues to survive. This cosmo-biological symbolism is a pervasive aspect of all cosmogonic myths. It makes clear the intimacy between the creator deity and the material form of man, but there is the insistence that the power of the deity is not absent even in this form. Though Judaism and Christianity do not derive their religious symbols primarily from nature, the notion of the body still remains a rich symbolic form in both religions. Later speculations concerning the nature of the body have led to some of the basic problems in the history of philosophy and theology. This is an example of the ontological dimension which is often brought to light through religious symbols.

Let us finally turn to art forms as another way in which the central structure of the cosmogonic myth is generalized. Maurice Leenhardt believes that artistic expression represents a diminution of the mythic dimension of human existence.[37] This diminution is described as a movement from the two-dimensional vision of the world of the mythic to the three-dimensional world of plastic expression. We agree with Leenhardt's judgment if he means that temporal-spatial objectification does not totally express the initial apprehension of reality. The meaning of the mythic imagination is not exhausted if its expression is restricted to these art forms. While agreeing with Leenhardt, we must insist on the necessity of these expressions and in this sense we cannot refer to religious art as a diminution. It is, rather, a correlate of the mythic apprehension, for experience tends to seek expression.

The artist lives in a cosmos. The creative intention of the artist and the use of the work are determined to a great degree by the actions of divine beings in the cosmogonic myth. Not only are the nuances and atmosphere of his world related to the cosmogonic myth, but often the tools which he uses and the technique which he employs are related to a structure of the cosmogonic myth. This is true whether the object has a cultic or utilitarian function. In many instances separate myths of origin of certain tools, techniques, or materials are present within the culture. These myths are in turn derivatives from a more central cosmogonic myth. The examples of religious art presented in the body of the text may convey something of the mythical world which forms the context for these expressions.

The relationship of the cosmogonic myth and art objects is another way in which the sacramental nature of existence is realized. Insofar as most tools and techniques have their meaning in relationship to a definite form of divine activity, the common life of the culture reveals a structure of sacredness. A. P. Elkin senses the relationship between the art forms and the religious life of the Australians when he says,

> The Aborigines live on two interrelated planes; one consists of the necessary daily events and actions of existence—food-gathering, eating, drinking, social intercourse and marriage; the other, which is basic to this, consists of ritual, symbolism and faith. So interrelated are these planes of living that they might be more exactly regarded as aspects of life. We may be tempted to distinguish them as practical and symbolic

respectively, but there is a sense in which both planes are practical and symbolic. . . . To those with eyes to see, rocks and trees, rivers and hills are "Dreamings," marking the journeyings, exploits and presence of the heroes, and the abiding places of the spirits of men and of natural species. For everything, including man, has its "shade," that which remains when the material shade cast by the sun or moon is no more seen. And it is that inner "shade," that soul, which must be conceived for itself, as distinct from its material vehicle, the object or body. The result is the symbolic representation in art and ritual. . . . But ritual implies art—at least for the Aborigines. Ritual is the ordered arrangement of symbols and symbolic actions, all of which express man's urge to conceive in outward forms the "shades," the inner life and meaning, the permanent element, in man and the world and his relationship to it—mundane though they often are. Here, then, is art.[88]

A vital religious life will tend to express itself in artistic forms. Art thus seems to be a necessary dimension of religion. In art forms the relationship of man to his world is objectified and made concrete.

The most impressive religious art is the type which has a cultic function. Such art might be in the form of masks, body tatooes, paintings on the ground or body. The cultic art may be designed for a role in a communal re-enactment of the myth, for sexual initiation, or for initiation into a secret society. In each instance, the actions and being of a specific structure, or structures, of the myth and the meaning of a divine being is given dramatic and precise embodiment.

Though the cultic art expresses the religious quality most decisively, the artistic quality of utilitarian art objects reveals a religious world. In many cases utilitarian objects carry the same designs and are shaped by the same techniques which produced the cultic art. The religious character of the cultic object is a function of its use in the ritual. But even when there is not a carry-over of design from the cultic object to the utilitarian object, the religious element still remains. The design and ornamentation remind us of the world which is present to the artist. It is a world which even on this level retains its spiritual quality.

We have made reference above to that character of the cosmogonic myth which enables it to pervade the universe which it describes. The cosmogonic myth always expresses power in one form or another, for creation must be understood as creation "over against" something. In the most general sense this "something" is often referred to as chaos or the void. On the specific historical level this "something" is the old world, the order before the irruption of the new. There must be a destruction of the old before a new creation can take place. This destruction may be seen as the creative power of action over against the inertia of the old order, or the power in the myth might represent the antagonism between two antithetical forms of order. The nonhistorical dimensions of life are often given expression as historical structures in this type of antagonism. For example, some myths may express the antagonism between matriarchal and patriarchal forms. These dimensions of life are not, however, simply historical. The cosmogonic myth is an attempt to resolve these antagonisms and to bring about a definitive structure of meaning for the entire culture. The cosmogonic myth is the myth *par excellence* precisely because the beginnings of all things within the culture are modeled on the pattern of this myth.

While this centeredness which is described in the cosmogonic myth orients, synthesizes, and integrates the world, a complete harmony is seldom achieved. The centrality given to a particular structure of meaning in the myth involves the possibility of greater tension between this structure and the other actual or possible structures adumbrated in the myth. Furthermore, there remains the threat of the older structure which the new creation ostensibly destroyed. There is also the threat of a return to chaos—a situation in which the meanings and energies of the cultural life are dissipated on trivial concerns. These threats and antagonisms are usually identifiable in the myth. As a matter of fact, they are made clearer in the light of the definitive structure of the cosmogonic myth.

This critique and qualification of the old cosmos by a new myth enables us to understand the history of mythological forms and symbols. Eliade believes that the oldest religious structures are symbols of sky phenomena.[39] These symbols are usually seen in the myth as supreme beings, creators and all-powerful gods. These symbols, in more advanced stages of cultures, are relegated to the background, their places being taken by deities of fertility, ancestor worship, and spirits and gods of nature. The appearance of these deities represents the thirst for concreteness and specificity over against the passivity of the celestial gods.

> The very structure of celestial supreme beings predisposes, one might say, their "religious inactuality." In fact, to understand the ejection of the supreme gods, we must take into consideration these factors: 1) the passivity of celestial gods, explainable by the sky's impassibility and infinite remoteness. . . . 2) the inactivity of the creator, his *otiositas*, after he finished the creation; 3) his "far off, distant and estranged character in the sense that he is not like human beings and does not take part in their drama; 4) the absence of any tragic elements in his existence (contrasted, for example, with the gods of vegetation. . . .)[40]

The movement away from cultic veneration of sky deities to the more concrete deities represents a humanizing tendency in religion, for the concrete deities participate to a degree in the life and activity of man. The homology between the life of plants, the fertility of earth, and the life of man is made possible. The religious life of man now takes on dramatic characteristics.

The old Sky Gods do not disappear completely; their

creative function is often taken over by the Sun, who becomes a giver of fertility; or the Sky Gods take on the
attribute of sovereignty, continuing to symbolize the existence of holiness and transcendence. When the creative role
of the Sky Gods is taken over by some form of solar symbolism, the attribute of omniscience, knowledge—light—
becomes a primary motif in the myths. The omniscience
and knowledge is in contrast with the symbolism of the
earth, which is usually understood to be dark and gloomy,
inhabited by beings grotesque in form and lacking intelligence. Finally, it is the union of earth and sun that forms
the new structure of completeness. The symbolism of union
between earth and sky combines transcendence, intelligence,
and light with darkness, chaos, and formlessness. This symbolism forms a basic structure of all cosmogonic myths of
agricultural societies. The earth becomes not only a womb
or repository, but a powerful goddess taking over some of
the creative attributes of the older Sky Gods. From this
basic symbolism many new structures of the religious life
emerge. However, we observe that the great monotheistic
religions have insisted on the older structure of the Sky God.
The union of earth and sky is rejected and the Sky Gods
create the world directly without the aid of the earth.

All of the religious structures referred to above are
related to specific historical periods. The Sky Gods are
usually found among nomadic pastoralists, whereas the symbolism of hierogamy (union of earth and sky) is found in
agricultural societies. The later valorization of sky deities
in the monotheistic religions is not the same symbolism as
that found among the early nomadic pastoralists. This later
monotheism is in tension with the fertility deities and
spirits, and on the religious level it represents the attempt
to place all the important structures in one deity without
identifying the deity with any one of these forms. In this

sense the deities of monotheistic religions are accessible within the forms of human existence, but they at the same time maintain a certain detachment from these forms. This is the reason the theological problem concerning the freedom of deity is so crucial in Judaism, Christianity, and Islam.

In the myths which follow, we shall not place our emphasis on the historical situation in which the myths occur. We shall be interested primarily in pointing up the various religious structures and symbolism in the cosmogonic myths. To be sure, a particular structure may be interpreted in different ways in various religious communities; however, certain enduring qualities remain regardless of the historical situation.

Our commentaries on each type of myth will highlight some of the general ideas mentioned here by pointing to the concrete symbols and structures in the myths. In many cases the mythical narratives relate events which follow from the act of creation. These portions of the myths have been included to illustrate the connection between creation and other religious meanings.

CHAPTER ONE

EMERGENCE MYTHS

O NE OF THE OLDEST and most widespread of religious symbols is the symbol of
Mother Earth. One can easily understand how the homology
between creation and woman occurs. It is the woman who
bears children; it is she who experiences the mysteries of
birth, growth, and change in ways more precise and profound than man. Echoes of this symbolism may be seen
in the following myths from the northwest frontier of India
and from the Thompson Indians of the Pacific Northwest.

At first Kujum-Chantu, the earth, was like a human being; she had a
head, and arms and legs, and an enormous fat belly. The original
human beings lived on the surface of her belly.

One day it occurred to Kujum-Chantu that if she ever got up and
walked about, everyone would fall off and be killed, so she herself died
of her own accord. Her head became the snow-covered mountains; the
bones of her back turned into smaller hills. Her chest was the valley
where the Apa-Tanis live. From her neck came the north country of
the Tagins. Her buttocks turned into the Assam plain. For just as the
buttocks are full of fat, Assam has fat rich soil. Kujum-Chantu's eyes
became the Sun and Moon. From her mouth was born Kujum-Popi,
who sent the Sun and Moon to shine in the sky.[1]

The structure of the Thompson Indian myth is similar.

A long time ago, before the world was formed, there lived a number of people together. They were the Stars, Moon, Sun, and Earth. The latter was a woman, and her husband was the Sun. The Earth-woman always found fault with her husband, and was disagreeable with him, saying he was nasty, ugly, and too hot. They had several children. At last the Sun felt annoyed at her grumbling, and deserted her. The Moon and Stars, who were relatives of the Sun, also left her, and moved over to where the Sun had taken up his abode. When the Earth-woman saw that her husband and his friends had all deserted her, she became very sorrowful, and wept much. Now Old-One appeared, and transformed Sun, Moon, and Stars into those we see in the sky at the present day, and placed them all so that they should look on the Earth-woman, and she could look at them. He said, "Henceforth you shall not desert people, nor hide yourselves, but shall remain where you can always be seen at night or by day. Henceforth you will look down on the Earth." Then he transformed the woman into the present earth. Her hair became the trees and grass; her flesh, the clay; her bones, the rocks; and her blood, the springs of water. Old-One said, "Henceforth you will be the earth, and people will live on you, and trample on your belly. You will be as their mother, for from you, bodies will spring, and to you they will go back. People will live as in your bosom, and sleep on your lap. They will derive nourishment from you, for you are fat; and they will utilize all parts of your body. You will no more weep when you see your children. . . . . When you die, you will return to your mother's body. You will be covered with her flesh as a blanket, under which your bones will rest in peace."[2]

The words of an Abyssinian woman quoted by Leo Frobenius describe the feminine in more concrete terms.

How can a man know what a woman's life is? A woman's life is quite different from a man's. God has ordered it so. A man is the same from the time of his circumcision to the time of his withering. He is the same before he has sought out a woman for the first time, and afterwards. But the day a woman enjoys her first love cuts her in two. She becomes another woman on that day. The man is the same after his first love as he was before. The woman is from the day of her first love another. That continues so all through life. The man spends a night by a woman and goes away. His life and body are always the same. The woman conceives. As a mother she is another person than the woman without child. She carries the fruit of the night nine months long in her body. Something grows. Something grows into her life that never again departs from it. She is a mother. She is and remains a mother even though her child dies, though all her children die. For at one time she carried the child under her heart. And it does not go out of her heart ever again. Not even when it is dead. All this the man does not know; he knows nothing.[8]

This experience of conceiving and giving birth marks one of the basic distinctions between man and woman and is the basis upon which the homology of woman and fertility symbols are made. A wide range of symbolism derives from this homology. First of all, there is the symbolism of the womb—the dark, hidden, chaotic, watery cavern from which life emerges. Woman is also the earth, the powerful matter from which all forms of life emerge and to which all forms eventually return. Another group of symbols show woman as the seducer, the mother, the wife. It is this basic symbolism which is alluded to in the statement by the Abyssinian woman.

Though the symbols of the Great Mother reach their climax in the great Neolithic cultures of the Near and Far East, they are not simply expressions of agricultural societies. The symbolism of mother as a transcendent reality can be seen in the art of Paleolithic societies. In these societies the symbolism is related to fertility magic, the magical-religious attempt to increase the food supply. While this may be looked upon as a purely economic motivation, it should be remembered that religious man always understands the material basis for his life as a gift from the gods. In all religious life the most important functions of life are never understood to be the result of deterministic laws.

In the Aurignacian culture of the late Paleolithic period in Europe, we find a number of statues in the form of women. The fertility organs are emphasized by the large breasts and buttocks (plates 1, 2). Some scholars have attributed a simple erotic intention to these statues, but given the entire complex of this culture, the burial rites, and climatic conditions, it is safe to assume that the religious-magical, procreative functions of these statues are the dominant meaning of these forms.

Mircea Eliade believes that it is possible to imagine a "primary intuition of the earth as a 'religious' form." This primary intuition is prior to the symbolism of the earth in the form of the Great Mother. Eliade is here referring to the intuition of the earth as the cosmic repository of all forms, latencies, and powers. It is the intuition of the earth as the fertile source of being. The Bambara statue of the Komo society gives us some idea of the powerful manifestation of the earth. The statue seems to be heavy with power waiting to break forth (plate 3).

The chthonic deities are specific manifestations of the powers and latencies present in the earth. When we say that the earth is the repository of all powers and latencies we mean that all later specifications of forms are present in the symbol of earth. A chthonic deity may represent at any one time many different aspects of the power of earth.

In the emergence myths the earth is described as containing within itself all of the potencies of life. The basic motif of these myths is not how the earth came into being but the symbol of earth as the source of all life and forms. Man and the forms of life are as seeds within the body of the earth. The birth of man and his world is described as a metamorphosis in which man progresses from the non-human form of life through the various worlds until he becomes a human being in a human world. A description of the beginning of this metamorphosis is given in Zuñi mythology.[4]

Anon is the nethermost of the four cave-wombs of the world, the seed
of men and creatures took form and increased; even as within eggs in
warm places worms speedily appear, which growing, presently burst
their shells and become as may happen, birds, tadpoles, or serpents, so
did men and all creatures grow manifoldly and multiply in many
kinds. Thus the lowermost womb or cave-world, which was Anosin
tehuli (the womb of sooty depth or of growth-generation because it
was the place of first formation and black as a chimney at night time,
foul too, as the internals of the belly), thus did it become overfilled
with being. Everywhere were unfinished creatures, crawling like reptiles one over another, one spitting on another or doing other in-
decency, insomuch that loud became their murmurings and lamenta-
tions, until many among them sought to escape, growing wiser and
more manlike.

The symbolism of Mother Earth is present in the emergence
myth, but the male element is given no prominence. There
is thus little tension or antagonism expressed in the myths
of this type. In the Navaho myth there is some antagonism
expressed in three of the worlds but, in the last analysis, this
antagonism, which is described as adultery between developing manlike beings and the inhabitants of the particular
world in which they find themselves, is the symbolic mecha-
nism which prompts them to seek another world. It also
points out the unsuitability of each of the worlds for the
beings who finally become men. One could then say that
the myths of emergence describe the process by which men
progress from incompleteness to completeness.

Let us examine some of the structures of these myths.
In the Hanelthnayhe Myths of the Navaho one is struck by
the emphasis placed on light and colors. The various worlds
are described in relationship to color. The beings who
direct them through the various worlds are also described
by their colors. These colors are, within the myth, associated with directions. The movement is from the blackness
of chaos in the first world through the various worlds of

specific colors to the world of light. In some emergence myths the movement through the various underworlds causes dizziness. In the lower worlds color replaces light. We are able to observe in these myths that the progressive evolution of man from the underworlds is at the same time an orientation—this orientation is physical, in the sense of an ordering in space and time (plates 7, 8).

The parallelism of directions and colors in the lower world indicates the incompleteness of these worlds. They are worlds of one color and one direction. The progress through these lower worlds is gradual rather than abrupt. There is no immediate change from darkness to light or from nonbeing to being. A certain type of harmony is present within the creative act. The emergence is also cumulative. The various worlds of specific color are finally harmonized in the final world of light, light being the harmony of the primary colors. Light is also a symbol of knowledge—knowledge which is complete in the last world. In the Pueblo myth described by Parsons, light and directions are aspects of a paradise myth. In paradise (long ago) Sun and Water produced order by finding directions and then leading the people from the underworld. The physical world of light and the ordering of the world in relationship to directions is one aspect of the orientation of man in the world.

In the account of the myth of emergence by Berard Haile, four columns of color are produced by First Man— a white column in the East, blue in the South, yellow in the West and black in the North. H. B. Alexander reports the following account of an emergence myth: "Then the people said to Ateseatine and Atseatsan, 'Raise the sun higher,'. . . . The couple then made four poles, two of turquoise and two of white shell beads, and each was put under the sun and with these poles the twelve men at each of the cardinal

PLATE 1. *"Venus of Lespugue." France.*

PLATE 2. *"The Lady of Sireuil." France.*

PLATE 3. *Komo Society Altar. Africa.*

PLATE 4. *Sky Goddess Nut. Egypt.*

PLATE 5. *Maori Deity.*

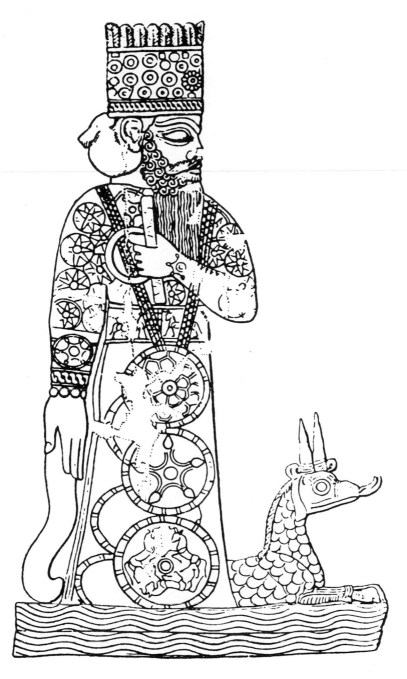

PLATE 6. *The God Marduk. Babylonian.*

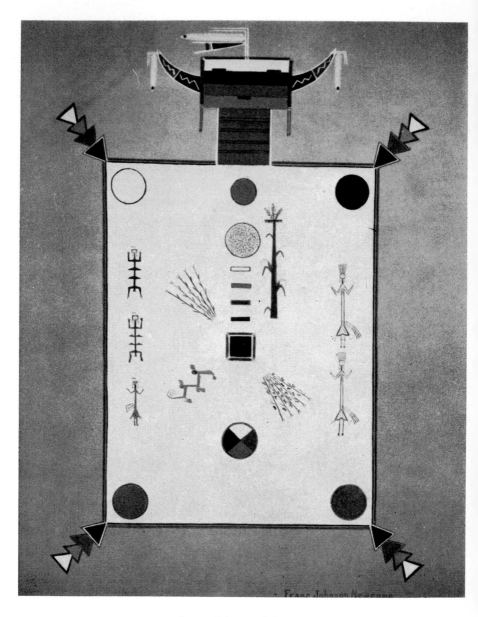

PLATE 7. *The White Spirit Land. Navajo.*

points raised it. They could not get it high enough to prevent the people and grass from burning. The people then said, 'Let us stretch the world'; so the twelve men at each point expanded the world. The sun is finally put in its proper place."[5]

This raising of the earth and sun is reminiscent of certain symbolic structures found in World-Parent myths. In the Polynesian myth Rangi and Papa, the primordial parents, are separated by Tane-mahuta, one of the children of the parents, permitting light to shine where there was darkness. Similar occurrences are to be found in Mesopotamia, Egypt, and India. Echoes of this separation are found in some versions of the emergence myths, but only echoes. The separation is rather mild and does not connote enmity between the offspring of the deities involved. It is quite possible for us to see the primordial male-female structure in the earth-sun structure of the myth, but such a structure is not so explicit. The separation does not constitute a violent act. It is, in keeping with the integrative character of these myths, a necessary but easily accomplished action.

In the myth of emergence recorded by Washington Matthews, the lower worlds are not only worlds of one color peopled by animals, but they represent the loci of human evil. In each of the underworlds, adultery is committed. In the last or fourth world no adultery is committed and the wanderers hold a council and resolve to mend their ways. Furthermore, they meet divine-like creatures who wish to create other beings like them. In this place corn is revealed to them and from this corn First Man and First Woman are born. Thus in the last world man is transformed; he discovers light, helpful divine beings, and corn—the source of life.

These emergence myths, which seem to be peculiar to the Southwestern American Indians, are intimately associated with rituals. The rituals are frequently performed and are highly stylized in terms of bodily actions and pictorial representations. Elaborate sand paintings are produced during each ceremony.

We find no hint in the myths that the process of metamorphosis is not reversible. As a matter of fact, the various worlds could be understood as experimental. The rituals and painting stabilize the last world and control the disruptive elements and beings encountered in the lower worlds. The emphasis is upon the harmonizing of many different elements. Gladys Reichard says that for the Navaho, "Good then . . . is control. Evil is that which is ritually not under control."[6] The world in which man lives is adequate but its structures do not seem to be final and definite. Laura Thompson, in a discussion of the Hopi, another Southwestern American Indian tribe, makes use of the phrase *logico-aesthetic*[7] to describe their cosmos. In using this phrase she emphasizes the manner in which emphasis is given to the immanence of law, the counterbalance of forces, and the internal relatedness of phenomena.

Men have emerged from the earth, but the potencies and latencies within the earth are still a part of his world. No fundamental break with the powers has taken place. The bonds of the earth constitute the immanent principle which operates in all phenomena. Certain deities have prominence in the emergence myth, e.g., the Sun and Corn in their various manifestations, but their pre-eminence is defined by their transformative power, rather than by their sovereignty and transcendence.

The principle of relatedness is the clue to the meaning of the emergence myths. The underworlds which are filled with various types of animals and colors demonstrate the great capacity of the earth to create and the revelation of corn in the final world shows the earth as a beneficent reality.

First Man and First Woman in one of the myths came into being from ears of corn. The earth is the mother of man, man in his totality—man who has completed his metamorphosis and who lives in a world of knowledge and light.

This metamorphosis, which is analogous to the developmental stage of the foetus, shows how the symbol of the earth gives specificity to the feminine element in the human being.[8]

Erich Neumann makes use of a word from Plato's *Timaeus*, the *uroboros*, to describe the static, eternal, unchanging, and nonhistorical origin of all creation.[9] In the emergence myth the *uroboros* is the earth itself. Creation of specific forms from this primordial reality is always accompanied by a display of power—a power which can break through the inertia of the static, nonchanging and undifferentiated character of this reality. As we saw above, this power is symbolized as the power which manifests itself in human birth—a gradual exfoliation of forms.

Even after the creation of man the symbolism of the primordial *uroboros* is still present. In the Navaho emergence myth the first human couple gives birth to five sets of twins, all hermaphrodites. The hermaphroditic nature of these first children carries through the notion of completeness of the level of sexuality and points to the divine origins of man. We shall have occasion to discuss hermaphroditism in the chapters dealing with the cosmic-egg motif.

In the South Pacific myth reported by W. W. Gill, the symbolism of the *uroboros* is expressed by a coconut shell. Not only is this symbolism analogous to the symbolism of earth, but also to the egg symbol. Unlike many of the egg myths, the antagonistic-twins element is omitted. In this myth emphasis is on the Great Mother, who creates from the lowest depths of the shell. She creates beings from her body by tearing out flesh from her sides. Vātea, the father of gods and men, is created by her, but he still bears a chthonic form, half man and half fish. The world is still under the dominance of a *uroboric* form. Vātea, though a creator, has not in this myth extricated himself from the creative structures of the Great Mother.

In these emergence myths we see in a well ordered form the symbolization of that "primary intuition of the earth as a religious form."

THE NAVAHO STORY OF THE EMERGENCE[10]

136. At To'bïlhaskï'di (in the middle of the first world), white arose in the east, and they regarded it as day there, they say; blue rose in the south, and still it was day to them, and they moved around; yellow rose in the west and showed that evening had come; then dark arose in the north, and they lay down and slept.

137. At To'bïlhaskï'di water flowed out (from a central source) in different directions; one stream flowed to the east, another to the south, and another to the west. There were dwelling-places on the border of the stream that flowed to the east, on that which flowed to the south, and on that which flowed to the west also.

138. To the east there was a place called Tan (Corn), to the south a place called Nahodoóla, and to the west a place called Lókatsosakád (Standing Reed). Again, to the east there was a place called Essalái (One Pot), to the south a place called To'hádzïtïl (They Come Often for Water), and to the west a place called Dsïllïtsíbehogán (House Made of the Red Mountain). Then, again, to the east there was a place called Léyahogán (Under-ground House), to the south a place called Tsïltsï'ntha (Among Aromatic Sumac), and to the west a place called Tse'-lïtsíbehogán (House Made of Red Rock).

139. Holatsí Dĭlyĭ'le (dark ants) lived there. Holatsí Lĭtsí (red ants) lived there. Tanĭlaí (dragon flies) lived there. Tsaltsá (yellow beetles) lived there. Woïntlĭ'zi (hard beetles) lived there. Tse'yoáli (stone-carrier beetles) lived there. Kĭnlĭ'zĭn black beetles) lived there. Maitsán (coyote-dung beetles) lived there. Tsápani (bats) lived there. Totsó' (white-faced beetles) lived there. Wonĭstsídi (locusts) lived there. Wonistsídikai (white locusts) lived there. These twelve people started in life there.

140. To the east extended an ocean, to the south an ocean, to the west an ocean, and to the north an ocean. In the ocean to the east lay Tiéholtsodi; he was chief of the people there. In the ocean to the south lived Thaltláhale (Blue Heron), who was chief of the people there. In the ocean to the west lay Tsal (Frog), who was chief of the people there. In the ocean to the north was Idni'dsĭlkaí (White Mountain Thunder), and he was chief of the people there.

141. The people quarrelled among themselves, and this is the way it happened. They committed adultery, one people with an-other. Many of the women were guilty. They tried to stop it, but they could not. Tiéholtsodi, the chief in the east, said: "What shall we do with them? They like not the land they dwell in." In the south Blue Heron spoke to them, and in the west Frog said: "No longer shall you dwell here, I say. I am chief here." To the north White Mountain Thunder said: "Go elsewhere at once. Depart from here!"

142. When again they sinned and again they quarrelled, Tiéhol-tsodi, in the east, would not speak to them; Blue Heron, in the south, would not speak to them; Frog, in the west, would say nothing; and White Mountain Thunder, in the north, would not speak to them.

143. Again, at the end of four nights, the same thing happened. Those who dwelt at the south again committed crime, and again they had contentions. One woman and one man sought to enter in the east (to complain to the chief), but they were driven out. In the south they sought to go in where Blue Heron lay, but

again they were driven out. In the west, where Frog was the chief, again they tried to enter; but again they were driven out. To the north again they were driven out. (The chief) said: "None of you (shall enter here). Go elsewhere and keep on going." That night at Nahodoóla they held a council, but they arrived at no decision. At dawn Tiéholtsodi began to talk. "You pay no attention to my words. Everywhere you disobey me; you must go to some other place. Not upon this earth shall you remain." Thus he spoke to them.

144. Among the women, for four nights, they talked about it. At the end of the fourth night, in the morning, as they were rising, something white appeared in the east. It appeared also in the south, the west, and the north. It looked like a chain of mountains, without a break, stretching around them. It was water that surrounded them. Water impassable, water insurmountable, flowed all around. All at once they started.

145. They went in circles upward till they reached the sky. It was smooth. They looked down; but there the water had risen, and there was nothing else but water there. While they were flying around, one having a blue head thrust out his head from the sky and called to them, saying: "In here, to the eastward, there is a hole." They entered the hole and went through it up to the surface (of the second world).

146. The blue one belonged to the Hastsósidïne', or Swallow People. The Swallow People lived there. A great many of their houses, rough and lumpy, lay scattered all around. Each tapered toward the top, and at that part there was a hole for entrance. A great many people approached and gathered around the strangers, but they said nothing.

147. The first world was red in color; the second world, into which the people had now entered, was blue. They sent out two couriers, a Locust and a White Locust, to the east, to explore the land and see if there were in it any people like themselves. At the end of two days the couriers returned, and said that in one day's

travel they had reached the edge of the world—the top of a great cliff that arose from an abyss whose bottom they could not see; but that they found in all their journey no people, no animals of any kind, no trees, no grass, no sage-brush, no mountains, nothing but bare, level ground. The same couriers were then dispatched in turn to the south, to the west, and to the north. They were gone on each journey two days, and when they returned related, as before, that they had reached the edge of the world, and discovered nothing but an uninhabited waste. Here, then, the strangers found themselves in the centre of a vast barren plain, where there was neither food nor a kindred people. When the couriers had returned from the north, the Swallows visited the camp of the newly arrived people, and asked them why they had sent out the couriers to the east. "We sent them out," was the reply, "to see what was in the land, and to see if there were any people like ourselves here." "And what did your couriers tell you?" asked the Swallows. "They told us that they came to the edge of the world, yet found no plant and no living thing in all the land." (The same questions were asked and the same answers given for the other points of the compass.) "They spoke the truth," said the Swallow People. "Had you asked us in the beginning what the land contained, we would have told you and saved you all your trouble. Until you came, no one has ever dwelt in all this land but ourselves." The people then said to the Swallows: "You understand our language and are much like us. You have legs, feet, bodies, heads, and wings, as we have: why cannot your people and our people become friends?" "Let it be as you wish," said the Swallows, and both parties began at once to treat each other as members of one tribe; they mingled one among the other, and addressed one another by the terms of relationship, as, my brother, my sister, my father, my son, etc.

148. They all lived together pleasantly and happily for twenty-three days; but on the twenty-fourth night one of the strangers made too free with the wife of the Swallow chief, and next

morning, when the latter found out what had happened, he said to the strangers: "We have treated you as friends, and thus you return our kindness. We doubt not that for such crimes you were driven from the lower world, and now you must leave this. This is our land and we will have you here no longer. Besides, this is a bad land. People are dying here every day, and even if we spare you, you cannot live here long." The Locusts took the lead on hearing this; they soared upwards; the others followed, and all soared and circled till they reached the sky.

149. When they reached the sky they found it, like the sky of the first world, smooth and hard with no opening; but while they were circling round under it, they saw a white face peering out at them,—it was the face of Nï'ltsi, the Wind. He called to them and told them if they would fly to the south they would find a hole through which they could pass; so off they flew, as bidden, and soon they discovered a slit in the sky which slanted upwards toward the south; through this slit they flew, and soon entered the third world in the south.

150. The color of the third world was yellow. Here they found nothing but the Grasshopper People. The latter gathered around the wanderers in great numbers, but said nothing. They lived in holes in the ground along the banks of a great river which flowed through their land to the east. The wanderers sent out the same Locust messengers that they had sent out in the second world to explore the land to the east, to the south, to the west, to the north, to find out what the land contained, and to see if there were any kindred people in it; but the messengers returned from each journey after an absence of two days, saying they had reached the end of the world, and that they had found a barren land with no people in it save the Grasshoppers.

151. When the couriers returned from their fourth journey, the two great chiefs of the Grasshoppers visited the strangers and asked them why they had sent out the explorers, and the strangers answered that they had sent them out to see what grew in the

land, and to find if there were any people like themselves in it. "And what did your couriers find?" said the Grasshopper chiefs. "They found nothing save the bare land and the river, and no people but yourselves." "There is nothing else in the land," said the chiefs. "Long we have lived here, but we have seen no other people but ourselves until you came."

152. The strangers then spoke to the Grasshoppers, as they had spoken to the Swallows in the second world, and begged that they might join them and become one people with them. The Grasshoppers consented, and the two peoples at once mingled among one another and embraced one another, and called one another by the endearing terms of relationship, as if they were all of the same tribe.

153. As before, all went well for twenty-three days; but on the twenty-fourth one of the strangers served a chief of the Grasshoppers as the chief of the Swallows had been served in the lower world. In the morning, when the wrong was discovered, the chief reviled the strangers and bade them depart. "For such crimes," he said, "I suppose you were chased from the world below: you shall drink no more of our water, you shall breathe no more of our air. Begone!"

154. Up they all flew again, and circled round and round until they came to the sky above them, and they found it smooth and hard as before. When they had circled round for some time, looking in vain for an entrance, they saw a red head stuck out of the sky, and they heard a voice which told them to fly to the west. It was the head of Red Wind which they saw, and it was his voice that spoke to them. The passage which they found in the west was twisted round like the tendril of a vine; it had thus been made by the wind. They flew up in circles through it and came out in the fourth world. Four of the Grasshoppers came with them; one was white, one blue, one yellow, and one black. We have grasshoppers of these four colors with us to this day.

155. The surface of the fourth world was mixed black and

white. The colors in the sky were the same as in the lower worlds, but they differed in their duration. In the first world, the white, the blue, the yellow, and the black all lasted about an equal length of time every day. In the second world the blue and the black lasted a little longer than the other two colors. In the third world they lasted still longer. In the fourth world there was but little of the white and yellow; the blue and the black lasted most of the time. As yet there was neither sun, moon, nor star.

156. When they arrived on the surface of the fourth world they saw no living thing; but they observed four great snow-covered peaks sticking up at the horizon,—one at the east, one at the south, one at the west, and one at the north.

157. They sent two couriers to the east. These returned at the end of two days. They related that they had not been able to reach the eastern mountain, and that, though they had travelled far, they had seen no track or trail or sign of life. Two couriers were then sent to the south. When they returned, at the end of two days, they related that they had reached a low range of mountains this side of the great peak; that they had seen no living creature, but had seen two different kinds of tracks, such as they had never seen before, and they described such as the deer and the turkey make now. Two couriers were next sent to the west. In two days these returned, having failed to reach the great peak in the west, and having seen no living thing and no sign of life. At last two couriers were sent to the north. When these got back to their kindred they said they had found a race of strange men, who cut their hair square in front, who lived in houses in the ground and cultivated fields. These people, who were engaged in gathering their harvest, the couriers said, treated them very kindly and gave them food to eat. It was now evident to the wanderers that the fourth world was larger than any of the worlds below.

158. The day following the return of the couriers who went to the north, two of the newly discovered race—Kisáni (Pueblos)

they were called—entered the camp of the exiles and guided the latter to a stream of water. The water was red, and the Kisáni told the wanderers they must not walk through the stream, for if they did the water would injure their feet. The Kisáni showed them a square raft made of four logs,—a white pine, a blue spruce, and yellow pine, and a black spruce,—on which they might cross; so they went over the stream and visited the homes of the Kisáni.

159. The Kisáni gave the wanderers corn and pumpkins to eat, and the latter lived for some time on the food given to them daily by their new friends. They held a council among themselves, in which they resolved to mend their manners for the future and do nothing to make the Kisáni angry. The land of the Kisáni had neither rain nor snow; the crops were raised by irrigation.

160. Late in the autumn they heard in the east the distant sound of a great voice calling. They listened and waited, and soon heard the voice nearer and louder. They listened still and heard the voice a third time, nearer and louder than before. Once more they listened, and soon they heard the voice louder still, and clear like the voice of one near at hand. A moment later four mysterious beings appeared to them. These were: Bĭtsís Lakaí, or White Body, a being like the god of this world whom the Navahoes call Hastséyalti; Bĭtsís Dotlĭ'z, or Blue Body, who was like the present Navaho god Tó'nenĭli, or Water Sprinkler; Bĭtsís Lĭtsói, or Yellow Body; Bĭtsís Lĭzĭ'n, or Black Body, who was the same as the present Navaho god of fire, Hastsézĭni.

161. These beings, without speaking, made many signs to the people, as if instructing them; but the latter did not understand them. When the gods had gone, the people long discussed the mysterious visit, and tried to make out what the gods meant by the signs they had made. Thus the gods visited four days in succession. On the fourth day, when the other three had departed, Black Body remained behind and spoke to the people in their own language. He said: "You do not seem to understand the signs

that these gods make you, so I must tell you what they mean. They want to make more people, but in form like themselves. You have bodies like theirs; but you have the teeth, the feet, and the claws of beasts and insects. The new creatures are to have hands and feet like ours. But you are uncleanly, you smell badly. Have yourselves well cleansed when we return; we will come back in twelve days."

162. On the morning of the twelfth day the people washed themselves well. The women dried themselves with yellow corn-meal; the men with white corn-meal. Soon after the ablutions were completed they heard the distant call of the approaching gods. It was shouted, as before, four times,—nearer and louder at each repetition,—and, after the fourth call, the gods appeared. Blue Body and Black Body each carried a sacred buckskin. White Body carried two ears of corn, one yellow, one white, each covered at the end completely with grains.

163. The gods laid one buckskin on the ground with the head to the west; on this they placed the two ears of corn, with their tips to the east, and over the corn they spread the other buckskin with its head to the east; under the white ear they put the feather of a white eagle, under the yellow ear the feather of a yellow eagle. Then they told the people to stand at a distance and allow the wind to enter. The white wind blew from the east, and the yellow wind blew from the west, between the skins. While the wind was blowing, eight of the Mirage People came and walked around the objects on the ground four times, and as they walked the eagle feathers, whose tips protruded from between the buck-skins, were seen to move. When the Mirage People had finished their walk the upper buckskin was lifted,—the ears of corn had disappeared; a man and a woman lay there in their stead.

164. The white ear of corn had been changed into a man, the yellow ear into a woman. It was the wind that gave them life. It is the wind that comes out of our mouths now that gives us life. When this ceases to blow we die. In the skin at the tips of

our fingers we see the trail of the wind; it shows us where the wind blew when our ancestors were created.

165. The pair thus created were First Man and First Woman (Atsé Hastín and Atsé Estsán). The gods directed the people to build an inclosure of brushwood for the pair. When the inclosure was finished, First Man and First Woman entered it, and the gods said to them: "Live together now as husband and wife." At the end of four days hermaphrodite twins were born, and at the end of four days more a boy and a girl were born, who in four days grew to maturity and lived with one another as husband and wife. The primal pair had in all five pairs of twins, the first of which only was barren, being hermaphrodites.

166. In four days after the last pair of twins was born, the gods came again and took First Man and First Woman away to the eastern mountain where the gods dwelt, and kept them there for four days. When they returned all their children were taken to the eastern mountain and kept there for four days. Soon after they all returned it was observed that they occasionally wore masks, such as Hastséyalti and Hastséhogan wear now, and that when they wore these masks they prayed for all good things,— for abundant rain and abundant crops. It is thought, too, that during their visit to the eastern mountain they learned the awful secrets of witchcraft, for the antíhi (witches, wizards) always keep such masks with them and marry those too nearly related to them.

NAVAHO EMERGENCE MYTH ACCORDING TO THE HANELTHNAYHE OR UPWARD-REACHING RITE[11]

There were nine people living there, six kinds of Ants and three kinds of Beetles; and at the east, the south, the west and the north they had four round houses four stories high, which were much like Ant Hills. The small Yellow-Black Ant was chief at the east, the Stag Beetle chief at the south, the Dark Red Ant chief at the west and the Red Ant chief at the north, and they all used the same speech. This world was known as Tsa-Tlai, the First Speech (or Action). They then built a house of four stories in the centre of that world and passed through the lower story to the second chamber or story called Tsa-Naki, the Second Action

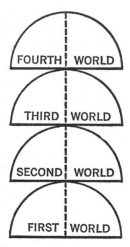

FIG. 1—Showing division of the dark world.

(or Speech). They explored this chamber, going out to its edge, but found the paths to the edge led nowhere. (The Beet Beetle— the Pot Carrier—forgot to bring his pots when passing from the first room and had to return to get them. This accounts for people's forgetfulness in this world.) This second chamber was also devoid of stones and vegetation. It was round like the first chamber, but larger, and there was no light, hence no days. They met two Locust People here and lived near them; eventually they all went up together to the third story or chamber called

Tsa-Trah (Third Speech or Action), but it was not fit to live in. The Locust tried to advise them what to do, but the rest of the people resented this and said that only the chiefs should be heard; after discussion they finally all agreed that the chiefs should settle the action for the people, and then they all moved up to the Fourth Chamber (this is the way people settle disputes now— by referring them to the chiefs.) This chamber was larger than the others and was called Tsa-Di; in this place there were people, but it was all dark, and from this chamber the Hanelthnayhe, the Moving Up or the Emergence, takes its origin. In this world there were two First Men and two First Women, and the First Made Man and the Second Made Man, First Boy and First Girl, also First Scolder, the Coyote. These nine people were living in this chamber and also the Fire God was there. The wealth of First Man was White Shell, Turquoise, Abalone, Jet and Red-White Stone.

First Man placed White Shell at the east and breathed upon it and out of it rose a White Cloud Column. Then he placed Turquoise at the south and when First Man had breathed upon it a Blue Column arose. He placed Abalone at the west and when the second First Man breathed on it a Yellow Column arose in that direction, and he placed Jet at the north. After the second First Man had breathed on it, it formed a Black Cloud Column. As the White East and Yellow West Columns grew, light came from them to the earth, and when these met overhead and crossed, it corresponded to our present mid-day, and this was the first form of Light. When the Blue and Black Columns grew and met overhead Night began and the people slept. First Man also placed Red-White Stone in the centre and breathed on it, and it grew into a Column of many colors. There were four Columns at the cardinal points: the east one was called Folding Dawn, the south one Folding Sky Blue, the west one Folding Twilight and the north one Folding Darkness. The Coyote went visiting to these Columns of light and changed his color to match theirs, so he is called Child of the Dawn, of the Sky Blue, of the Twilight, and of the Darkness, and his power increased as he absorbed these different colors. In each of the directions were baskets covering disks of Holy White Shell, Turquoise, Abalone, and Jet, and these Holy Stones were the food of the nine people living in that world. The basket placed in the centre contains Sickness, Smallpox, Whooping Cough, Nervousness, Paleness and all evil diseases, and First Man and his companions were all evil people practicing witchcraft, they say. The Ant People did not know that these people were evil and the Spider Ant who came with them was also very wicked.

Now the Columns of various colors descended back to the baskets placed at the cardinal points and the central Column descended back to the centre and turned black at the bottom. Above that it became blue, then yellow, and then white, while its upper tip was many-colored. This is the beginning of the Hanelthnayhe Rite of Prayer coming from all directions including the zenith and the nadir, and this movement of the Columns typifies the movement of the prayers from all the holy directions. The black portion of the pillars of light represents the Dark Medicine against Evils (Hanelthnayhe Rite); the yellow portion of the pillar of light and prayer is for other purposes and the white refers to the Blessing Rite, which corrects the effects of the chants against evil. The Blessing Rite may be used in war as well as in rites of witchcraft.

The Spider Ant made friends with the people, particularly with Coyote, who explained the secrets to him, and the Ant people talked with the people of this world and consulted with them on how they should go upward. First Man said he knew how this should be done, that they should move up by the pillars of light and prayers of the different directions; so First Man and Coyote, followed by the rest, grasped the central Column, and it raised them upward. They brought with them all the evils contained in this Column of light and from this they entered the next world, which was red.

THE EMERGENCE, AND THE NEXT WORLD (PUEBLO)[12]

"Long ago when the earth was soft" all the relations with the Spirits were more intimate. Everything could talk, animals, plants, even wood or stone. The kachina came in person to dance or, as at Acoma, to fight. Coyote was a well-behaved messenger between the underworld and White House. The War Brothers begotten by Sun or Water not only produced order by finding the directions or making mountains and valleys but led the migrant people or borrowed curing societies or freed people from dangerous personages or from monsters the women had borne in the lower world after they quarreled with the men. Sun became a handsome man to appear on earth to his sons. It was a golden age. Water gushed from rocks (Isleta). Dew Boy made corn grow for the people of Oraibi in a single day, giving the seeds to the Corn clan. The seeds the Keresan Mothers obtained from their skin were planted at sunrise, ripened at noon, and were dry at sunset. It was only after the trouble with P'ashaya'ni that corn had to be planted as it is planted today. In those days all growth was miraculously rapid. The War Brothers as well as other children begot by the gods grew up overnight or rather in four days. Even human persons were wonderful. The two girls who played hide and seek with Ne'wekwe and perched invisible on his hair plumes were able to do this "because the world was still new. When the world was raw, people used to be like this. They were very wonderful in those days, the old people tell us."

The underworld, the four underground wombs or levels, was

dark (Zuni); Sun sent emissaries to the underworld people to bid them come up into the light. Sun wanted company and prayer-sticks and prayer-meal. In Keresan myth (Acoma excepted) the upper world was dark, the sun was a secondary creation. The "Mothers" send out Ma'sewi to look for the sun and, having found it, to place it properly. Tewa emissaries to the upper world seek for the proper "directions," but they are not aided by Sun. In Tewa, Isleta, and Jemez myth Sun does not figure at all in the Emergence. Hopi make their sun by throwing upward a back tablet or shield covered with buck-skin or cotton cloth together with a fox skin and a parrot tail, for the lights of dawn.

THE BEGINNING OF ALL THINGS AS FOUND IN A SOUTH PACIFIC MYTH OF CREATION[13]

The universe of these islanders is to be conceived of as the hollow of a vast cocoa-nut shell. . . .

The interior of this imaginary shell is named Avaiki. At the top is a single aperture communicating with the upper world, where mortals (i.e. Mangaians) live. At various depths are different floorings, or lands, communicating with each other. But at the very bottom of this supposed cocoa-nut shell is a thick stem, gradually tapering to a point, which represents the very beginning of all things. This point is a spirit or demon, without human form, and is named Te-aka-ia-Roê, or *The-root-of-all-existence*. The entire fabric of the universe is constantly sustained by this primary being (fig. 2).

Above this extreme point is Te-tangaengae, or Te-vaerua; that is to say, *Breathing*, or *Life*. This demon is stouter and stronger than the former one. But the thickest part of the stem is Temanava-roa, or *The-long-lived,* the third and last of the primary, ever-stationary, sentient spirits, who themselves constitute the foundation, and insure the permanence and well-being of all the rest of the universe.

We advance now to the *interior* of the supposed cocoa-nut shell.

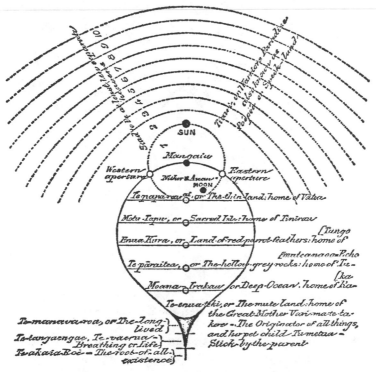

FIG. 2—Diagram of coconut as the model for the cosmos.

In the lowest depth of Avaiki, where the sides of the imaginary shell nearly meet, lives a woman—a demon, of flesh and blood—named Vari-ma-te-takere, or *The-very-beginning.* Such is the narrowness of her territory that her knees and chin touch, no other position being possible. Vari-ma-te-takere was very anxious for progeny. One day she plucked off a bit of her *right* side, and it became a human being—the first man Avatea, or Vātea (the elision of the *a* in Avatea is compensated by the elongation of the second vowel).

Now Vātea, the father of gods and men, was half man and half fish, the division being like the two halves of the human body. The species of fish to which this great divinity was allied being the taairangi (*Cetacea*), or great sea monsters, i.e. porpoises, whose

Fig. 3—Drawing of Vatea, god of the underworld.

sides are covered with pure fat, and whose home is the boundless ocean. Thus one eye of Vātea was human, the other a fish-eye. His right side was furnished with an arm; the left with a fin. He had one proper foot, and half a fish-tail (fig. 3).

But there is another, and probably far more ancient, account of Vātea, or Avatea, which means *noon* in all the dialects of Eastern Polynesia. Vātea is a man possessed of two magnificent eyes, rarely visible at the same time. In general, whilst one, called by mortals the sun, is seen here in this upper world, the other eye, called by men the moon, shines in Avaiki. (A contradictory myth represents the sun and moon as living beings.)

The land assigned by the Great Mother to Vātea was Te-papa-rairai, or *The-thin-land*. Another designation for his home was Te enua mārama o Vātea, or *The-bright-land-of-Vātea*, implying the perfect contrast between the brightness of *noon-day*, or Avatea, and the utter gloom of Po, or *night*, which is equivalent to Avaiki.

On another occasion Vari-ma-te-takere tore off a second bit from that same right side, and it became Tinirau, or *Innumerable*, who, like his brother, had a second and fishy form. The sort of fish which composed his half fish body, was of the *sprat*-kind. The Great Mother gave him the land of Motu-Tapu, or *Sacred Isle* as his own domain. There were his celebrated ponds full of all kinds of fish. Tinirau was lord of the finny inhabitants of the sea, from the shark downwards.

Another day Vari-ma-te-takere took a bit off her *left* side, and it became Tango, or *Support*, who went to live at Enua-Kura, or *The-land-of-red-parrot-feathers*.

A fourth child was produced from a bit of the same left side, and was named Tumuteanaoa, or *Echo*, whose home was Te-pārai-tea, or *The-hollow-grey-rocks*. Echo is represented as a female.

A fifth child originated from a bit of that same left side of the Great Mother, and was designated Raka, or *Trouble*, who presides, like Aeolus, over the winds. Raka found a congenial home in Moana-Irakau, or *Deep-ocean*. Raka received from Vari-ma-te-takere a great basket in which the winds were hidden; also the knowledge of many useful inventions. The children of Raka are the numerous winds and storms which distress mankind. To each child is allotted a hole at the edge of the horizon, through which he blows at pleasure.

Vari, or *The-very-beginning*, finding that her left side had been more injured than her right, resolved to make both sides alike by taking a third bit from the *right* side, and named this, her last child, Tu-metua, *Stick-by-the-parent*. Now, this sixth and most beloved child, as the name implies, lives with the Great Mother in that narrow strip of territory constituting the very bottom of Avaiki, and which is designated Te-enua-te-ki, or *The-mute-land*. Do what you may to the attached mother and daughter, you cannot provoke an angry reply; for the only language known in The-mute-land is that of signs—such as nods, elevated eye-brows, grimaces, and smiles.

Tu-metua is usually shortened into *Tu,* a principal god in most of the Polynesian mythologies, to whom the fourteenth night in every "moon" was sacred. On Cook's second visit to Tahiti, he found the king to be Otoo, ancestor of the present Pomare. Otoo should be written *Tu,* the *O* being a mere prefix to all proper names. This mythological name was adopted in order to secure for its owner the superstitious reverence due to the gods which are unseen by mortals. Tu was the tutelar goddess of Moorea. On Mangaia Tu was invariably linked with her nephew Tangaroa; but was little regarded. The second islet of Hervey's Island is known as "the kingdom of Tu" (au-o-Tu).

At Raiatea Tu-papa = *Tu-of-the-lowest-depths* (the same as Tu-metua) becomes the wife of Rā, the Sun-god, whose too frequent visits to her home required to be checked by Māui.

It was deemed by Vari very unseemly that Vātea's land, which originally was immediately above her own, should be underneath, and so to speak invaded by, his younger brothers.' The-very-beginning, therefore, altered the relative position of The-thin-land, placing it directly under the opening from this upper world; so that the law of primogeniture was established, the lands of all the younger brothers thus lying *underneath* the territory of Noon-day.

Vātea in his dreams several times saw a beautiful woman. On one happy occasion he succeeded in clutching her in his sleep, and thus detained the fair sprite as his wife in his home in Te-papa-rairai. Another account asserts that on Vātea's waking from sleep he could discover no trace of the fair one. He searched in all directions for her—but in vain. At length it occurred to him that her home might be in some dark cavern communicating with a land lower than his own, from which the fair one was in the habit of ascending to The-thin-land to pay him nocturnal visits. To test the correctness of this supposition, Vātea scraped a quantity of cocoa-nuts and scattered handfuls down all the chasms in his territory. Some time afterwards he found that from the bottom of one cave, named Taeva-rangi, or *The-celestial-aperture,* the rich white food had entirely disappeared. A fresh lot of the same dainty food was now thrown down, whilst Vātea from behind a projecting crag cautiously peered down. It was not long before a slender hand, very unlike his own, was slowly extended towards the coveted morsels. Vātea at once concluded that this must belong to the woman he had seen in his dreams. With a favouring current of wind, he descended to the bottom, and caught the fair thief. His visions were realized; this lovely one confessed that she had again and again ascended to his house above in The-thin-land in order to win him as her future husband. She correctly guessed that Vātea would never rest until he had discovered the whereabouts of the fair coquette, and made her his wife. She informed her lover that she was Papa, or *Foundation,* the daughter of Timātekore, or *Nothing-more,* and his wife Tamaiti-ngava-ringa-vari, or *Soft-bodied.* The famed Papa thus became the cherished wife of Vātea; both ascended by another eddy of wind through the chasm to The-bright-land-of-Vātea!

CHAPTER TWO

WORLD-PARENT MYTHS

W E HAVE ALREADY referred in our Introduction to the movement from sky deities to the
concrete deities of fertility in the history of religion. We infer
such a development from the myths and symbols which
are at our disposal. We have no knowledge of a religion
which consists only in the veneration of sky deities; at whatever stage we find religion, the transformation has already
taken place. Even among the Paleolithic people the cave
paintings and statues of mother goddesses support the notion
that cultic activities centered around concrete fertility deities.

In a similar manner we observed in the emergence
myths how the earth as a primordial symbol takes on the
forms of woman and how this form develops into the more
concrete symbolism of the womb, the cave, mother goddesses, etc. Thus in both cases, we observe the movement from
symbols expressive of totality and possibility to those which
give expression to actuality and definiteness.

For purposes of our analysis, we may posit an intermediate stage between the symbols of primordial unity and
the symbols of actuality and concreteness. This intermediate
stage is constituted by that form of symbolism which depicts

the primordial unity of reality, not in terms of either earth or sky alone, but in terms of the union of earth and sky. Here the symbolism of the earth is that of the feminine. It is the coming together of those opposites which expresses the totality from which all other powers and realities finally emerge.

As a matter of fact, the origin of the primordial parents is understood to be the primal chaos in either the form of earth or of a watery chaos. Eldson Best reports that the Maori have a word, *Po*, which has four interrelated definitions. These definitions are: 1) The period of time prior to the existence of the universe; 2) the period of labor of the earth-mother; 3) the period of time after death; and 4) the spirit world—underworld.[1] This notion of *Po* among the Maori refers to the stuff out of which and the method by which creation comes into being. When the *Po* element is emphasized, the creation is seen as a gradual development from embryonic to mature forms in much the same manner as we saw in the emergence myths. The term *Po* in all of its connotations is a symbol of the earth mother who is before all things, who brings all things into being, nurtures them, and receives them at death. The World Parents, Rangi and Papa, appear only at the end of a long genealogy which carries the basic symbolism of emergence.

One cosmogonic condition or phase resulted in another, until they culminated in Earth and Sky, and one of the supernatural offspring of these primal parents became the progenitor of man. Inasmuch as all the foregoing offspring were of the male sex, woman had to be created from the body of Earth Mother ere man could be begotten.[2]

A similar situation occurs in Egypt. The first divine beings emerge from a primordial chaos and give birth to more precise deities who are personifications of natural phenomena. From these beings the sun god Amon emerges. We see here the same genealogical motif as we observed among the Maori. Alongside of this genealogical myth there is present among the Maori and the Egyptians a cosmogonic myth which attributes creation to a Supreme Being (see chapters on Creation from Chaos and Creation from Nothing). In these myths the symbolism of sovereignty of the sky deities reasserts itself in relationship to a social elite. Among the Maori the genealogical version of the myth was the most popular version; the Supreme Being myth remained esoteric. But before the myth of creation by a Supreme Being, we must deal with the World-Parent myth.

The symbol of sky-earth in union is expressive of completeness, totality. For this reason, the myths which present us with this motif never stop at this point, for creation means a qualification of totality whether this totality is conceived of as chaos or primordial unity. The myths which portray the World-Parent motif always relate how and why the parents have been separated. First of all, the union itself is described in chthonic terms. In the Polynesian myth we read, "Darkness then rested upon the heaven and upon the earth and they still both clove together, for they had not been rent apart." In the Babylonian myth the union of heaven and earth is characterized by a type of inactivity and inertia. The noise and activity of the offspring of the primordial couple disturbs the parents. They are threatened by the activity and actuality of their offspring, preferring to remain in the quiet passive stage of very limited activity. Furthermore, Tiamat is a dragon or snakelike monster, conveying in her form many of the chthonic nuances of both earth and the feminine. Heidel argues against the interpretation of Tiamat as a dragon. For Heidel this interpretation is derived from extraliterary sources (Babylonian and Assyrian art) and is not supported by the texts.

No conclusive proof has yet been found for the idea that Tiamat was a dragon, or a similar being, while against it can be cited the testimony of Berossus and of *Enuma elish* to the effect that Tiamat was a woman, the mother of the gods, who had a husband and a lover. . . . Apsu and Tiamat were not simply the ancestors of the gods. They represented at the same time the living, uncreated world-matter; Apsu was the primeval sweet-water ocean, and Tiamat the primeval salt-water ocean. They were matter and divine spirit united and coexistent, like body and soul.[8]

Heidel fails to understand the multivalent nature of symbolism. There is no reason to think that the symbol of the feminine is exhausted by the forms of mother and lover. Tiamat is a symbol of the Great Mother, not only as wife and lover, but also as the avenger and devourer. As avenger and devourer she is related to the dragon symbolism.

We have stated that the symbolism of World Parents represents a limited conception from the indeterminancy of chaos. The important aspect of the World Parents is not just this limited conception but the more radical concretion of forms which are spoken of in the myths as the separation of the World Parents.

K. Numazawa, in his discussion of the separation motif, lists two categories of separation agents.[4] There is, first of all, separation of the World Parents by a woman who is pounding grain. In this myth the low-hanging sky prevents the woman from pounding her grain properly. He relates the myth to a matriarchal complex and to the development of the status of women in agricultural societies. Where this motif is found, Numazawa feels that he can identify some aspect of the matriarchal sphere.

The second category of agents includes sun, fire, and wood. The emphasis of these agents is on the bringing of light to a world which is dark. Often the agents take on the form of solar deities. Marduk, for example, in *Enuma elish* is the symbol of the rising sun, and the prominence of

Amon, the sun god among the Egyptians, attests to this fact. But curiously enough, Numazawa concludes his discussion of this category by saying, "In other words, the sun and light are not the cause of the separation, but rather the result."[5]

This statement by Numazawa does not take account of the dynamic element involved in the separation. The myths, whether among the Polynesians, Egyptians, or Babylonians, convey a sense of urgency regarding the separation. It is a matter of necessity, and while light does not appear before the separation, the *drive* toward light is already present before it becomes a reality. Involved in this drive toward light is insistence upon a precise order and structure of the world over against the rather indeterminate symbolism of the union of the divine couple. Numazawa hints at this interpretation when he refers us to the matriarchal motif in the separation, but this motif does not account for the very complex structure of these myths. One can see in the myths that the separation of the World Parents is followed by a proliferation of forms of beings and cultural activity. In some myths, earth and sky are relegated to the background; in others, these parents suffer some mutilation or destruction. The separation (which is already a disruption) is carried out by the children of the primordial pair who now insist on a life of their own away from the darkness of the parents. New life and new knowledge is the ideology behind the separation motif. But if life is no longer to emerge from the World Parents, what is the new source of creativity and fertility? It is the symbolism of sun god that now takes over the fecundity role. Just as the sun god gives specificity to the symbolism of the sky, different forms of earth or feminine symbolism emerge. In other words, the cosmogonic myth, which emphasizes the separation of earth and sky, at the same time insures continued procreation and fertility in its reference to the creativity which comes into being through the younger gods who now take over the spheres of power.

In one of the American Indian emergence myths we learn of a mass separation of the sexes in primordial time.[6] The men and women could not get along amicably, so they decided to separate. The men agreed to live on one side of a river, the women on the other. During this period of time:

> a young woman, not a maid, was sitting in her house in great misery; her body was hardly covered, for her gown only hung over her in ragged shreds; she was very lousy and was picking the vermin off and scratching herself. While thus engaged her person was almost wholly exposed, and the sun-rays coming through a crevice in the wall, fell upon her vulva, and she moved with pleasure and then fell asleep. She told of this occurrence to some elder women, and it came on to rain, and the water began to drip through the roof, and the elder women said to her, "Lie over yonder and let the rain drops fall upon you," and she went over and the rain drops fell upon her vulva, and again she moved with pleasure and fell asleep. She conceived and gave birth to twins . . .

In this story we see the power of the sun as a fertilizing agent, even after the separation of the sexes.

Konarak, the great Indian temple in Orissa, is dedicated to the sun god. The sculpture of this temple in the words of Coomaraswamy ". . . is a hymn of life, a frank and equisitive glorification of creative forces."[7] The erotic sculpture of this temple symbolizes the creative and pro-creative role of the sun (plates 30 and 31).

We have mentioned the following general characteristics of world parent myths: 1) the union of sky father and earth mother is a symbol of primordial unity; 2) the offspring of this union insists on a separation; and 3) the separation of the parents brings light.

Let us now turn to a more detailed analysis of these

characteristics as they are found in the myths which follow in this chapter.

1) The Symbol of Primordial Unity in the Union of Sky Father and Earth Mother

We have already referred to Neumann's use of the term *uroboros* to describe the unity out of which all life emerges. We have also said that the sexual connotations of this unity represent a more precise designation of the "primary stuff" of creation than the symbolism of water and chaos. In the symbolism of unity which involves the sexual designation, we observe the discovery of sexuality as a mode of expressing transcendence. It should be made clear that feminine and masculine do not in this symbolism refer simply to the male and the female, but to the creative functioning involved in sexuality as a dimension of humanness. The fact that the symbolism of the myth refers to an eternal union of the feminine and masculine makes this point clear. Unity on the level of sexuality has reference to that completeness in which feminine and masculine are in complete harmony without tension or ambiguity. Though the mention of sexual principles adds a degree of specificity to the symbolism, the emphasis of the symbolism falls on potentiality rather than on actuality and definiteness. In the Babylonian creation narrative, *Enuma elish,* we read:

> When on high the heaven had not been named,
> Firm ground below had not been called by name,
> Naught but primordial Apsu, their begetter,
> (And) Mummu-Tiamat, she who bore them all,
> Their waters commingling as a single body;
> No reed hut had been matted, no marsh land had appeared,
> When no gods whatever had been brought into being,
> Uncalled by name, their destinies undetermined—[8]

In the Polynesian myth of Rangi and Papa we confront a similar orientation.

> According to the traditions of our race, Rangi and Papa, or Heaven and Earth, were the source from which, in the beginning, all things originated. Darkness then rested upon the heaven and upon the earth, and they still both clove together, for they had not yet been rent apart; and the children they had begotten were ever thinking amongst themselves what might be the difference between darkness and light; they knew that beings had multiplied and increased, and yet light had never broken upon them, but it ever continued dark.[9]

The other myths in this chapter do not express this chthonic potency as explicitly as do the Babylonian and Polynesian myths, but it is still present nevertheless. In the Egyptian myth related to Hermopolis in Middle Egypt, chaos is conceived of in terms of eight primordial creatures who live in the primeval slime. They are in the form of snakes, frogs, and toads and are both males and females. The sun is the offspring of these primordial creatures. The sun is supposed to retreat at each sunset into the primordial chaos and to be reborn from this chaos at each sunrise.

This symbolism of completeness is made clearer as the myth progresses. The notion of sexuality as a sign of definiteness does not occur until after the separation of the parents; before this time sexuality is a sign of absolutness, passivity, completeness. Neumann relates this harmony of sexual principles to the psychological development of the child.

> It is the same with the pair of opposites male and female. Man's original hermaphroditic disposition is still largely conserved in the child. Without the disturbing influences from outside which foster the visible manifestation of sexual differences at an early date, children would be children; and actively masculine features are in fact as common and effective in girls as are passively feminine ones in boys. It is only cultural influences, whose differentiating tendencies govern the child's early upbringing, that lead to an identification of the ego with the

monosexual tendencies of the personality and to the suppression, or regression, of one's congenital contrasexuality.[10]

The same point is made by Bruno Bettelheim.[11] As we have seen, Bettelheim interprets the mutilation of sexual organs in initiation rites as an attempt on the part of the male to recover the pregenital hermaphroditic childhood principle before a definite emphasis is given to one sexual principle. Neumann believes that it is the influence of culture which makes definite one principle of sexuality over against the other. While this is true, it does not go far enough in its explanation. Since all humans have culture, we must say that there is something in the human condition which insists on emphasis and definiteness. The form of the culture will determine the mode by which this explicitness is made, but the cultural situation does not by itself produce this drive toward explicitness. This drive toward explicitness and concreteness may be related to the development of the psychic structure, but such an interpretation does not account for the total situation involved in the myth. While the cultural situation is not totally explanatory of the phenomenon under discussion, it cannot be dismissed. The mythological material symbolizes not only the cultural situation, the psychic orientation, but relates these dimensions to a notion of reality which one is forced to recognize as religion. By religion, we have reference to the fact that in and through the modes of expression we observe the need for an ontological or transcendental base for the explicitness and concreteness which breaks forth from the primordial unity.

2) The Offspring of Earth and Sky as Agents of Separation

Generally speaking, the offspring of earth and sky insist on the separation of the parents, because they do not wish to be crushed, or they desire light in place of the darkness of their abode. Thus, in one of the Minyong myths from India we read, ". . . Wiyus, men and animals held a Kebang to consider how they could save themselves from being crushed between them."[12] In the Polynesian myth it is the problem of darkness, and in the Babylonian myth it is the desire for freedom of activity. The characteristics may all be subsumed under the more general notion of actuality. As long as the parents are in union, their offspring are not "real." Their being is dominated by the union of the parents; they live in darkness without room for the expression of their unique modes of being. They represent potential modes of being. The separation of the World Parents is the action which will allow them to become concrete and actual or free beings.

In the Polynesian myth the offspring do not all agree to the separation. We read in the myth that Tawhiri-ma-tea, the father of winds and storms, refused to consent to the separation proposed by Tane-mahuta. After the separation, warfare ensues between the forces of Tane-mahuta and Tawhiri-ma-tea.[13] Eldson Best sees in this struggle the contest between Light and Darkness.[14] While this is certainly an ingredient in the struggle, the ethical emphasis of Best should be supplemented. The struggle represents the attempt of the primordial parents to adjust to a new situation. In other words, the relationship of man to the earth after the separation is the crux of the problem.

We mentioned in our Introduction the change which took place regarding sky deities. With the appearance of more concrete deities, the sky deities retreat to the background. However, the symbolism of sovereignty remains and continues to inform religious symbolism. The same situation obtains in relationship to the symbolism of the earth mother. The separation of the parents and the ascendancy of the deities of light do not entirely destroy the symbolism of the older sky deities or the earth mother. These deities remain, sometimes in a subordinate role, but nevertheless they are there as a residue—a residue which still orders the limits of any new form of creativity. In the Babylonian myth, Marduk, after defeating Tiamat, "paused to view her dead body that he might do artful works." From the dead body of Tiamat he reconstructs the universe. In the account of the Egyptian creation, which we have from Adolph Erman,[15] Re, the sun god, is on the verge of slaughtering all the people. He is advised by Nun not to take such drastic action, but to send forth his eye to frighten the people. Nun is the primeval matter which surrounds and supports the earth. She is a symbol of the feminine, and in this instance, she shows her beneficent character. In the Zuñi myths we see also this beneficent character of the earth mother manifesting itself.[16] The earth mother in these two myths is concerned for the welfare of the offspring, and she convinces the sky father to help her in providing for their security. A new mode of being for the feminine dimension of human life results from the separation of the World Parents.

The separation of the World Parents is often spoken of in terms of its sociological meaning; that is, it is interpreted as the triumph of the patriarchy over a matriarchy. Insofar as new dimensions of sexuality are discovered, it is not strange that they should find expression in the life of society, but we should bear in mind that neither patriarchy nor matriarchy means the absolute elimination of either sex. It refers to the dominance of one sex in some areas of cultural life. The dominance in some areas of cultural life leaves other areas open for the exploration of the other sex. It is quite possible that new dimensions of sexuality as a mode of being occur precisely because of the dominance of one sex in the affairs of culture.

One other aspect of the agents of separation remains to

be discussed. In both the Polynesian and the Babylonian accounts several of the offspring participate in the various phases of the separation before it is completed. In the Polynesian myth, several of the offspring attempt to perform the separation before it is accomplished by Tane-mahuta, and in the Babylonian account, Tiamat conquers several of the offspring before she is defeated by Marduk. In a version of the Egyptian creation myth given by Erman, Shu, the god of the atmosphere, shoved himself between Nut, the goddess of heaven, and Seb, the earth god. This section of the myth ends with the sentence, "Only the bones of Shu, those wonderful arms which support Nut, connect the upper and lower world."[17]

This aspect of the myth makes it clear that the bringing about of the new order is not an easy task. The inertia and passivity of the primordial couple are almost imponderable and only an extreme exertion of power can separate them. Furthermore, the offspring who manages to separate them, or defeat one of them, as in the case of Marduk, shows himself to be the most powerful of the offspring. Any subsequent fight with this offspring is bound to fail, for he has already shown himself to be the most powerful of the offspring. The absoluteness of his power is made manifest. The new structure which he creates is thus undergirded by great power—power which gives stability to the new order.

3) Separation, Light, and Knowledge

The separation of the parents allows light to shine where previously there was darkness. "There was darkness from the first division of time, unto the tenth, to the hundredth, to the thousandth."[18] These words are from the Polynesian myth. In the Egyptian, Zuñi, Polynesian, and Northeast Indian myths the union of the World Parents is a synonym for confusion and chaos. But the two symbols of the union are related. Light and order occur when the parents are separated. Light is a symbol of knowledge and order. It is for this reason that solar deities—bringers of light—dominate after the separation of the World Parents.

We find the sun symbolism in its highest form in Egypt. Frankfort lists the various names which are given to the sun by the Egyptians:

Re was an almost neutral term for the sun; Atum, meaning possibly "the All" or the "Not (Yet?) Being," referred to the sun as demiurge; Khepri ("He Who Becomes"), appearing as a beetle, applied mostly to the morning sun, while the Aten proclaimed to be the one god by Akhenaten, was for the Egyptians in general the actual heavenly body, the orb of the sun. Harakhte, the falcon, as we have seen, referred to the ancient sky god Horus as manifest in the most powerful object of the sky. . . .[19]

Frankfort quotes an Egyptian hymn to the sun which conveys some of the religious aura surrounding this symbolism:

Hail to thee, sun disk (Aten) of the day!
Creator of all,
Who made their life;
Great falcon, feathered in many hues,
Who came into being to lift himself;
Who came into being by himself, without sire;
Eldest Horus who dwellest upon Nut;
Whom one acclaims when he shines forth
And likewise at his setting.

Thou who shapest what the earth produces,
Khnum and Amon of men;
Who hast taken possession of the Two Lands
From the greatest to the smallest of that which is in them;
Patient artist,
Great in perseverance at innumerable works;
Courageous shepherd driving his sheep and goats,
Their refuge, made so that they may live.

Hurrying, approaching, running,
Khepri, highly born,
Who lifts his beauty to the body of Nut

And illuminates the Two Lands with his disk;
Primeval god who created himself,
Who sees what he should do; Sole Lord
Who reaches daily the ends of the lands
And views those who walk there;
Who rises in the sky in the shape of the sun,
That he may create the seasons out of the months—
Heat when he wants it, cold when he wills it.
He lets the limbs grow faint and then embraces them;
Every land prays daily at his rising in his praise.[20]

The movement of the sun through the heavens each day is a sign of order and regularity. It symbolizes the victory of the sun over chaos and is simultaneously a symbol of immortality. The inflexibility of its order is furthermore given an ethical interpretation so that the king as a representation of the sun is the guardian of justice. As the god of justice, the sun is also an omniscient deity. He is, in the words of Pettazzoni, an All-Knowing God.[21] The identification of the sun with every other concrete deity is a way of expressing his omnipotence and omniscience.

The light of the sun is at the same time the light of knowledge. This knowledge may finally be identified in abstract ethical terms and related to a supreme deity (see Chapter Four). This can be seen in the identification of the Egyptian sun god, Re, with justice and omnipotence. These attributes are synonymous for order. Ananda Coomaraswamy relates the notion of knowledge and ethics to the religious idea of spiritual paternity.[22] He cites many examples to show how the sun as the progenitor of life is also the source of knowledge and judgment. The life of man imitates the divine life because the divine life has been implanted in him through the "kiss of the sun." He cites the following texts from Indian literature to illustrate his point.

". . . Where is the maker? Whence has it arisen? How will it perish?" (Sanigatha Nikaya 1:134). The answers to all these questions had long since been given: "The Sun is the fastening to which these worlds are linked . . . He strings these worlds to himself by a thread, the thread of the Gale." (Satapatha Brahmana VI:7.117 and VIII:7.3.10). So it is that "all this universe is strung on Me, like rows of gems on a thread;" (Bhagavad Gita VII:7; cf. Tripura Rahasya) and, "verily, he who knows *that* thread, and the Inner Controller who from within controls this and the other world and all beings, he knows Brahma, he knows the Gods, the Vedas, Being, Self, and everything." Brhadarangaka Upanishad III:7.1).[23]

The fight between the offspring in the Polynesian myth finally determines the new order which is established. The solar deities establish and guarantee the new order which has come into being. In the first instance the solar deities become fertilizing deities. The solar deities take over this function and are thus related to the concrete symbolism of feminine fertility symbols.

In the Zuñi myth reported by Cushing, we read,

Then did the Sun-father take counsel within himself, and casting his glance downward espied, on the great waters, a Foam-cap near to the Earth-mother. With his beam he impregnated and with his heat incubated the Foam-cap, whereupon she gave birth to Uanam Achi Piahkoa, the Beloved Twain. . . .[24]

The remainder of this myth shows how specific modes and techniques are given to man from the knowledge and power of the Sun-father. "And of men and all creatures he gave them the fathership and dominion, also as a man gives over the control of his work to the management of his hands."[25]

Generally speaking, among the American Indians the symbolism of the sun plays a paramount role. The myths and ceremonies related to this symbol express fertility and procreation. In the ceremonies and rites of the sun dance, prominence is given to the use of tobacco, sweet grass, sage, the fat of animals, colors of the world quarters, and furs. Equally important is the homology of the sun to the tree of life and its fertility. Among the Plains Indians the symbolism of the sun is related to the bison. The bison is the symbol of sustenance, abundance, and procreation. H. B. Alexander reports that in the Arapaho sun dance buffalo robes are worn by the impersonators of the Creator. One of the prayers recited during the ceremony is as follows:

> My Father, have pity upon us! Remember we are your children since the time you created the heavens and earth, with a man and woman!
>
> Our Grandfather, the Central-Moving-Body who gives light, watch us in the painting of the belt which our Father directed. . . . May our thought reach to the sky where there is holiness.
>
> Give us good water and an abundance of food![26]

The relationship of the solar deity to procreation in the form of cattle is also present in Egypt. The rising and setting of the sun already carried the symbolism of birth and rebirth. This symbolism of rebirth was reinforced by its relationship to cattle. "The sun is a powerful bull; the sky is a cow. . . . So we see the cow of heaven studded with stars and with the sun-boat sailing along her body, a woman bending over the earth upon which the sun, whom she has borne, falls down merely to take wing as a beetle"[27] (plates 4 and 6). The bull and the cow are thus more concrete symbols of fertility in Egyptian mythology, and these symbols are related to the overpowering fertility of the sun god.

In the Polynesian myth, Tane-mahuta is a personification of the sun. He produced trees, but he is also spoken of as the producer of water, stones, snow, hail, and other atmospheric phenomena. Tane-mahuta is in some Polynesian myths the progenitor of birds. He renders the forest fertile and enables trees to reproduce their species.

The solar deities are not only procreative but are equally guarantors of the new cosmic order. We have already cited the enmity between Re, the Egyptian sun god, and his progeny. They work to overthrow his order, but Re upholds the order by a display of his eye—his light. In the myth from the Dhammai of northeast India, Shuzanghu rescues her off-spring from the body of the worm Phangnalomang, and the various trials of the offspring of earth and sky, before a suc-cessful separation and victory is accomplished by the solar deity, points to this deity as an all-powerful being able to uphold his creation in the face of any threat.

The separation of the World Parents signals the birth of a new cosmic order. It is not strange that this type of sym-bolism is found in agricultural societies. These societies made possible the discovery of new dimensions of sexuality and sacredness. A corresponding diminution of the earth and sky deities results from this new discovery. The symbolism of the earth and sky are not lost. They remain on new and differ-ent levels. The earth still remains a source of birth, but in a different form, and the sky deities still express sovereignty and power, but on a level removed from the concreteness of the life of man. When the sky deities appear again, they carry with them monotheistic tendencies. But even then the earth symbolism is not completely lost. While more concrete deities, those deities who are primarily the agents of the separation, appear . . . the tension between these deities and the pri-mordial parents still remains. In the last analysis the pri-mordial World Parents seem to be eternal structures, setting the limits within which the symbolism of the more concrete and precise symbols must manifest themselves.

THE BABYLONIAN CREATION EPIC[28]

TABLET 1

When on high the heaven had not been named,
Firm ground below had not been called by name,

Naught but primordial Apsû, their begetter,
(And) Mummu-Tiamat, she who bore them all,
Their waters commingling as a single body;
No reed hut had been matted, no marsh land had appeared,
When no gods whatever had been brought into being,
Uncalled by name, their destinies undetermined—
Then it was that the gods were formed within them.
Lahmu and Lahamu were brought forth, by name they were
    called.
For aeons they grew in age and stature.
Anshar and Kishar were formed, surpassing the others.
They prolonged the days, added on the years.
Anu was their son, of his fathers the rival;
Yea, Anshar's first-born, Anu, was his equal.
Anu begot in his image Nudimmud.
This Nudimmud was of his fathers the master;
Of broad wisdom, understanding, mighty in strength,
Mightier by far than his grandfather, Anshar.
He had no rival among the gods, his brothers.
The divine brothers banded together,
They disturbed Tiamat *as they surged back and forth.*
Yea, they troubled the mood of Tiamat
By their *hilarity* in the Abode of Heaven.
Apsû could not lessen their clamor
And Tiamat was speechless at their [*ways*].
Their doings were loathsome unto [. . .].
Unsavory were their ways; they were *overbearing.*
Then Apsû, the begetter of the great gods,
Cried out, addressing Mummu, his vizier:
"O Mummu, my vizier, who rejoicest my spirit,
Come hither and let us go to Tiamat!"
They went and sat down before Tiamat,
Exchanging counsel about the gods, their first-born.
Apsû, opening his mouth,
Said unto *resplendent* Tiamat:

"Their ways are verily loathsome unto me.
By day I find no relief, nor repose by night.
I will destroy, I will wreck their ways,
That quiet may be restored. Let us have rest!"
As soon as Tiamat heard this,
She was wroth and called out to her husband.
She cried out aggrieved, as she raged all alone,
Injecting woe into her mood:
"What? Should we destroy that which we have built?
Their ways indeed are most troublesome, but let us attend
    kindly!"
Then answered Mummu, giving counsel to Apsû;
[*Ill-wishing*] and ungracious was Mummu's advice:
"Do destroy, my father, the mutinous ways.
Then shalt thou have relief by day and rest by night!"
When Apsû heard this, his face grew radiant
Because of the evil he planned against the gods, his sons.
As for Mummu, by the neck he embraced him
As (that one) sat down on his knees to kiss him.
(Now) whatever they had plotted between them
Was repeated unto the gods, their first-born.
When the gods heard (this), they were astir,
(Then) lapsed into silence and remained speechless.
Surpassing in wisdom, accomplished, resourceful,
Ea, the all-wise, saw through their scheme.
A master design against it he devised and set up,
Made artful his spell against it, surpassing and holy.
He recited it and made it subsist in the deep,
As he poured sleep upon him. Sound asleep he lay.
When Apsû he had made prone, drenched with sleep,
Mummu, the adviser, was *impotent to move.*
He loosened his band, tore off his tiara,
Removed his halo (and) put it on himself.
Having fettered Apsû, he slew him.

Mummu he bound and left behind lock.
Having thus upon Apsû established his dwelling,
He laid hold on Mummu, holding him by the nose-rope.
After he had vanquished and trodden down his foes,
Ea, his triumph over his enemies secured,
In his sacred chamber in profound peace he rested.
He named it "Apsû," for shrines he assigned (it).
In that same place his cult hut he founded.
Ea and Damkina, his wife, dwelled (there) in splendor.
In the chamber of fates, the abode of destinies,
A god was engendered, most potent and wisest of gods.
In the heart of Apsû was Marduk created,
In the heart of holy Apsû was Marduk created.
He who begot him was Ea, his father;
She who conceived him was Damkina, his mother.
The breasts of goddesses he did suck.
The nurse that nursed him filled him with awesomeness.
Alluring was his figure, sparkling the lift of his eyes.
Lordly was his gait, commanding from of old.
When Ea saw him, the father who begot him,
He exulted and glowed, his heart filled with gladness.
He rendered him perfect and endowed him with a double god-
    head.
Greatly exalted was he above them, exceeding throughout.
Perfect were his members beyond comprehension,
Unsuited for understanding, difficult to perceive.
Four were his eyes, four were his ears;
When he moved his lips, fire blazed forth.
Large were all four hearing organs,
And the eyes, in like number, scanned all things.
He was the loftiest of the gods, surpassing was his stature;
His members were enormous, he was exceeding tall.
"My little son, my little son!
My son, the Sun! Sun of the heavens!"

Clothed with the halo of ten gods, he was strong to the utmost,
As their (awe)some flashes were heaped upon him.
[. . .] the four winds Anu begot
To restrain the griffin, leader of the host.
[. . .] . . . to disturb Tiamat.
Disturbed was Tiamat, astir day and night.
[*The gods*], in malice, *contributed to the storm.*
Their insides having plotted evil,
To Tiamat these brothers said:
"When they slew Apsû, thy consort,
Thou didst not aid him but remainedst still.
Although he fashioned the awesome Saw,
Thy insides are diluted and so we can have no rest.
Let Apsû, thy consort, be in thy mind
And Mummu, who has been vanquished! Thou art left alone!
[. . .] thou pacest about hurriedly,
[. . . without ce]ase. Thou dost not love us!
[. . .] clouded are our eyes,
[. . .] without cease. Let us have rest!
[. . . *to batt*]*le.* Do thou avenge them!
[. . .] and render (them) as the wind!"
[When] Tiamat [heard] (these) words, she was pleased:
"[. . .] you have given. Let us make *monsters.*
[. . .] and the gods in the mid[st . . .]
[. . . let us do] battle and against the gods [. . .]!"
They thronged and marched at the side of Tiamat.
Enraged, they plot without cease night and day,
They are set for combat, growling, raging,
They form a council to prepare for the fight.
Mother Huber, she who fashions all things,
Added matchless weapons, bore monster-serpents,
Sharp of tooth, unsparing of *fang.*
[With venom] for blood she has filled their bodies.
Roaring dragons she has clothed with terror,

Has crowned them with haloes, making them like gods,
So that he who beholds them shall perish abjectly,
(And) that, with their bodies reared up, none might turn [them
    back].
She set up the Viper, the Dragon, and the *Sphinx,*
The Great-Lion, the Mad-Dog, and the Scorpion-Man,
Mighty lion-demons, the Dragon-fly, the Centaur——
Bearing weapons that spare not, fearless in battle.
Firm were her decrees, past withstanding were they.
Withal eleven of this kind she brought [forth].
From among the gods, her first-born, who formed [her Assembly],
She elevated Kingu, made him chief among them.
The leading of the ranks, command of the Assembly,
The raising of weapons for the encounter, advancing to combat,
In battle the command-in-chief—
These to his hand she entrusted as she seated him in the Council:
"I have cast for thee the spell, exalting thee in the Assembly of
    the gods.
To counsel all the gods I have given thee full power.
Verily, thou art supreme, my only consort art thou!
Thy utterance shall prevail over all the Anunnaki!"
She gave him the Tablets of Fate, fastened on his breast:
"As for thee, thy command shall be unchangeable, [Thy word]
    shall endure!"
As soon as Kingu was elevated, possessed of [the rank of Anu],
For the gods, his [*var.* her] sons, [they decreed] the fate:
"Your word shall make the fire subside,
Shall humble the 'Power-Weapon,' so potent in (its) *sweep!"* . . .

TABLET IV

They erected for him a princely throne.
Facing his fathers, he sat down, presiding.

"Thou art the most honored of the great gods,
Thy decree is unrivaled, thy command is Anu.
Thou, Marduk, art the most honored of the great gods,
Thy decree is unrivaled, thy word is Anu.
From this day unchangeable shall be thy pronouncement.
To raise or bring low—these shall be (in) thy hand.
Thy utterance shall come true, thy command shall not be
    doubted.
No one among the gods shall transgress thy bounds!
Adornment being wanted for the seats of the gods,
Let the place of their shrines ever be in thy place.
O Marduk, thou art indeed our avenger.
We have granted thee kingship over the universe entire.
When in Assembly thou sittest, thy word shall be supreme.
Thy weapons shall not fail; they shall smash thy foes!
O lord, spare the life of him who trusts thee,
But pour out the life of the god who seized evil."
Having placed in their midst a piece of cloth,
They addressed themselves to Marduk, their first-born:
"Lord, truly thy decree is first among gods.
Say but to wreck or create; it shall be.
Open thy mouth: the cloth will vanish!
Speak again, and the cloth shall be whole!"
At the word of his mouth the cloth vanished.
He spoke again, and the cloth was restored.
When the gods, his fathers, saw the fruit of his word,
Joyfully they did homage: "Marduk is king!"
They conferred on him scepter, throne, and palū;
They gave him matchless weapons that ward off the foes:
"Go and cut off the life of Tiamat.
May the winds bear her blood to places undisclosed."
Bel's destiny thus fixed, the gods, his fathers,
Caused him to go the way of success and attainment.
He constructed a bow, marked it as his weapon,

Attached thereto the arrow, fixed its bow-cord.
He raised the mace, made his right hand grasp it;
Bow and quiver he hung at his side.
In front of him he set the lightning,
With a blazing flame he filled his body.
He then made a net to enfold Tiamat therein.
The four winds he stationed that nothing of her might escape,
The South Wind, the North Wind, the East Wind, the West
    Wind.
Close to his side he held the net, the gift of his father, Anu.
He brought forth Imhullu, "the Evil Wind," the Whirlwind, the
    Hurricane,
The Fourfold Wind, the Sevenfold Wind, the Cyclone, the
    Matchless Wind;
Then he sent forth the winds he had brought forth, the seven of
    them.
To stir up the inside of Tiamat they rose up behind him.
Then the lord raised up the flood-storm, his mighty weapon.
He mounted the storm-chariot irresistible [and] terrifying.
He harnessed (and) yoked to it a team-of-four,
The Killer, the Relentless, the Trampler, the Swift.
Sharp were their teeth, bearing poison.
They were versed in ravage, in destruction skilled.
[.] . . they smote, they were fearsome in battle.
To the left of [the right] *they will not open* [.] . .
For a cloak he was wrapped in [an armor] of terror;
With his fearsome halo his head was turbaned.
The lord went forth and followed his course,
Towards the raging Tiamat he set his face.
In his lips he held [*a* . . .] of red paste;
A plant to put out poison was grasped in his hand.
Then they milled about him, the gods milled about him,
The gods, his fathers, milled about him, the gods milled about
    him.

The lord approached to scan the inside of Tiamat,
(And) of Kingu, her consort, the scheme to perceive.
As he looks on, his course becomes upset,
His will is distracted and his doings are confused.
And when the gods, his helpers, who marched at his side,
Saw the valiant hero, blurred became their vision.
Tiamat emitted [a cry], without turning her neck,
Framing savage defiance in her lips:
"Too [imp]ortant art thou [for] the lord of the gods to rise up
    against thee!
Is it in their place that they have gathered, (or) in thy place?"
Thereupon the lord, having [raised] the flood-storm, his mighty
    weapon,
[To] enraged [Tiamat] he sent word as follows:
"[*Mightily*] art thou risen, art haughtily exalted;
[Thou hast] charged thine own heart to stir up conflict,
[So that] sons reject their own fathers,
[And thou], who has born them, dost hate . . [.]!
Thou has aggrandized Kingu to be (thy) consort;
[A rule], not rightfully his, thou has substituted for the rule of
    Anu.
Against Anshar, king of the gods, thou seekest evil;
[Against] the gods, my fathers, thou hast confirmed thy wickedness.
[Though] drawn up be thy forces, girded on thy weapons,
Stand thou up, that I and thou meet in single combat!"
When Tiamat heard this,
She was like one possessed; she took leave of her senses.
In fury Tiamat cried out aloud.
To the roots her legs shook both together.
She recites a charm, keeps casting her spell,
While the gods of battle sharpen their weapons.
Then joined issue Tiamat and Marduk, wisest of gods.
They *swayed* in single combat, locked in battle.
The lord spread out his net to enfold her,

The Evil Wind, which followed behind, he let loose in her face.
When Tiamat opened her mouth to consume him,
He drove in the Evil Wind that she close not her lips.
As the fierce winds charged her belly,
Her body was distended and her mouth was wide open.
He released the arrow, it tore her belly,
It cut through her insides, splitting the heart.
Having thus subdued her, he extinguished her life.
He cast down her carcass to stand upon it.
After he had slain Tiamat, the leader,
Her band was shattered, her troupe broken up;
And the gods, her helpers who marched at her side,
Trembling with terror, turned their backs about,
In order to save and preserve their lives.
Tightly encircled, they could not escape.
He made them captives, and he smashed their weapons.
Thrown into the net, they found themselves ensnared;
Placed in cells, they were filled with wailing;
Bearing his wrath, they were held imprisoned.
And the eleven creatures which she had charged with awe,
The band of demons that marched.[. .] before her,
He cast into fetters, their hands [. . .].
For all their resistance, he trampled (them) underfoot.
And Kingu, who had been made chief among them,
He bound and accounted him to Uggae.
He took from him the Tablets of Fate, not rightfully his,
Sealed (them) with a seal and fastened (them) on his breast.
When he had vanquished and subdued his adversaries,
Had wholly established Anshar's triumph over the foe,
Had . . . the vainglorious foe,
Nudimmud's desire had achieved, valiant Marduk
Strengthened his hold on the vanquished gods,
And turned back to Tiamat whom he had bound.
The lord trod on the legs of Tiamat,

With his unsparing mace he crushed her skull.
When the arteries of her blood he had severed,
The North Wind bore (it) to places undisclosed.
On seeing this, his fathers were joyful and jubilant,
They brought gifts of homage, they to him.
Then the Lord paused to view her dead body,
That he might divide the monster and do artful works.
He split her like a shellfish into two parts:
Half of her he set up and ceiled it as sky,
Pulled down the bar and posted guards.
He bade them to allow not her waters to escape.
He crossed the heavens and surveyed (its) regions.
He squared Apsû's quarter, the abode of Nudimmud,
As the lord measured the dimensions of Apsû.
The Great Abode, its likeness, he fixed as Esharra,
The Great Abode, Esharra, which he made as the firmament.
Anu, Enlil, and Ea he made occupy their places.

TABLET V

He constructed stations for the great gods,
Fixing their astral likenesses as constellations.
He determined the year by designating the zones;
He set up three constellations for each of the twelve months.
After defining the days of the year [by means] of (heavenly) figures,
He founded the station of Nebiru to determine their (heavenly)
     bands,
That none might transgress or fall short.
Alongside it he set up the stations of Enlil and Ea.
Having opened up the gates on both sides,
He strengthened the locks to the left and the right.
In her belly he established the zenith.
The Moon he caused to shine, the night (to him) entrusting.

He appointed him a creature of the night to signify the days:
"Monthly, without cease, form designs with a crown.
At the month's very start, rising over the land,
Thou shalt have luminous horns to signify six days.
On the seventh day be thou a [half]-crown.
At full moon stand in opposition in mid-month.
When the sun [overtakes] thee at the base of heaven,
Diminish [thy crown] and retrogress in light.
[At the time of disappearance] approach thou the course of the
    sun,
And [on the twenty-ninth] thou shalt again stand in opposition to
    the sun."

THE CHILDREN OF HEAVEN AND EARTH (POLYNESIA) [29]

Men had but one pair of primitive ancestors; they sprang from the vast heaven that exists above us, and from earth which lies beneath us. According to the traditions of our race, Rangi and Papa, or Heaven and Earth, were the source from which, in the beginning, all things originated. Darkness then rested upon the heaven and upon the earth, and they still both clave together, for they had not yet been rent apart; and the children they had begotten were ever thinking amongst themselves what might be the difference between darkness and light; they knew that beings had multiplied and increased, and yet light had never broken upon them, but it ever continued dark. Hence these sayings are found in our ancient religious services: "There was darkness from the first division of time, unto the tenth, to the hundredth, to the thousandth," that is, for a vast space of time; and these divisions of times were considered as beings, and were each termed a Po;

and on their account there was yet no world with its bright light, but darkness only for the beings which existed.

At last the beings who had been begotten by Heaven and Earth, worn out by the continued darkness, consulted amongst themselves, saying, "Let us now determine what we should do with Rangi and Papa, whether it would be better to slay them or to rend them apart." Then spoke Tu-matauenga, the fiercest of the children of Heaven and Earth, "It is well, let us slay them."

Then spake Tane-mahuta, the father of forests and of all things that inhabit them, or that are constructed of trees, "Nay, not so. It is better to rend them apart, and to let the heaven stand far above us, and the earth lie beneath our feet. Let the sky become as a stranger to us, but the earth remain close to us as a nursing mother."

The brothers all consented to this proposal, with the exception of Tawhiri-ma-tea, the father of winds and storms, and he, fearing that his kingdom was about to be overthrown, grieved greatly at the thought of his parents being torn apart. Five of the brothers willingly consented to the separation of their parents, but one of them would not consent to it.

Hence, also, these sayings of old are found in our prayers, "Darkness, darkness, light, light, the seeking, the searching, in chaos, in chaos;" these signified the way in which the offspring of heaven and earth sought for some mode of dealing with their parents, so that human beings might increase and live.

So, also, these sayings of old time, "The multitude, the length," signified the multitude of the thoughts of the children of Heaven and Earth, and the length of time they considered whether they should slay their parents, that human beings might be called into existence; for it was in this manner that they talked and consulted amongst themselves.

But at length their plans having been agreed on, lo, Rongo-ma-tane, the god and father of the cultivated food of man, rises up, that he may rend apart the heavens and the earth; he struggles, but he rends them not apart. Lo, next, Tangaroa, the god and father of fish and reptiles, rises up, that he may rend apart the heavens and the earth; he also struggles, but he rends them not apart. Lo, next, Haumia-tikitiki, the god and father of the food of man which springs without cultivation, rises up and struggles, but ineffectually. Lo, then, Tu-matauenga, the god and father of fiery human beings, rises up and struggles, but he, too, fails. Then, at last, slowly uprises Tane-mahuta, the god and father, of forests, of birds, and of insects, and he struggles with his parents; in vain he strives to rend them apart with his hands and arms. Lo, he pauses; his head is now firmly planted on his mother, the earth, his feet he raises up and rests against his father the skies, he strains his back and limbs with mighty effort. Now are rent apart Rangi and Papa, and with cries and groans of woe they shriek aloud, "Wherefore slay you thus your parents? Why commit you so dreadful a crime as to slay us, as to rend your parents apart?" But Tane-mahuta pauses not, he regards not their shrieks and cries; far, far beneath him he presses down the earth; far, far above him he thrusts up the sky.

Hence these sayings of olden time, "It was the fierce thrusting of Tane which tore the heaven from the earth, so that they were rent apart, and darkness was made manifest, and so was the light."

No sooner was heaven rent from earth than the multitude of human beings were discovered whom they had begotten, and who had hitherto lain concealed between the bodies of Rangi and Papa.

Then, also, there arose in the breast of Tawhiri-ma-tea, the god and father of winds and storms, a fierce desire to wage war with his brothers, because they had rent apart their common parents. He from the first had refused to consent to his mother being torn from her lord and children; it was his brothers alone that wished for this separation, and desired that Papa-tu-a-nuku, or the Earth alone, should be left as a parent to them.

The god of hurricanes and storms dreads also that the world

should become too fair and beautiful, so he rises, follows his father to the realms above, and hurries to the sheltered hollows in the boundless skies; there he hides and clings, and nestling in this place of rest he consults long with his parent, and as the vast Heaven listens to the suggestions of Tawhiri-ma-tea, thoughts and plans are formed in his breast, and Tawhiri-ma-tea also understands what he should do. Then by himself and the vast Heaven were begotten his numerous brood, and they rapidly increased and grew. Tawhiri-ma-tea despatches one of them to the westward, and one to the southward, and one to the eastward, and one to the northward; and he gives corresponding names to himself and to his progeny the mighty winds.

He next sends forth fierce squalls, whirlwinds, dense clouds, massy clouds, dark clouds, gloomy thick clouds, fiery clouds, clouds which precede hurricanes, clouds of fiery black, clouds reflecting glowing red light, clouds wildly drifting from all quarters and wildly bursting, clouds of thunder storms, and clouds hurriedly flying. In the midst of these Tawhiri-ma-tea himself sweeps wildly on. Alas! alas! then rages the fierce hurricane; and whilst Tane-mahuta and his gigantic forests still stand, unconscious and unsuspecting, the blast of the breath of the mouth of Tawhiri-ma-tea smites them, the gigantic trees are snapt off right in the middle; alas! alas! they are rent to atoms, dashed to the earth, with boughs and branches torn and scattered, and lying on the earth, trees and branches all alike left for the insect, for the grub, and for loathsome rottenness.

From the forests and their inhabitants Tawhiri-ma-tea next swoops down upon the seas, and lashes in his wrath the ocean. Ah! ah! waves steep as cliffs arise, whose summits are so lofty that to look from them would make the beholder giddy; these soon eddy in whirlpools, and Tangaroa, the god of the ocean, and father of all that dwell therein, flies affrighted through his seas; but before he fled, his children consulted together how they might secure their safety, for Tangaroa had begotten Punga, and he had begotten two children, Ika-tere, the father of fish, and Tu-te-wehi wehi, or Tu-te-wanawana, the father of reptiles.

When Tangaroa fled from safety to the ocean, then Tu-te-wehi wehi and Ika-tere, and their children, disputed together as to what they should do to escape from the storms, and Tu-te-wehi wehi and his party cried aloud, "Let us fly inland;" but Ika-tere and his party cried aloud, "Let us fly to the sea." Some would not obey one order, some would not obey the other, and they escaped in two parties: the party of Tu-te-wehi wehi, or the reptiles, hid themselves ashore; the party of Punga rushed to the sea. This is what, in our ancient religious services, is called the separation of Ta whiri-ma-tea. Hence these traditions have been handed down:—"Ika-tere, the father of things which inhabit the water, cried aloud to Tu-te-wehi wehi, 'Ho, ho, let us all escape to the sea.'

"But Tu-te-wehi wehi shouted in answer, 'Nay, nay, let us rather fly inland.'

"Then Ika-tere warned him saying, 'Fly inland, then; and the fate of you and your race will be, that when they catch you, before you are cooked, they will singe off your scales over a lighted wisp of dry fern.'

"But Tu-te-wehi wehi answered him, saying, 'Seek safety, then, in the sea; and the future fate of your race will be, that when they serve out little baskets of cooked vegetable food to each person, you will be laid upon the top of the food to give a relish to it.'

"Then without delay these two races of beings separated. The fish fled in confusion to the sea, the reptiles sought safety in the forests and scrubs."

Tangaroa, enraged at some of his children deserting him, and, being sheltered by the god of the forests on dry land, has ever since waged war on his brother Tane, who, in return, has waged war against him.

Hence, Tane supplies the offspring of his brother Tu-ma-tauenga with canoes, with spears and with fish-hooks made from his trees, and with nets woven from his fibrous plants, that they may destroy the offspring of Tangaroa; whilst Tangaroa, in return, swallows up the offspring of Tane, overwhelming canoes with the surges of his sea, swallowing up the lands, trees, and houses that are swept off by floods, and ever wastes away, with his lapping waves, the shores that confine him, that the giants of the forests may be washed down and swept out into his boundless ocean, that he may then swallow up the insects, the young birds and the various animals which inhabit them,—all which things are recorded in the prayers which were offered to these gods.

Tawhiri-ma-tea next rushed on to attack his brothers Rongo-ma-tane and Haumia-tikitiki, the gods and progenitors of cultivated and uncultivated food; but Papa, to save these for her other children, caught them up, and hid them in a place of safety; and so well were these children of hers concealed by their mother Earth, that Tawhiri-ma-tea sought for them in vain.

Tawhiri-ma-tea having thus vanquished all his other brothers, next rushed against Tu-matauenga, to try his strength against his; he exerted all his force against him, but he could neither shake him or prevail against him. What did Tu-matauenga care for his brother's wrath? he was the only one of the whole party of brothers who had planned the destruction of their parents, and had shown himself brave and fierce in war; his brothers had yielded at once before the tremendous assaults of Tawhiri-ma-tea and his progeny—Tane-mahuta and his offspring had been broken and torn in pieces—Tangaroa and his children had fled to the depths of the ocean or the recesses of the shore—Rongo-ma-tane and Haumia-tikitiki had been hidden from him in the earth —but Tu-matauenga, or man, still stood erect and unshaken upon the breast of his mother Earth; and now at length the hearts of Heaven and of the god of storms became tranquil, and their passions were assuaged.

Tu-matauenga, or fierce man, having thus successfully resisted his brother, the god of hurricanes and storms, next took thought how he could turn upon his brothers and slay them, because they had not assisted him or fought bravely when Tawhiri-ma-tea had attacked them to avenge the separation of their parents, and because they had left him alone to show his prowess in the fight. As yet death had no power over man. It was not until the birth of the children of Taranga and of Makea-tu-tara, of Maui-taha, of Maui-rota, of Maui-pae, of Maui-waho, and of Maui-tikitiki-o-Taranga, the demi-god who tried to deceive Hine-nui-te-po, that death had power over men. If that goddess had not been deceived by Maui-tikitiki, men would not have died, but would in that case have lived for ever; it was from his deceiving Hine-nui-te-po that death obtained power over mankind, and penetrated to every part of the earth.

Tu-matauenga continued to reflect upon the cowardly manner in which his brothers had acted, in leaving him to show his courage alone, and he first sought some means of injuring Tane-mahuta, because he had not come to aid him in his combat with Tawhiri-ma-tea, and partly because he was aware that Tane had had a numerous progeny, who were rapidly increasing, and might at last prove hostile to him, and injure him, so he began to collect leaves of the whanake tree, and twisted them into nooses, and when his work was ended, he went to the forest to put up his snares, and hung them up—ha! ha! the children of Tane fell before him, none of them could any longer fly or move in safety.

Then he next determined to take revenge on his brother Tangaroa, who had also deserted him in the combat; so he sought for his offspring, and found them leaping or swimming in the water; then he cut many leaves from the flax-plant, and netted nets with the flax, and dragged these, and hauled the children of Tangaroa ashore.

After that, he determined also to be revenged upon his brothers Rongo-ma-tane and Haumia-tikitiki; he soon found them by their peculiar leaves, and he scraped into shape a wooden hoe, and plaited a basket, and dug in the earth and pulled up all kinds of plants with edible roots, and the plants which had been dug up withered in the sun.

Thus Tu-matauenga devoured all his brothers, and consumed the whole of them, in revenge for their having deserted him and left him to fight alone against Tawhiri-ma-tea and Rangi.

When his brothers had all thus been overcome by Tu', he assumed several names, namely, Tu-kariri, Tu-ka-nguha, Tu-ka-taua, Tu-whake-ticke-tangata, Tu-mata-what-iti, and Tu-ma-tauenga; he assumed one name for each of his attributes displayed in the victories over his brothers. Four of his brothers were entirely deposed by him, and became his food; but one of them, Tawhiri-ma-tea, he could not vanquish or make common, by eating him for food, so he, the last born child of Heaven and Earth, was left as an enemy for man, and still, with a rage equal to that of man, this elder brother ever attacks him in storms and hurricanes, endeavouring to destroy him alike by sea and land.

Now the meanings of these names of the children of the Heaven and Earth are as follows:—

Tangaroa signifies fish of every kind; Rongo-ma-tane signifies the sweet potato, and all vegetables cultivated as food; Haumia-tikitiki signifies fern root, and all kinds of food which grow wild; Tane-mahuta signifies forests, the birds and insects which inhabit them, and all things fashioned from wood; Tawhiri-ma-tea signifies winds and storms; and Tu-matauenga signifies man.

Four of his brothers having, as before stated, been made common, or articles of food, by Tu-matauenga, he assigned for each of them fitting incantations, that they might be abundant, and that he might easily obtain them.

EGYPTIAN WORLD PARENTS:
SEB AND NUT

The god Seb (or, Keb) and his spouse, the goddess Nut, are very important figures throughout the development of Egyptian religion. They play a very prominent role in mythology, art, and in the rituals for the dead. The mythological structure of Seb and Nut as World Parents cannot be presented in any one myth because of the fragmentation of the texts. It is possible, however, to reconstruct from various texts a definite narrative concerning their role and action in the Egyptian mythology of creation. Their prominence in creation is witnessed to by the many art forms showing their position in the creation of the cosmos.

We shall follow Adolf Erman's[30] description of this mythic action.

The cosmos which had been created from primeval water (chaos) remained quite confused. This was so because heaven and earth had not yet been separated. The goddess of heaven, Nut, was still lying upon her spouse the earth god, Seb, (or, Keb). Then the god of the atmosphere (or, air), her father Shu, shoved himself between them and lifted her up along with everything which had been created i.e., *every god with his boat*. Nut took possession of them, counted them all and made them stars. The sun itself was no exception to this and now they all travel upon the body of Nut in their boats. This was the actual creation of our present world. Since the separation of heaven (Nut) and earth (Seb) all things have kept their present order. Only the bones of Shu, those wonderful arms which support Nut, connect the upper and lower world.

Since the Sun god was separated from the earth he appointed Seb (god of earth) to take over his own governorship. He handed over to Seb his heritage and the entire Nine (i.e., the great Gods). Now, say the Gods, Seb is our Prince, the Prince of the gods. If he calls us we shall come and be his companions. He rules at the top of the nine as well as his father and mother. He is more powerful than any god. Thus Seb rules over the gods on earth while Nut, who is in heaven, has power over the gods of heaven, their heritage, their life and all their possessions.

An earlier version is given by Erman,[31] in which the above structure of Seb, Shu, and Nut are the result of a revolt which happened during the rule which Re (or, Ra; the first creator, and sun god) had established.

At one time Re had governed both gods and men. In time however he became old, his bones were silver, his limbs golden and his hair was the color of pure sapphire. The people noted this change in him and began to think evil things about him.

He knowing this, called his Eye, Shu and Tefnut (i.e., the parents of Seb and Nut), Seb and Nut, and Nun (i.e., the primeval water from which Re arose.)[32]

He had decided to slaughter all the people because of their thoughts of revolting against him. He wanted, however, to confer with the gods before taking action. Nun proposed that he send forth his eye; for this would in itself make the people respect him, since this fear of him was great. Following Nun's advice, Re sent forth his eye and the people fled in terror into the desert, as Nun had predicted. The gods, however, advised Re that he should send his eye after them and slaughter them all. Re followed their advice again and many of the people were killed.

The old god nevertheless did not want to rule over his

ungrateful creatures any longer. He was tired of living with them. Then old Nun laid himself once more in the middle (a return to chaos?) and called his daughter, the cow-formed Nut, next to himself. He seated himself upon her back and she lifted him up and thus built heaven. When Nut looked down she trembled because of the dizzy heights she had reached. Then Re called Shu and said, "My son Shu, place yourself underneath my daughter Nut, put her upon your head." Shu did as he was asked and has supported ever since the heavenly Cow upon whose belly the stars twinkle and upon which the sun travels in his boat.

In the narrative by E. A. Budge[33] we find added to the above:

(and) when Shu had taken up his place beneath the cow and was bearing up her body, the heavens and earth beneath came into being, and the four legs of the cow became the four props of heaven at the four cardinal points; and thus it came to pass that the god Seb and his female counterpart Nut began their existence.

Nut and Seb are the creators of things on earth and in the sky. The earth is the "house of Seb"; it forms his body. In Budge's *Book of the Dead,* Chapter XXXI 5, we read, "My father is Seb and my mother is Nut." In Egypt they are the gods *par excellence* of earth and sky.

THE BIRTH FROM THE SEA OF THE TWAIN DELIVERERS OF MEN (ZUÑI)[84]

Then did the Sun-father take counsel within himself, and casting his glance downward espied, on the great waters, a Foam-cap near to the Earth-mother. With his beam he impregnated and with his heat incubated the Foam-cap, whereupon she gave birth to Úanam Achi Píahkoa, the Beloved Twain who descended; first, Úanam Éhkoma, the Beloved Preceder, then Úanam Yáluna, the Beloved Follower, Twin brothers of Light, yet Elder and Younger, the Right and the Left, like to question and answer in deciding and doing. To them the Sun-father imparted, still retaining, control-thought and his own knowledge-wisdom, even as to the offspring of wise parents their knowingness is imparted and as to his right hand and his left hand a skillful man gives craft freely surrendering not his knowledge. He gave them, of himself and their mother the Foam-cap, the great cloud-bow, and for arrows the thunderbolts of the four quarters (twain to either), and for buckler the fog-making shield, which (spun of the floating clouds and spray and woven, as of cotton we spin and weave) supports as on wind, yet hides (as a shadow hides) its bearer, defending also. And of men and all creatures he gave them the fathership and dominion, also as a man gives over the control of his work to the management of his hands. Well instructed of the Sun-father, they lifted the Sky-father with their great cloud-bow into the vault of the high zenith, that the earth might become warm and thus fitter for their children, men and the creatures. Then along the trail of the sun seeking Póshaiyank'ya, they sped backward swiftly on their floating fog-shield, westward to the Mountain of Generation. With their magic knives of the thunderbolt they spread open the uncleft depths of the mountain, and still on their cloud-shield—even as a spider in her web descendeth— so descended they unerringly, into the dark of the under-world. There they abode with men and the creatures, attending them, coming to know them, and becoming known of them as masters and fathers, thus seeking the ways for leading them forth.

THE GENESIS OF MEN AND THE CREATURES (ZUÑI)[35]

From the lying together of these twain upon the great world waters, so vitalizing, terrestrial life was conceived; whence began all beings of earth, men and the creatures, in the Four-fold womb of the World (Á wi-ten Téhu'hlnakwi).

Thereupon the Earth-mother repulsed the Sky-father, growing big and sinking deep into the embrace of the waters below, thus separating from the Sky-father in the embrace of the waters above. As a woman forebodes evil for her first-born ere born, even so did the Earth-mother forbode, long withholding from birth her myriad progeny and meantime seeking counsel with the Sky-father. "How," said they to one another, "shall our children, when brought forth, know one place from another, even by the white light of the Sun-father?"

Now like all the surpassing beings (*pikwaiyin áhái*) the Earth-mother and the Sky-father were *'hlimna* (changeable), even as smoke in the wind; transmutable at thought, manifesting themselves in any form at will, like as dancers may by mask-making.

Thus, as a man and woman, spake they, one to the other. "Behold!" and the Earth-mother as a great terraced bowl appeared at hand and within it water, "this is as upon me the homes of my tiny children shall be. On the rim of each world-country they wander in, terraced mountains shall stand, making in one region many, whereby country shall be known from country, and within each, place from place. Behold, again!" said she as she spat on the water and rapidly smote and stirred it with her fingers. Foam formed, gathering about the terraced rim, mounting higher and higher. "Yea," said she, "and from my bosom they shall draw nourishment, for in such as this shall they find the substance of life whence we were ourselves sustained, for see!" Then with her warm breath she blew across the terraces; white flocks of the foam broke away, and, floating over above the water, were shattered by the cold breath of the Sky-father attending, and forthwith shed downward abundantly fine mist and spray! "Even so, shall white clouds float up from the great waters at the borders of the world, and clustering about the mountain terraces of the horizons be borne aloft and abroad by the breaths of the surpassing of soul-beings, and of the children, and shall hardened and broken be by thy cold, shedding downward, in rain-spray, the water of life, even into the hollow places of my lap! For therein chiefly shall nestle our children mankind and creature kind, for warmth in thy coldness."

Lo! even the trees on high mountains near the clouds and the Sky-father crouch low toward the Earth-mother for warmth and protection! Warm is the Earth-mother, cold the Sky-father, even as woman is the warm, man the cold being!

"Even so!" said the Sky-father; "Yet not alone shalt thou helpful be unto our children, for behold!" and he spread his hand abroad with the palm downward and into all the wrinkles and crevices thereof he set the semblance of shining yellow corn-grains; in the dark of the early world-dawn they gleamed like sparks of fire, and moved as his hand was moved over the bowl, shining up from and also moving in the depths of the water therein. "See!" said he, pointing to the seven grains clasped by his thumb and four fingers, "by such shall our children be guided; for behold, when the Sun-father is not nigh, and thy terraces are as the dark itself (being all hidden therein), then shall our children be guided by lights—like to these lights of all the six regions turning round the mid-most one—as in and around the mid-most place, where these our children shall abide, lie all the other regions of space! Yea! and even as these grains gleam up from the water, so shall seed-grains like to them, yet numberless, spring up from thy bosom when touched by my waters, to nourish our children." Thus and in other ways many devised they for their offspring.

PLATE 8. *Emergence Sand Painting. Navajo.*

PLATE 9. *Air-god Shu.*

PLATE 10. *Ritual Marriage of god and goddess. Iraq.*

PLATE 11. *Dogon Ancestor Figures. Africa.*

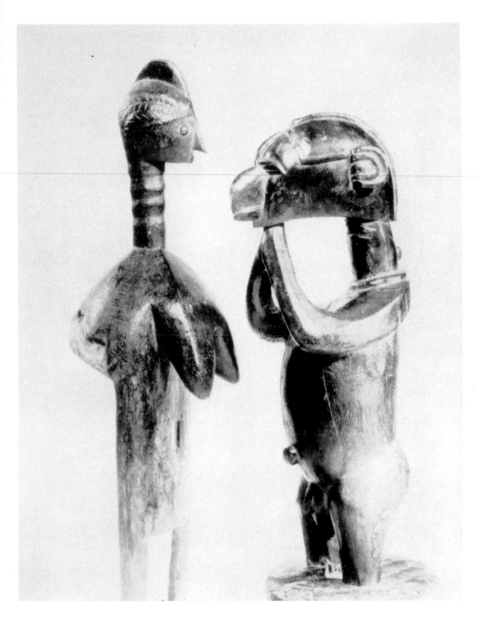

PLATE 12a. *Baga shoulder mask. Africa.*

PLATE 12b. *Nimba fertility statue. Africa.*

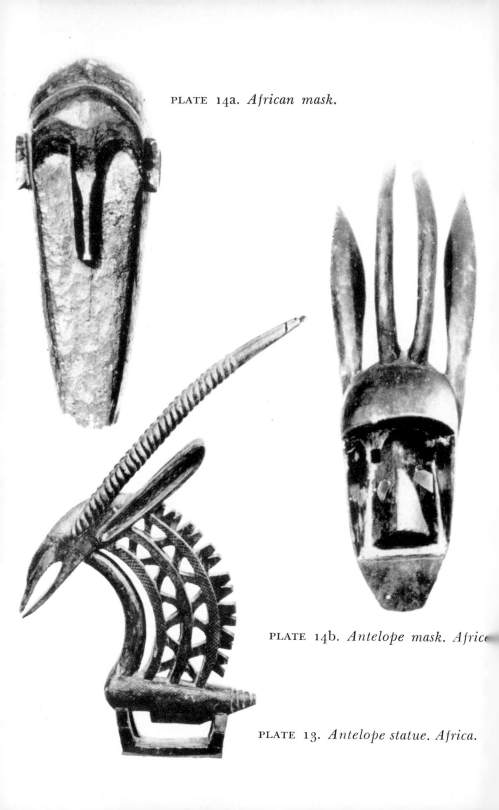

PLATE 14a. *African mask.*

PLATE 14b. *Antelope mask. Afric*

PLATE 13. *Antelope statue. Africa.*

PLATE 15. *Stone Tiki*.

PLATE 16. *House detail. Melanasia.*

MYTH FROM THE DHAMMAI (MIJI)[36]

At first there was neither earth nor sky. Shuzanghu and his wife Zumiang-Nui lived above. One day Shuzanghu said to his wife, "How long must we live without a place to rest our feet?" Zumiang-Nui said, 'What can I say to you? You always live apart from me and don't love me. But if you truly love me and will stay with me, I will tell you what to do.' So Shuzanghu went to his wife and she conceived.

In due time Zumiang-Nui gave birth to a baby-girl, Subbu-Khai-Thung, who is the Earth and to a baby-boy, Jongsuli-Young-Jongbu, who is the Sky. But there was no place for them. So they fell down, down to where Phangnalomang the Worm and his wife were living, and the Worm swallowed them both.

Zumiang-Nui tried to find her children and asked her husband, 'What has happened to them? Where have they gone?' But he could not tell her. Then she said, 'Next time I have a child, make a clear flat place when I can keep him safely and set traps all round it.' Shuzanghu made such a place and when his wife was delivered of her next child, there was somewhere for him to stay. And now when Phangnalomang came to devour the child he was caught in one of the traps. Shuzanghu found him there and split his body open. The two children were still in his belly and the lower part of his body became the Earth and the upper the Sky.

Now Earth and Sky lived together. The Sky went to his wife, the Earth, and she gave birth to a son, Sujang-Gnoi-Rise and a daughter, Jibbi-Jang-Sangne. These were gods but they had the shape of mountains. After they were born Earth and Sky separated and as they were parting Earth gave birth to two other children, a boy, Lujjuphu, and a girl named Jassuju, who had the form of frogs. They mated and from them a boy and a girl in human form, Abugupham-Bumo and Anoi-Diggan-Juje, were born. They were human but were covered with hair. They married each other and in time had three sons, Lubukhanlung, Sangso-Dungso and Kimbu-Sangtung.

MYTH FROM THE MINYONG[37]

Sedi is the earth; Melo is the Sky. The Earth is a woman, the Sky is a man. These two married, and when they came together, Wiyus, men and animals held a Kebang to consider how they could save themselves from being crushed between them. Sedi-Diyor, one of the greatest of the Wiyus, caught hold of the Sky and beat him so that he fled far up into the heavens leaving the Earth behind. As he went away, the Earth gave birth to two daughters. But she was so sad at losing her husband that she could not bear to look at them. Sedi-Diyor, therefore, found a woman to nurse them.

When the little girls were old enough to walk, light began to shine for them, and day by day the light grew brighter. After a while the nurse died and Sedi-Diyor buried her in the ground. The children wept for her as for their mother: they wept so much that they died, and the light they gave died with them.

Now it was dark again, and Wiyus, men and animals were afraid. The Wiyus thought that the nurse must have stolen something from the children and that it was this that had made them weep so much. So they dug up her body to see what it was. They found that it had rotted away, all except the eyes. They saw the eyes great and shining in the darkness, and their own reflection was mirrored in them. They thought that they saw the dead children in the eyes. They took them to a stream and washed them in the water for five days and five nights, and made them shine more brightly. But they could not remove the images looking back at them from the eyes.

The Wiyus sent for a carpenter and he cut the eyes open with great care and removed the reflections, which turned into living children. They called one girl Sedi-Irkong-Bomong and the other Sedi-Irkong-Bong. They did not let them go out of their house.

But one day, when they were grown up, the elder girl, Bomong, dressed herself in gaily-coloured clothes and many ornaments, and went out in her beauty to wander through the world. As she came out of the house, there was light all round her, and it was day. She went across the hills and did not return.

After a long time, her sister Bong went to look for her, tracing the path for her footsteps. But when she came out, there was so much light that she caused the rocks to break, the trees to wither and men to faint in the heat.

Wiyus, men and animals held yet another Kebang and decided that the only thing to do was to kill one of the sisters. They were afraid to do it and argued for a long time, but at last the frog went to sit by the path and waited, bow in hand, for the girl to come. When Bong came shining and lovely he shot her with an arrow in each side and she died. Then it was not so hot, the light was not so dazzling. The trees revived and men went again about their work.

But the girl's body lay where it had fallen. Then there came along Kirte, a Wiyu in the form of a rat; he dragged the corpse to Bomong on his back. As he went along, he fell over and ever since the rat's legs have been crooked. But he got up and took the body to a river where Bomong was due to pass. He showed her sister's body and she wept for sorrow and fear that she herself would be killed. She took a path that no one knew and sat down, placing a big stone on her head. With the shadow of the stone, the world became dark.

At this, Wiyus, men and animals were afraid and they went to search for light. For a long time they found nothing. Then Nginu-Botte caught a rat, a wild bird and a cock and sent them to find Bomong. The cock went first, but its parts were so heavy that it could not walk. It met Banjibanman and told him its trouble, and he cut off its organ and threw it away. Its testes went into its body. This is why the cock has no parts outside its body.

The cock's organ turned into the earthworm.

The cock went on and at last found Bomong and begged her to come back. 'No', she said, 'they killed my sister and they'll kill me. Tell them that I will only come if they make my sister alive.' The cock returned and told Nginu-Botte what the girl had said. He found a carpenter who fashioned Bong's body, making it small and putting life into it. When Bomong heard that her sister was alive again, she threw the stone down from her head and stood up. The day returned and as the light blazed out, the cock cried *'Kokoko-kokoko'*; the wild bird sang *'Pengo-pengo'*; the rat squeaked *'Taktak-taktak.'* For they were glad at the light and heat.

CHAPTER THREE

CREATION FROM CHAOS

AND FROM THE COSMIC EGG

IN THIS CHAPTER we have combined two cosmogonic structures—chaos and the cosmic egg. We have taken this liberty not simply because these structures often appear together in the same myth, but also because we hope to point out some of the relations existing between these two types of myths. Let us first set forth our understanding of the chaos symbolism.

In the Babylonian creation myth which appears in the chapter on World Parents, we learn that Apsû and Mummu are the primordial World Parents. Their names mean sweet water and salt water respectively, but since they appear in union they represent a mixture of salt and sweet water. In Egypt there is a myth which attributes creation to a primeval hillock. Around this hillock are the waters of chaos and within this chaos four pairs of procreative deities emerge. Though the idea of form or structure is implied in the emergence of deities, the deities in this myth seem to be abstractions of the qualities of chaos.

These four pairs of gods persisted in the mythology as the "Eight" who were before the beginning. They were Nun, the primordial waters, and his consort Naunet, who became the counter-heaven; Huk, the boundless stretches of primordial formlessness, and his consort Kauket; and Amun, that is Amon, "the hidden," representing the intangibility and imperceptibility of chaos with his consort Amanuet.[1]

Chaos, which is described in terms of confusion, darkness, and water, carries with it the notions of indeterminacy and potentiality. This is a reflection on the condition of reality before the "centering" of the cosmos by a definite conception and form of reality. It may even refer to a historical period before the birth of the new gods. In Egypt the primeval hillock is related to Hermopolis. Chaos could be here understood as the vestiges of predynastic Egypt. This, however, is not the primary religious meaning. What is being expressed here is the eternity of the stuff of creation. That is to say, the stuff from which creation finally arises has always existed. Even in its indeterminate form of chaos, the possibilities of a cosmos were always present.

We saw above in the Egyptian myth that the first emergent deities from the water were still indistinct. In the version of the Babylonian myth given by Damascius and Berossus, grotesque beings are the first to emerge from the chaos. They are described as "strange and peculiarly shaped creatures . . . with two wings, some also with four wings and two faces; (some) also having one body but two heads, the one of a man, the other of a woman, being likewise in their genitals both male and female; and that there were other human beings with legs and horns of goats. . . ."[2]

In the above narrative all of the possibilities inherent in chaos are actualized without a controlling principle of order. Though this myth as reported by Damascius and Berossus is a late account, it probably belongs to a rather early strata of mythological structures. In one version of the Egyptian myth the sun emerged from the primeval ocean, Nun, and in Chinese myth light comes forth from chaos. The abrupt emergence of light is related to the development of an esoteric form of the myth and is parallel to certain cultic and priestly forms in the religious community. The same trend in the mythological structures can be observed among the Polynesians, and among the Indian myths from the Satapatha Brahmana, the Chandogya Upanishad, and the Laws of Manu. The more popular myth is one which is formed in terms of a genealogical structure. In this mythological structure there is a movement from chaos to more definite but still confused and indeterminate beings, then to earth-mother and sky-father and their offspring, and finally to man.

In any case, the primary motif of the myths which begin with chaos is the story of the development of order out of disorder. In the Babylonian myth, Marduk finally defeats Tiamat; in the Egyptian myth the sun as a harbinger of order gives ·structure to the cosmos. Nevertheless, the water still remains as a primordial symbol of reality. It remains as providence and threat. It is formless chaos and the reality out of which all structures emerge. Water is thus a blessing and a curse. Its power of renewal and purification is never completely forgotten. In Marcel Griaule's conversations with the old Dogon philosopher Ogotemmêli, we see very clearly the meaning of the symbolism of water. In describing the creation of the world, Ogotemmêli at a certain point relates the following narrative:

God had again intercourse with his wife and this time nothing disturbed their union, for the excision had done away with the cause of the first trouble. Water, the divine semen, penetrated into the womb of the earth, and generation went on, in accordance with the regular cycle of procreation, through twins. Two beings were formed.

God has created them in the form of water. They were green coloured and had the shape of a human being and a serpent. From the head to the loins they were human; the lower part had the shape of a serpent.

The red eyes were almond-shaped like those of man and their tongue was forked like the one of serpents. The arms were flexible and had no joints. Their whole body was green and smooth, slithery like a water surface, and covered with short, green hair, foretelling the vegetations and germinations-to-come.

So these genii, called Nommo, were two homogeneous products of God, of divine essence like He, conceived without adventures and developed according to the norms that are prevalent in the matrix of the earth. Their destiny brought them to heaven where they received instruction from their father. Not that it has been necessary for God to teach them the Word, which is indispensable to all beings as well as to the system of the universe: the couple was born complete and perfect; because of their eight members, their number was eight, which is the symbol of speech.

They were also in possession of the essence of God, for they were made out of his semen, which is at the same time support, form and substance of the vital power of the world, the source of movement and of perseverance in a living being. And this power is water. The couple is present in all water, they *are* water, the water of the seas, of the most remote places, of the streams, of the thunderstorms and of the spoonful of liquid one drinks.

Ogotemmêli used indiscriminately the terms "water" and "Nommo."

"If it were not for Nommo," he said, "the earth could not even have been created, for the earth was kneaded and it was only through the water (through the Nommo) that it came to life."

"What sort of life is there in the earth?" asked the white man.

"The vital power of the earth is water. God has kneaded the earth with water. In the same way He makes the blood with water. Even in stone this power is present, for there is moisture in everything."

But even though the Nommo is water, he produces also copper. One can see how, in a clouded sky, the sunrays materialize on the hazy horizon; these rays, excrements of the genii, consist of copper and they are light. They consist also of water, for they support the moisture of the earth on its way upward. The couple discharges light, because they are also light.[3]

A similar form of schematization of the water symbolism is hinted in the Indian myth from the Laws of Manu: "The waters are called *narah* (for) the waters are, indeed, the off-spring of Nara; as they were the first residence, he thence is named Narayana.[4]

In many of the myths which refer to water or chaos as

the primary condition of reality, we find the motif of an egg. In some cases the waters produce the egg, as in the Indian myths from the Laws of Manu and the Satapatha Brahmana. In the Polynesian myths, Ta'aora, the supreme being, exists within the egg and in the African myth the supreme being Amma produces the egg. In the Japanese myth, chaos itself is likened to an egg and the Orphic version states that time (Chronos) created the silver egg of the cosmos. Does this symbolism in the form of the egg point to a definite structure which is not represented by the symbolism of water and chaos?

One can immediately see the relationship of this form of symbolism to ideas of fertility. The egg is the potential source of all life. It is the incubator and therefore a homologue of the womb. This symbolism can be extended to cover shells, caverns, dark places, the earth, etc. We are obviously dealing with an aspect of the feminine principle as a source of life and vitality. In the Introduction to the emergence myths (p. 35) we discussed some of the characteristics of this symbolism. In the Mande Creation myth from Africa we read, "The twins are thus conceived as twins of opposite sex in the 'Egg of God' which is also called 'egg of the world' or 'placenta of the world.'" The symbolism of the womb is made quite explicit in this myth. Similarly, among the Polynesians the fertility symbols of parturition are combined in the cosmic-egg structure. We have reproduced illustrations of the Tuamotuan cosmogonic myths. The "stuff" out of which life emerges is called sometimes earth, other times shells, and in some myths it is an egg. The structure of these myths is related very closely to the American Indian emergence myths (plates 7 and 8; figs. 1, 2, 3, 4, on pp. 54, 59, 60, 118.

Mircea Eliade has pointed out how shells may express fecundity,[5] and we have already shown how the earth is an expression of this same meaning. At the substratum of the cosmic-egg symbolism lies the structure of fertility and fecundity. There is, however, something more than the old Mother Earth or watery-chaos symbolism in this structure. For example, we have abundant evidence of the feminine-earth-fertility forms in Hesiod's theogony, but neither Hesiod nor Homer mention the cosmic-egg motif in their cosmogonies.[6] It is in the Orphic cosmogony that this structure is made explicit. It is possible that neither Hesiod nor Homer knew of this mythological motif, but it is more likely that the importation of this structure in their mythological fabrications would defeat the purposes of their productions. Not only in Greece, but in many other cultures the cosmic egg represents a rather definite meaning which is something more than the Mother Earth or chaos as a latent reservoir of all life.

Hermann Baumann believes that the symbolism of bisexuality (which is an aspect of the egg myth) is a late mythological development concerning sexuality.[7] The earliest sexual notions, according to Baumann, are those which conceive of the earth as mother and female and the heavens as father and male. In the next development the godhead is understood as world parents having bisexual characteristics. The cosmic-egg symbol represents the next development of sexual symbolism and is related to the megalithic cultural complex. The later stages in the development of the sexual symbolism consist in the working out of the sexual notions in more abstract categories, and Baumann finally interprets the last stage of this mythological structure as a reversion to the dualistic antagonism between the sexes as this antagonism was expressed in the first stage. This last stage of sexual antagonism is, however, more sophisticated and refers not only to the general primordial antagonism of two distinct and external principles, but also to the internal sexual antagonism in every human being, male or female.

In Baumann's interpretation, the cosmic-egg symbolism, insofar as it includes bisexuality, represents the attempt to come to terms with the religious meaning of the powerful antithetical symbols of sexuality. In the egg symbolism the union of the sexual principles in twins as in a bisexual deity is an attempt to overcome the dualism involved in the revelation of the sacred in one or the other sexes. This is not the old primordial union of earth mother and sky father. In this symbolism the emphasis is on the passive togetherness of the sexes. Though the myths always state that the World Parents have offsprings, the full meaning of sexuality as unique and separable principles is not emphasized. The symbolism of the World Parents is shrouded in chaos and passivity. The World Parents do not wish to be separated. Once the separation takes place, the tension between the sexes is acute. The problem of the dominance of one sexual principle over the other becomes a central issue. Baumann, Numazawa, and others see this tension expressed historically in a matriarchal circle which later yielded to the patriarchal.

The theory of a matriarchal circle which spread by diffusion to various parts of the world has not yet been proved. We are, nevertheless, justified in understanding the cosmic-egg symbolism as a reconciliation of the antagonism involved in the dominance of one form of sexual symbolism over the other. This meaning is borne out in the Japanese myth. After Izanami and Izanagi go around the heavenly pillar, Izanami speaks first. Izanagi then says that it was unlucky for the woman to speak first. As a result of this action their first child is abnormal.

When he visits the underworld after the death of Izanami he is pursued by the Ugly Females of Yomi (underworld). Through various magical gestures he is able to escape their wrath. He is, however, finally overtaken by Izanami, but he blocked up the pass to the underworld with a great rock at the same time pronouncing the formula of divorce. The defeat, the subjugation of matriarchal chthonic powers, is complete.

In the myth from Kalevala, a beautiful bird lays the cosmic egg in the waters. The bird is a solar male symbol but in so far as he lays eggs he is androgynous. Like the god, Amma, in the Mande myth a predetermined plan of action is implied in this gesture.

Several scholars attribute the type of symbolism found in the cosmic-egg myth to the "pre-classical" periods of the respective cultures.[8] It is in this sense that the cosmic-egg motif is spoken of as an older form. Norman Brown says that Hesiod's theogony (see Chapter Four) moves "from a natural to an anthropocentric order and from the primacy of the female to the primacy of the male."[9] We have already noted the fact that Hesiod's theogony does not include the Orphic cosmic-egg symbolism.

In the cosmic-egg symbolism the beginning of things is spoken of as a totality which includes the opposite modes of sexuality in relation. This is a *coincidentia oppositorum,* a form of symbolism which is different from that of the primordial World Parents. Sexuality is not represented here by World Parents but by the precise creative power of each sex, who, though related, are capable of independence and separate determination. In other words, the actual *power of creativity* is already present in the beginning. In the World-Parent myths, there is a reluctance on the part of the parents to acknowledge their creative role. In the Mande Myth of Creation from Africa, one of the twins in the egg leaves the egg before maturation and attempts to create a world independent of his partner. This "will to power" of the twins in the egg is unthinkable in the World-Parent myths. In some versions of the Polynesian myths the bursting of the egg is a creative process which brings about the evolution of all other forms of life. There is movement and life in the egg already. In one version of the African myth, the egg itself is created by a kind of ovoid movement—a movement which defines both time and space and has become the archetypal symbol for agriculture, sky phenomena, and the cosmo-biology of man.[10]

In the cosmic egg the concrete forms of the two sexual principles are united. This unity is a symbol of perfection. Again we must emphasize that this unity is not the same as the unity of the primordial World Parents; rather, it is the unity of sexuality which has expressed its potentiality and power as separate from the other sexual principle.

In one sense the cosmic-egg myths present us with two conflicting tendencies. In the Polynesian myth from Tahiti, Ta'aroa is a supreme being who lived alone in a shell (fig. 4). After breaking out of the shell he creates by himself the god, Tu, who becomes his companion in creation. In the other Tahitian version, Ta'aroa creates the world out of his body— his spine becomes a mountain ridge, his vitals floating clouds, his arms and legs strength for the earth, etc. A similar form of transmutation is found in the Indian myth from the Laws of Manu. "He (that is, the Self-Existent) desiring to produce beings of many kinds from his own body, first with a thought created the waters and placed his seed in them."[11] The same account is found in the myth from the Chandogya Upanishad; and finally in the myth from the Satapatha Brahmana, Prajapati, the supreme being born from the waters, creates the universe. In the Orphic myths, Zeus swallows Phanes and renews the world.

Thus then engulfing the might of Ericapaeus, the First born, he held the body of all things in the hollow of his own belly; and he mingled with his own limbs the power and strength of the god. Therefore to-

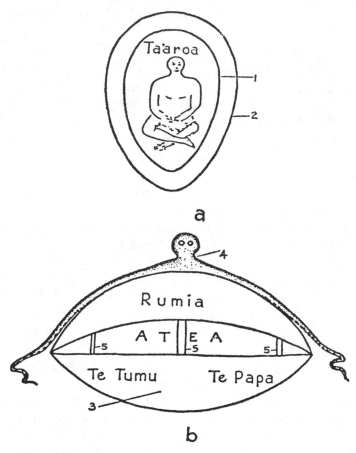

FIG. 4—Main points of Tahitian creation graphically represented.

Based on accounts in *Ancient Tahiti*, by Teuira Henry. *a*, The world in the beginning (in the form of an egg spinning in space in absolute darkness). The god Ta'aroa, called Te Tumu (The Foundation), dwells in Fa'a-iti (Little Valley), the region within the shell Tumu-iti (Little-foundation), 1, enclosed within an outer shell, Rumia, 2. *b*, The developing world, primal Hava'k'i Ta'aroa's inner shell, 1, was taken by Ta'aroa for 3, a *tumunui* (main foundation) and a *papa* (stratum rock) of this world. His outer shell, 2, was taken for the sky Rumia, held close to the earth by the octopus, 4, Tumu-ra'i-fenua (Foundation-of-the-earth's-sky). Ta'aroa has Te Tumu (The Foundation) into which he has put his spirit, and Te Papa brings props, 5, to prop the sky Rumia. He invokes a spirit to pervade the resulting space *atea*, and so the god Atea comes into being. Ta'aroa dwells in the lower world of darkness, 3, known as *te po*.

gether with him all things in Zeus were created anew, the shining height of the broad Aither and the sky, the seat of the unharvested sea and the noble earth, great Ocean and the lowest depths beneath the earth, and rivers and the boundless sea and all else, all immortal and blessed gods and goddesses, all that was then in being and all that was come to pass, all was there, and mingled like streams in the belly of Zeus.[12]

In like manner an Orphic hymn addressed to Zeus sings his praises as the supreme being.

Zeus was first and Zeus last, he with the glittering lightning; Zeus is the head, Zeus is the middle, all things are accomplished out of Zeus. Zeus is the foundation of earth and of the starry heavens. Zeus became a man, Zeus became an immortal woman. Zeus is the breath of all things, Zeus is the impulse of the unwearying fire. Zeus is the root of the sea, Zeus is the sun and the moon. Zeus is king, Zeus is the ruler of all things, he with the gleaming lighting.[13]

There seems to be in the myths a movement toward monotheism—the supremacy of one god. If we understand monotheism as it is expressed in classical historical forms of Judaism, Christianity, and Islam, the monotheistic tendency does not reach its goal in these myths. The forms of monotheism in Judaism, Christianity, and Islam represent the triumph and dominance of a celestial deity as the absolute and supreme being. In the myths of the cosmic egg the essential complementary relationship of the sexual modes of being is emphasized. The existence of these modes of being is from the beginning. Neither man nor the world is complete without them. Though the movement in the myths has monotheistic tendencies, the supreme being cannot extricate himself from the religious structures of fertility and Mother Earth. He does not create from "nothing," but from the creative stuff of the feminine structures of being. He is thus a bisexual or androgynous deity possessing within himself the creative forms of the male and the female.

This does not mean that in the cosmic-egg myths we have a complete equilibrium of religious power on the level of sexuality. It does mean that equilibrium expressed in terms of sexuality is understood as absolute perfection. The tension between the two sexual modes of being finds expression in the myths. In the West African myth the world which is created by Pemba is incomplete; it is dry and barren. Pemba then realizes that he needs his female counterpart and returns to the cosmic egg to get her. She had been changed into the sun, and Pemba could not take her. In lieu of this he steals male seeds from the egg. The seeds are planted in the earth (the placenta of the egg), but they make the earth impure. Faro, Pemba's twin, is sacrificed and his body falls to the earth, purifying it. Later we read that the first human beings, like Faro himself, had a common vital force (*nyama*) and complementary spiritual forces *ni* and *dya,* each of which possessed male and female principles.

Walter Wili, in his interpretation of the Orphic legend of the dismemberment of Dionysus by the Titans, places emphasis on the Orphic ethical evaluation of this religious dualism.

> When man rose from the ashes of the Titans, it was not only the evil Titanic nature that he inherited. The Titans had eaten the boy Dionysus; thus the ashes, and hence man as well, contained a divine Dionysian part. The evaluation of man as a good and evil creature of Titanic and Dionysian origin is essential to Orphism and occurs for the first time in Greece.[14]

The cosmic-egg symbolism seems to express a movement toward monotheism, but a monotheism which cannot extricate itself from the structure of the chthonic forms of creation and procreation. Jane Harrison, in her discussion of the cosmic egg in the Orphic cosmogony, fails to come to a definite conclusion as to its significance. She does say that it played a definite role in the Orphic ritual. "In ordinary ceremonial it served two purposes: it was used for purification, it was an offering to the dead."[15]

We are probably on the right track if we continue along the lines suggested by Harrison. In the cosmic-egg symbolism a cosmological dualism comes to the fore. The myths of this type posit the dualism, but they show at the same time the necessary relation between the two active principles. W. K. C. Guthrie, in pointing to the new element in the Orphic cosmogony, says, ". . . the conception which seems to me to have the best right to be called an Orphic idea is that of a creator."[16] Phanes thus becomes in one of the Orphic cosmogonies the creator and is later swallowed by Zeus. Insofar as creation may be an expression of chthonic powers which are later to be dominated by Zeus, this explanation is sound, but it does not go far enough. It does not explain why the creator has to be born from a cosmic egg. Is not the egg a symbol of procreation and rebirth? The egg is a continual resource of life and renewal. The return to the egg is the return to the source. Pemba in the Mande myth returns to the egg to resuscitate the universe which he had created. W. W. Gill reports a Polynesian myth from Raratonga in which Mani, the Polynesian civilizing hero, brings Tangaroa, god of darkness, back to life by shaking his hands in a coconut shell.[17] In the Brahmanic version of Indian religion, salvation is understood as a realization of the Self-Existent, and in the Orphic mysteries man is saved by the devaluation of his Titanic nature through his ecstatic participation in his Dionysiac nature.

The Brahmanic and Orphic traditions have at their core an ideal of personal salvation. The dual principles are immanent in man and he can through various means achieve the dominance of one over the other. Eliade speaks of *prakṛtilagas* or superhuman beings who, sunk in meditation on *prkṛti,* pierce the cosmic egg and thereby attain the situation of the divinity.[18] He makes reference to the same symbolism in another context. The laying of an egg is a metaphor for the first birth—the natural birth of man; the hatching of the egg corresponds to supernatural birth.[19]

> Thus the act of transcending time is formulated by a symbolism that is both cosmological and spatial. To break the shell of the egg is equivalent, in the parable of the Buddha, to breaking out of *samsara,* out of the wheel of existence—that is, to the transcending *both of cosmic space and cyclic Time.*[20]

In the Orphic and Indian traditions an effort is made to defeat natural time and space. The egg symbolism is a sign of the natural ordering of the world. The emphasis is on an esoteric kind of knowledge or technique or rather it is on the symbolism of light and the male principle. This is the more sophisticated form of the tension between the sexual principles mentioned by Baumann. In the Polynesian and African Mande traditions the procreative activity is still paramount, at least in the myths we have reproduced. In the symbolism of the Maori myth from Polynesia (see Chapter Four), light becomes paramount and completely dispels through its power all shades of darkness. The egg symbolism is not mentioned at all in this myth. The most thorough cosmology involving egg symbolism as the immanent power in all creative and procreative activity is found in Africa among the Bambara and the Dogon peoples. The egg symbolism is assimilated to all vital activities, to the physiological and spiritual qualities of man, and to agriculture and fishing (fig. 5).

We have seen in this analysis of the egg symbolism how a particular religious structure takes on definite meaning in various religious traditions. The basic symbolism of the egg as the creative source of life and rebirth, however, remains the same.

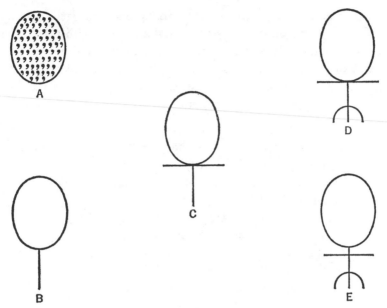

FIG. 5.—Ball of the World.

A. Ball of the World
B. The Way
C. Way of the Twins

D. The Way Extended
E. Man, Principle of the World

A. (Ball of the World) is an oval circle containing the germ of all things in the form of tadpoles.
B. The line underneath the circle shows the germ leaving the egg (world).
C. A second germ, twin of the first, is placed across the vertical shaft.
D. A third germ, extending the first, takes it place. The first germ follows its leaving and turns without closing itself, making the circle of the world incomplete.
E. This is man the microcosm, principle of the world. The arms separate the celestial placenta (the head) from the terrestrial placenta (the legs and sexual organs) which is incomplete because of the opening in the egg.

THE ORPHIC CREATION MYTH[21]

In the beginning time created the silver egg of the cosmos. Out of this egg burst Phanes-Dionysus. For them (the Orphics) he was the first god to appear, the firstborn, whence he early became known as Protogonos. He was bisexual and bore within him the seeds of all gods and men. He was also the creator of heaven and earth, of the sun, the stars, and the dwelling of the gods. The sixth Orphic hymn, dated to be sure in the Christian era but preserving old elements, represented him in epic hexameters:

> O mighty first-begotten, hear my prayer,
> Twofold, egg-born, and wandering through the air;
> Bull-roarer, glorying in thy golden wings,
> From whom the race of Gods and mortals springs.
> Ericapaeus, celebrated power,
> Ineffable, occult, all-shining flower.
> 'Tis thine from darksome mists to purge the sight,
> All-spreading splendor, pure and holy light;
> Hence, Phanes, called the glory of the sky,
> On waving pinions through the world you fly.

Phanes first created his daughter Nyx, the Night; in his bisexual quality, he was her father and mother at once. With Nyx, who alone was privileged to behold him, Phanes at vast intervals of time begat Gaea, Uranus, and Cronus, who after Uranus became lord of the world.

CREATION MYTH AS FOUND IN THE LAWS OF MANU[22]

8. He (that is the Self-existent) desiring to produce beings of many kinds from his own body, first with a thought created the waters and placed his seed in them. 9. That (seed) became a golden egg, in brilliancy equal to the sun; in the (egg) he himself was born as Brahman, the progenitor of the whole world. 10. The waters are called *narah* (for) the waters are, indeed, the

offspring of Nara; as they were his first residence, he thence is named Narayana. From that cause, which is indiscernible, eternal, and both real and unreal, was produced that male (Purusha) who is famed in this world (under the appelation of) Brahma. 12. The divine one resided in that egg during a whole year, then he himself by his thought (alone) divided it into two halves; 13. and out of those two halves he formed heaven and earth, between them the middle sphere, the eight points of the horizon, and the eternal abode of the waters.

The epic then continues to describe what was created from the Purusha himself.

A VERSION OF THE BABYLONIAN MYTH BASED ON EXCERPTS FROM DAMASCIUS AND BEROSSUS[23]

He says there was a time in which all was darkness and water, wherein strange and peculiarly shaped creatures came into being; that there were born men with two wings, some also with four wings and two faces; (some) also having one body but two heads, the one of a man, the other of a woman, being likewise in their genitals both male and female; and that there were other human beings with legs and horns of goats; that some had horses' feet; that others had the limbs of a horse behind, but before were fashioned like men, resembling hippocentaurs; that, likewise, bulls with the heads of men bred there; and dogs with fourfold bodies and the tails of fish; also horses with the heads of dogs; and men and other creatures with the heads and bodies of horses and the tails of fishes; and other creatures with the shapes of every species of animals; that besides these there were fishes, and reptiles, and serpents, and still other wondrous creatures, which had appearances derived from one another; that of these are set up appearances derived from one another; that of these are set up images in the temple of Bêl; (and) that over all these (creatures) ruled a woman named Omorka. This in Chaldean is *thamte,* meaning in Greek "the sea," but in numerical value it is equal to "moon."

He says that all things being in this condition, Bêl came and clove the woman in two; and that out of one half of her he formed the earth, but with the other half the sky; and that he destroyed the creatures within her; but that this was an allegorical description of nature; for while the whole universe consisted of moisture and such living creatures had been born therein, Bêl, who is identified with Zeus, divided the darkness in two, separated heaven and earth from one another, and reduced the universe to order; but that the living things, not being able to bear the strength of the light, perished; that this Bêl, upon perceiving that the land was desolate and bearing no fruit, commanded one of the gods to cut off his head, (that he also commanded the other gods) to mix the blood which flowed forth with earth, and to form men and animals capable of bearing the air; that this Bel also formed the stars, the sun, the moon, and the five planets. These things, according to Alexander Polyhistor, Berossus told in his first book: that this god cut off his own head, and that the other gods mixed the blood which flowed forth with earth and formed men; that on this account they are rational and partake of divine understanding.

A VERSION OF CREATION IN CHINESE MYTH AND LEGEND[24]

In the beginning there was chaos. Out of it came pure light and built the sky. The heavy dimness, however, moved and formed the earth from itself. Sky and earth brought forth the ten thousand creations, the beginning, having growth and increase, and all of them take the sky and earth as their mode. The roots of Yang and Yin—the male and female principle—also began in sky and earth.

Yang and Yin became mixed, the five elements separated themselves from it and a man was formed. As he looked about he perceived how the sun sank in a red haze in the west and in the east he saw the silver moon ascending, enveloped in the pale fog and all the stars were circling a great star which was in the middle of the world. Out of this illuminating pattern a brilliant ray fell to the earth and standing in front of this amazed man appeared someone like him yet different, he was completely golden in color. The Gold Colored One bowed to the man and honored him. He taught him how to make a garment from grass in order to cover his naked body. He gave him a name, "Huang-lao" (The Yellow Old Man), and showed him how to nourish himself from the roots of plants. He explained to him the journey of the stars, the year long path of sun and moon.

Huang-lao asked about the beginning of all things, about the form of heaven and earth. The Gold Shining form answered:

"In the beginning out of heaven and earth was produced that which is equivalent to blood which flows through the arteries of man. The earth bore fire which produces breath in man. Wind and clouds, rain and snow spread themselves between water and fire. When Yin and Yang diminish or increase in their power, heat and cold are produced. The sun and moon trade their light. This also produces the expiration of the year and the five opposites of the sky: east, south, west, north and midpoint. Thus sky and earth produce the form of man. Yang gives and Yin receives."

Huang-lao asked more questions concerning the nature of that which is beyond the earth and the Gold Colored One answered:

"In the middle of the earth grows a huge boulder which reaches up into the sky and there supports a mighty sphere. At the foot of this mountain flows a source which divides itself into ten thousand rivers and streams and all of these waters empty into the eight seas. The world is encircled by eight poles. The great earth, however, lies in the middle of the world sea in which are found four islands. Thus the water flows around all the sides of the great earth as the juicy meat surrounds the seed of fruit, as the white surrounds the yoke of an egg. In this way everything corresponds to the great in the small and the small in the great. The sun and moon, however, circle the earth in an endless movement and give light to the top and bottom of earth by their brightness."

The story continues from here telling of the populating of the earth and moves from there to the divine-hero, P'an-Ku, who orders the world and teaches men many things and finally vanishes. When he does, suffering appears on earth.

CREATION MYTH AS FOUND IN TAHITIAN FOLKLORE[25]

Ta'aroa (unique) was the great supreme being, who existed alone in a little world, in a shell like an egg, revolving in dark empty space for ages. At length, he burst forth from confinement, and finding himself quite alone he conjured forth the famous god Tu, who became his companion and artisan in the great work of creation. When the universe was completed, gods innumerable were conjured into existence to fill every region, and, last of all creatures, man was made to inhabit the earth, which was prepared for him.

Ta'aroa was known under four titles according to his attributes: Ta'aroa of the heaven, said to be ten in number; Ta'aroa the great foundation, in a rock in the centre of the earth, from which land grew; Ta'aroa of the surface of the earth; and Ta'aroa of the netherlands, supposed to be down in the earth, the entrance to which was an extinct crater called Te Mehani, in the island of Ra'iatea, near Tahiti. This crater is visited by tourists that pass that way; for a description of it, see "Na Motu," a book in the Honolulu Library, written by a sailor named Perkins, who descended into it and found chambers and winding passages extending into unknown regions of thick darkness, and he heard the fall and rush of a mighty stream of water, which in mythology is called Te-vai-tu-po-Ta-a'aroa (the river in darkness of Ta'aroa). Perkins carried a torch with him, which, to his regret, soon went out in the damp atmosphere, and with difficulty he groped his way out again.

The first man that was created was Ti'i, clothed in sand, whom Ta'aroa conjured from out of the earth, and then pronounced him perfect. Then was born a wife for Ti'i, Hina, to extricate and mitigate many things, a demi-goddess, whose parents were Te-fatu (the lord) and Fa'ahotu (be fruitful), and she had a face before and behind, and was full of goodness. Ti'i was malicious and had a white heron to bewitch and slay mankind.

After the creation, peace and harmony everywhere existed for a long time. But at last, discontentment arose and there was war among the gods in their different regions, and among men, so Ta'aroa and Tu uttered curses to punish them.

They cursed the stars, which made them blink; and they cursed the moon, which caused it to wane and go out. But Hina, the mitigator of many things, saved their lives since which the host of stars are ever bright, but keep on twinkling; and the moon always returns after it disappears.

They cursed the sea, which caused low tide; but Hina preserved the sea, which produced high tide; and so these tides have followed each other ever since.

They cursed the rivers, which frightened away the waters, so that they hid beneath the soil; but Hina reproduced the shy waters, which formed springs, and so they continue thus to exist.

They cursed the trees, which caused their leaves to turn yellow and their fruit to go out of season; but Hina saved their lives, which caused new leaves ever to succeed the old and the fruit to return in their seasons. An so it would have been with people, they would have withered under the curse of the gods, while Hina would have saved their lives, had it not been that Ti'i conjured them to death.

Hina said, "Oh, Ti'i! do not persist in invoking man to death! When he suffers under the curse of the gods, I shall resuscitate him. Behold, my moon and glittering stars, my budding trees and my fruit that come in seasons, are they not more comely than thy dying men?"

But her husband was unyielding, and he replied, "My master, Ta'aroa, whose curse is death, loves to slay, and I shall conjure to death all whom I cause my white heron to enter." So, according to the Tahitians, the man and not the woman caused people to lose eternal life, and at length he fell and died beneath his own curse.

BRAHMAN CREATION FROM EGG[26]

1. Verily, in the beginning this (universe) was water, nothing but a sea of water. The waters desired, "How can we be reproduced?" They toiled and performed fervid devotions (or, they toiled and became heated). When they were heated, a golden egg was produced. The year, indeed, was not then in existence; this golden egg floated about for as long as the space of a year.

2. In a year's time a man, this Prajapati, was produced therefrom; and hence a woman, a cow, or a mare brings forth within the space of a year; for Prajapati was born in a year. He broke open this golden egg. There was then, indeed, no resting-place: only this egg, bearing him, floated about for as long as the space of a year.

3. At the end of a year he tried to speak. He said: *"bhuh;"* this (word) became this earth;—*"bhuvah;"* this became this air;—

"*svah;*" this became yonder sky. Therefore a child tries to speak at the end of a year, for at the end of a year Prajapati tried to speak.

4. When he was first speaking Prajapati spoke (words) of one syllable and of two syllables; whence a child, when first speaking, speaks (words) of one syllable and of two syllables.

5. These (three words consist of) five syllables; he made them to be the five seasons, and thus there are these five seasons. At the end of the (first) year, Prajapati rose to stand on these worlds thus produced; whence a child tries to stand up at the end of a year, for at the end of a year Prajapati stood up.

6. He was born with a life of a thousand years; even as one might see in the distance the opposite shore, so did he behold the opposite shore (the end) of his own life.

7. Desirous of offspring, he went on singing praises and toiling. He laid the power of reproduction into his own self. By (the breath of) his mouth he created the gods; the gods were created on entering the sky; and this is the godhead of the gods that they were created on entering the sky. Having created them, there was, as it were, daylight for him; and this also is the godhead of the gods, that, after creating them, there was, as it were, daylight for him.

8. And by the downward breathing he created the Asuras; they were created on entering the earth. Having created them there was, as it were, darkness for him.

9. He knew, "verily, I have created evil, for myself since, after creating there has come to be, as it were, darkness for me." Even then he smote them with evil, and owing to this it was that they were overcome; whence people say, "Not true is that regarding (the fight between) the gods and Asuras which is related partly in the tale and partly in the legend, for it was even then that Prajapati smote them with evil, and it was owing to this that they were overcome."

The myth continues telling how Prajapati as well as the gods which he created continue creating through the performance of certain sacrifices.

BIRTH OF VÄINÄMÖINEN (KALEVALA)[27]

Short the time that passed thereafter;
Scarce a moment had passed over,
Ere a beauteous teal came flying
Lightly hovering o'er the water,
Seeking for a spot to rest in,
Searching for a home to dwell in.
Eastward flew she, westward flew she,
Flew to north-west and to southward,
But the place she sought she found not,
Not a spot, however barren,
Where her nest she could establish,
Or a resting-place could light on.
Then she hovered, slowly moving,
And she pondered and reflected,
"If my nest in wind I 'stablish
Or should rest it on the billows,
Then the winds will overturn it,
Or the waves will drift it from me."
Then the Mother of the Waters,
Water-Mother, maid aërial,
From the waves her knee uplifted,
Raised her shoulder from the billows,
That the teal her nest might 'stablish,
And might find a peaceful dwelling.
Then the teal, the bird so beauteous,
Hovered slow, and gazed around her,

And she saw the knee uplifted
From the blue waves of the ocean,
And she thought she saw a hillock,
Freshly green with spinging verdure.
There she flew, and hovered slowly,
Gently on the knee alighting,
And her nest she there established,
And she laid her eggs all golden,
Six gold eggs she laid within it,
And a seventh she laid of iron.
  O'er her eggs the teal sat brooding,
And the knee grew warm beneath her;
And she sat one day, a second,
Brooded also on the third day;
Then the Mother of the Waters,
Water-Mother, maid aërial,
Felt it hot, and felt it hotter,
And she felt her skin was heated,
Till she thought her knee was burning,
And that all her veins were melting.
Then she jerked her knee with quickness,
And her limbs convulsive shaking,
Rolled the eggs into the water,
Down amid the waves of ocean,
And to splinters they were broken,
And to fragments they were shattered.
In the ooze they were not wasted,
Nor the fragments in the water,
But a wondrous change came o'er them,
And the fragments all grew lovely.
From the cracked egg's lower fragment,
Rose the lofty arch of heaven,
From the yolk, the upper portion,
Now became the sun's bright lustre;

From the white, the upper portion,
Rose the moon that shines so brightly;
Whatso in the egg was mottled,
Now became the stars in heaven,
Whatso in the egg was blackish,
In the air as cloudlets floated.

ACCOUNT OF CREATION FROM THE CHANDOGYA UPANISHAD III, 19[28]

In the beginning this (universe) was non-existent. It became existent. It grew. It turned into an egg. The egg lay for the period of a year. Then it broke open. Of the two halves of the eggshell, one half was of silver, the other of gold. That which was of silver became the earth; that which was of gold, heaven. What was the thick membrane (of the white) became the mountains; the thin membrane (of the yolk), the mist and the clouds. The veins became the rivers; the fluid in the bladder, the ocean. And what was born of it was yonder Aditya, the sun. When it was born shouts of "Hurrah" arose, together with all beings and all objects of desire. Therefore at its rise and its every return shouts of "hurrah!" together with all beings and all objects of desire arise.

THE MANDE CREATION MYTH[29]

God, *Mangala,* first created the *balāzā (Acacia albida)* seed, which was, however, a failure. So he abandoned it in order to create twin varieties of eleusine seed, *fani berere* and *fani ba;* thus, as the Keita say, he "made the egg of the world in two twin parts which were to procreate." God then created six more seeds and associated with this group of eight seeds the four elements and the "cardinal points" in order to mark out the organization of the world and its expansion. Thus there was: in the west *(klebi)*: *fani berere* and *fani ba;* in the east *(koro)*: *sañõ* and *Keninge;* in the north *(kanaga)*: *so* and *kende;* in the south *(worodugu)*: *kaha* and *malo*. Finally the whole was enfolded in a hibiscus seed.

The seeds are thus conceived as twins of opposite sex in the "Egg of God" which is also called "egg of the world" or "placenta of the world." They are often represented in drawings as an open flower with four petals which are also sometimes called the four "clavicles" of God.

In the same egg, according to the myth, there were in addition two pairs of twins, each consisting of one male and one female, archetypes of the future men. One of the males, Pemba, desiring to dominate the creation, emerged prematurely, before gestation was complete, tearing away a piece of his placenta as he did so. He came down through empty space; the piece of placenta became the earth, but it was dry and barren and he could do nothing with it. Seeing this, he went back to heaven and tried to resume his place in the placenta and find his twin. In this he could not succeed, for God had changed the remaining part of his placenta into the sun. So Pemba then stole from one of God's clavicles the eight male seeds which he carried down in a calabash flask *(bara)*.

He sowed these seeds in the piece of placenta which had become the earth. In this first field, which the Keita locate near Bounan (a village not far from Lake Debo), only the *fani berere*—one of the eleusine seeds—germinated in the blood of the placenta; the other seeds died for want of water. Because of Pemba's theft and his incestuous act (for Pemba had put the seed in his own placenta, that is, in his mother's womb) the earth became impure and the eleusine seed turned red as it is today.

The other male twin, Faro, assumed, while in heaven, the form of twin *mannogo* fishes, which are represented in the Niger river today by the *mannogo ble* and the *mannogo fi.* The first represented his strength and his life, the second his body. In order to atone for Pemba's sin and purify the earth, Faro was sacrificed in heaven and his body was cut into sixty pieces which were scattered throughout space. They fell on the earth where they became trees, symbols of vegetal resurrection. God then brought Faro back to life in heaven and, giving him human shape, sent him down to earth on an ark made of his celestial placenta.

The ark came to rest on the mountain called Kouroula, in the area called *kele koroni* "ancient space," which lies between Kri and Kri Koro. This area was then given the name of Mande which the inhabitants translate as "son of the person" *(ma)* or more explicitly "son of the *mannogo*," the "person" being Faro whose first bodily form was that of a silurian fish. The place is also called "the mountain that encircles the world," it is said that "faro came out of this mountain, he took his life from the cloudy sky of Mande."

Where the ark came to rest near Kri there was a cave called *kaba koro,* or more commonly *ka.* Near this cave appeared a hollow in the earth which became the first pool, *ko koro* or *ko ba.* On the ark stood Faro, brought back to life, and also the eight original ancestors of men, created from Faro's placenta, that is to say four pairs of male and female twins called *mogo si segi.* The males of these twins were called: kanisimbo ("from Ka's womb"), Kani yogo simbo ("from the same Ka's womb"), Simboumba Tangnagati ("the big remaining part of the womb which took command"), Nounou (from *nono,* milk). In the ark were also all the animals and plants that were going to multiply on earth.

The first human beings, like Faro himself, had a common vital force *(nyama)* and complementary spiritual forces *ni* and *dya,* each of which had both a male and a female form. Also, in their clavicles were deposited the symbols of the eight seeds created by God. Emerging from the ark they watched, for the first time, the rising of the sun.

The bardic ancestor, Sourakata, then came down from heaven at Kri Koro holding in his hands the skull of the sacrificed Faro. This skull became the first drum. He played on it only once to ask, in vain, for rain. He then put the drum in a cave. The ancestral smith then came down to Kri, while Mousso Koroni Koundye, Pemba's female twin, came down "on the wind" at Bounan.

When he saw the prevailing drought the smith struck a rock with his hammer to ask for rain and water poured down from heaven, filling the hollow *ko koro* with purifying and fertilizing water. Two fishes then came down: *mannogo ble* and *mannogo fi*, manifestations of Faro. *Mannogo fi* is the archetype of man who was to be Faro's "son;" *mannogo ble* represents Faro himself, and on earth and in the water was to be the intermediary between him and mankind. This is why, for the Mande, this fish has become the basic taboo of a great number of people including the Keita.

Revelation of the Word and Building of the First Sanctuary

Simboumba Tangnagati, one of the male twins, who had entered the pool with the first fall of rain, was then given by Faro the first thirty words and the eight female seeds from God's clavicle. Now, coming out of the water, Simboumba said: "*nko* (I speak)." In order to plant out the seeds he had received, Simboumba Tangnagati left the area of the pool and, that very day at sunset, built a sanctuary on a hill near Kri Koro. This building, called *lu daga blo* (hall of the upper house), stood on the top of a hill; it was regarded as the "egg of the world" and was consecrated to the *mannogo ble*. It was made of black earth from the original pool, and its roof was made of bamboo from the same place which represented Faro's hair. The roof had six edges symbolizing the *mannogo ble's* beard, Faro's speech, and the spilling of water; inside the building Simboumba Tangnagati drew the sign of the *mannogo ble.*

From the door of the sanctuary Simboumba Tangnagati, who thence-forward was to be responsible for the seeds, the rain, and speech, gave men the first thirty words while the seeds were still in the sanctuary. He talked the whole night, ceasing only when he saw the sun and Sirius rising at the same time. This sun was what remained of Pemba's placenta, while Sirius, *sigi dolo,* was the image of Faro's placenta. During this night-long speech, the bard who was present carried a staff, symbol of Faro's resurrection, made of *ñogoñogo* wood which had grown in the first pool.

The following night the *mannogo ble,* coming out of the Kri pool where he had been hidden among the rice, entered the sanctuary. The next day Simboumba Tangnagati put the seeds on the *mannogo ble*'s head, at a place where there were signs. Then the rain started to pour down on the hill where the *blo* was. The *mannogo ble* then left the sanctuary and went back to the Kri pool. Then the rain, bringing down earth from the hill, spread it out near the pool.

The first human ancestor, Kanisimbo, now sowed in this earth some of the seeds which Simboumba Tangnagati had put in the *blo.* This first field was called *kanisimbo foro.* It was rectangular like the ark and orientated in an east-west direction. Kanisimbo marked off its limits with the rope made of *ñogoñogo* fibres from which the ark had been suspended during its descent to earth. The field was 80 "cubits" long and 60 "cubits" wide. The "cubits" marked out the work and also represented the length of a man's fore-arm. Kanisimbo then gave the rope to Simboumba who used it to tie down the roof of the sanctuary.

In the middle of the field Kanisimbo built a shrine made of three upright stones supporting a fourth. On the east he sowed the *fani berere,* on the west, the *fani ba,* on the north, the small millet *sãnõ,* on the south rice, *malo,* and in the centre maize, *kaba.* Finally hibiscus seeds, *da,* were sown all round the field.

After the first storm that followed upon the building of the *blo,* two stars began to circle round Sirius (*sigi dolo*). They represented the two descents of the seeds: the one, called *no dolo,* symbolized Pemba's male seeds, the second, called *dyi dolo,* Faro's female seeds.

The Building of the Second Sanctuary

During this period Mousso Koroni Koundye, Pemba's female twin, left Kri and fled to Bounan. There she grew the impure *fani berere* seeds and she and Pemba ate back part of the crop. Between Bounan and Kri, however, she dropped seeds all along her way, "sowing at night and cultivating by day." The wild animals sent by Faro tried with varying success to stop her.

Back in Kri, Mousso Koroni, in her fear, hid the *fani berere* brought from Bounan for seven years. Then, on a moonless night (*kalo laba*), she sowed it "when the sun was in the south." She kept trying "to catch the sun" which was made of the rest of her and Pemba's placenta. By sowing when the sun was in the south, at the time when it looked as if it were going to "fall," she thought "it would dry her field if Faro should attempt to flood it." But the moon when it rose revealed what she had done. The pool *kokoro* overflowed, poured down the hill, and flooded her field and the *mannogo ble* swallowed the seeds. It sowed part of them on the same spot and turned the rest into fishes' roe.

Men then came down to reap the field which Mousso Koroni had sown and thus, by recovering the seeds, witnessed to Faro's victory. They first built a second Mande *blo* which was an exact copy of the original one. In order to find the right place for it, Simboumba Tangnagati, the third ancestor, took his own seeds in a flask (*bara*) and followed the path the water had made when it flowed out of the pool. The *mannogo ble* showed the way. The place where the water had stopped in Mousso Koroni's field lay between Kaba and Kela and this spot became Faro's first seat (*faro tyn*). The second *blo* was built near it, at sunset, after rain had fallen. It was dedicated to the *mannogo fi*.

Inside this second sanctuary, also made of earth from the pool, Simboumba Tangnagati drew the sign of the *mannogo ble*, including all the marks he had on his head, and then the sign of the *mannogo fi*. The bamboo roof had six edges representing the beard of the *mannogo fi*.

The two stars which circled roung *sigi dolo*—*ño dolo* and *dyi dolo*—were symbolized by two balls of earth from the pool, dried and hung from the roof of the sanctuary; other signs represented Sirius, the sun, the moon, and the move from the first to the second sanctuary; each word was associated with a star and also had its sign.

A well (*kolo*) was dug near the sanctuary for Faro and for the *mannogo* which is thought to enter it whenever the roof is being repaired. To draw water from the well and pour it on the sown fields is called "to take the *mannogo* and put it in the field." Round the second sanctuary a field of *fani berere* was made to replace the one made by Mousso Koroni. Afterwards it was changed into a maize-field, maize (*kaba*) being a basic seed for the Keita. While his brothers went back to the hill, Simboumba Tangnagati, the third ancestor, settled down at the foot of the hill and took command "because of the word."

The first village was laid out at the four cardinal points round the central field which contained the sanctuary and was called Kaba, thus recalling that its centre was a maize-field, *keba*. Keba is also the name of the place where Faro came down to earth in the Kouroula mountains and in other contexts means "cloudy sky."

ANOTHER VERSION OF THE CREATION FROM POLYNESIA[30]

For a long period Ta'aroa dwelt in his shell (crust). It was round like an egg and revolved in space in continuous darkness.

There was no sun, no moon, no land, no mountain, all was in a confluent state. There was no man, no beast, no fowl, no dog, no living thing, no sea, and no fresh water.

But at last Ta'aroa was filliping his shell, as he sat in close confinement, and it cracked, and broke open. Then he slipped out and stood upon the shell, and he cried out, "Who is above there? Who is below there?" No voice answered! "Who is in front there? Who is in back there?" No voice answered! Only the echo of his own voice resounded and nothing else.

Then Ta'aroa said, "O rock, crawl hither!" But there was no rock to crawl to him. And he said, "O sand, crawl hither!" But there was no sand to crawl to him. Then he got vexed because he was not obeyed.

So he overturned his shell and raised it up to form a dome for the sky and called it Rumia. And he became wearied and after a short period he slipped out of another shell that covered him, which he took for rock and for sand. But his anger was not yet appeased, so he took his spine for a mountain range, his ribs for mountain slopes, his vitals for broad floating clouds, his flare and his flesh for fatness of the earth, his arms and legs for strength for the earth; his finger nails and toe nails for scales and shells for the fishes; his feathers for trees, shrubs, and creepers, to clothe the earth; and his intestines for lobsters, shrimps, and eels for the rivers and the seas; and the blood of Ta'aroa got heated and drifted away for redness for the sky and for rainbows.

But Ta'aroa's head remained sacred to himself, and he still

lived, the same head on an indestructible body. He was master of everything. There was expansion and there was growth.

Ta'aroa conjured forth gods, but it was much later that man was conjured, when Tu was with him.

As Ta'aroa had crusts, that is, shells, so has everything a shell.

The sky is a shell, that is, endless space in which the gods placed the sun, the moon, the Sporades, and the constellations of the gods.

The earth is a shell to the stones, the water, and plants that spring from it.

Man's shell is woman because it is by her that he comes into the world; and woman's shell is woman because she is born of woman.

One cannot enumerate the shells of all the things that this world produces.

A JAPANESE CREATION NARRATIVE[31]

Of old, Heaven and Earth were not yet separated, and the In and Yo not yet divided. They formed a chaotic mass like an egg, which was of obscurely defined limits, and contained germs. The purer and clearer part was thinly diffused and formed Heaven, while the heavier and grosser element settled down and became Earth. The finer element easily became a united body, but the consolidation of the heavy and gross element was accomplished with difficulty. Heaven was therefore formed first, and Earth established subsequently. Thereafter divine beings were produced between them.

The seventh generation consisted of two deities, Izanagi and Izanami. It is with them that Japanese myth really begins, all that precedes being merely introductory and for the most part of comparatively recent origin.

Izanagi and Izanami stood on the floating bridge of Heaven, and held counsel together, saying "Is there not a country beneath?" Thereupon they thrust down the "Jewel-Spear of Heaven" (Ame no tama-boko) and groping about with it, found the ocean. The brine which dripped from the point of the spear coagulated and formed an island which received the name of Onogoro-jima or the "Self-Coagulating Island." The two deities thereupon descended and dwelt there. Accordingly they wished to be united as husband and wife, and to produce countries. So they made Onogoro-jima the pillar of the centre of the land.

The two deities having descended on Onogoro-jima erected there an eight fathom house with an august central pillar. Then Izanagi addressed Izanami, saying: "How is thy body formed?" Izanami replied, "My body is completely formed except one part which is incomplete." Then Izanagi said, "My body is completely formed and there is one part which is superfluous. Suppose that we supplement that which is incomplete in thee with that which is superfluous in me, and thereby procreate lands." Izanami replied, "It is well." Then Izanagi said, "Let me and thee go round the heavenly august pillar, and having met at the other side, let us become united in wedlock." This being agreed to, he said, "Do thou go round from the left, and I will go round from the right." When they had gone round, Izanami spoke first and exclaimed, "How delightful! I have met a lovely youth." Afterwards he said, "It was unlucky for the woman to speak first." The child which was the first offspring of their union was the Hiruko (leech-child), which at the age of three was still unable to stand upright, and was therefore placed in a reed-boat and sent adrift.

Next they gave birth to the island of Tsukushi. This island likewise has four faces, and each face has a name. So the land of Tsukushi is called Shira-bi-wake (white-sun-youth); the land of

Toyo is called Toyo-bi-wake (rich-sun-youth); the land of Hi is called Take-hi-mukahi-toyo-kuji-hine-wake (brave-sun-confronting-rich-wondrous-lord-youth); the land of Kumaso is called Take-bi-wake (brave-sun-youth).

In the time of flowers the inhabitants worship her (Izanami) mitana by offerings of flowers. They also worship her with drums, flutes, singing and dancing.

When she died Izanami went to the land of Yomi, or darkness.

Thereafter Izanagi went after Izanami, and entered the land of Yomi. When he rejoined her, they conversed together. Izanami said: "My lord and husband, why is thy coming so late? I have already eaten of the cooking-furnace of Yomi. But I am about to lie down to rest. Do not thou look on me." Izanagi did not give ear to her, but secretly took his many-toothed comb, and breaking off its end-tooth made of it a torch and looked at her. Her body was already putrid, maggots swarmed over it, and the eight thunder-gods had been generated in her various members. Izanagi, greatly shocked, exclaimed, "What a hideous and polluted land I have come to unawares!" So he speedily ran away. Izanami was angry, and said, "Why didst thou not observe that which I charged thee? Now am I put to shame." So she sent the Ugly Females of Yomi to pursue and slay him. Izanagi, in his flight, threw down his many-toothed comb, which forthwith became changed into bamboo-shoots. The Ugly Females pulled them up and ate them. When they had done eating them they again gave chase. He then threw down his headdress, which became changed into grapes, and so once more delayed his pursuers. On reaching the foot of the "Even Pass of Yomi" he gathered three peaches that were growing there, and smote his pursuers with them, so that they all fled back. Moreover, he said to the peaches, "As ye have helped me, so must ye help all living people in the Central Land of Reed-plains when they are in trouble." And he gave them the title Oho-kamu-dzu-mi no mikoto (their augustness great-divine fruit).

This was the origin of the custom of exorcising evil spirits by means of peaches.

At the Even Pass of Yomi, Izanagi was overtaken by Izanami herself. He took a great rock and blocked up the pass with it, pronouncing at the same time the formula of divorce—namely, "Our relationship is severed." He also said, "Come no further," and threw down his staff, which was called Funado no Kami (pass-not-place-deity), or Kunado no Kami (come-not-place-deity). Moreover, he threw down his girdle, which was called Nagachiha no Kami. Moreover, he threw down his upper garment, which was called Wadzurahi no Kami (God of disease). Moreover, he threw down his trousers, which were called Aki-guhi no Kami. Moreover, he threw down his shoes, which were called Chishiki no Kami.

CHAPTER FOUR

CREATION FROM NOTHING

IN THE PREVIOUS CHAPTER we noted that in some myths our attention is focused on chaos as the primordial reality out of which the cosmos finally emerges. The beginning is spoken of as an undifferentiated mass existing in water and darkness. The first emergents from this chaotic mass are grotesque beings or an egg. The cosmos as a habitation for man is not created until much later. Indeed, the beings or gods who create the human cosmos are themselves born at a very late stage in the emergence process. We spoke in our introductory chapter of the persistence of the symbolism of the Sky Gods even after the concrete deities bearing the image of the sun appear. The *otiositas* character of Sky Gods is a way of speaking of their detachment, but also of their transcendence and sovereignty. This dimension of religious reality is hardly, if ever, lost by religious communities, even though the symbolism and cultic activity may center around more concrete manifestations of sacredness in the form of earth deities, chthonic powers, cultural heroes, or ancestors. When the Sky Gods reappear they are discovered anew as Supreme Beings, taking into themselves all of the powers and structures of the more concrete deities.

The reappearance or rediscovery of the Supreme Beings is usually a late development in the history of a religious system or religious-cultural area. Father Wilhelm Schmidt and his followers made the mistake of identifying the old Sky Gods with their later reappearance as Supreme Beings. The "urmonotheism" of Schmidt is really not a monotheism at all, for the true monotheistic deity takes into himself all of the previous religious structures.

Even in the classical types of monotheism which we find in Judaism and Islam, we are able to see vestiges of a notion of creation which emphasizes the struggle of the deity against the powers of chaos. For example, in Psalm 74:13-14 we read,

Thou didst divide the sea by thy might;
Thou didst break the heads of the dragons on the waters.
Thou didst crush the heads of Leviathan,
Thou didst give him as food for the creatures of the wilderness.

Furthermore, in the creation story in the second chapter of Genesis, God creates man from the earth. The Hebrews probably took over these notions from the other religious systems of the Ancient Near East. The fact that the Hebrews made use of them points to their persistence as religious symbols. Similar notions are to be found in the Islamic tradition.[1]

We have already made reference to Eldson Best's theory that the genealogical-type myth is the popular myth among the Polynesians while the myth which introduces the notion of a Supreme Being is the property of an esoteric cult of priests.

Ananda Coomaraswamy relates the water symbolism which is present in the Indian tradition to a very old and probably pre-Aryan period of Indian culture. We know that the Upanishads are by and large of a later period than the four principal Vedas.[2] The myths of the Ancient Egyp-

tians do not present us with a clear-cut picture. In Frankfort's work we *l*earn that Akhenaten, a pharaoh during
the seventeenth dynasty, broke with the Amon priesthood
of Thebes "when he persisted in his plan to dedicate the
Soil Festival not to the kings of the gods, Amon or Ptah . . .
but to the peculiar form of solar deity whose exclusive
worship he wanted to establish."[3] This Akhenaten cult
elevated one god, Aten, to a position of supremacy.

We are also aware of the long proto- and pre-history
of Greek religion before the time of Homer and Hesiod.
Zeus as the supreme deity appears only during the period
of the formation of the Greek city-states. Prior to this time,
Greek religion is filled with the worship of chthonic deities.
As a matter of fact, W. K. Guthrie thinks that the Orphic
religion serves as the bridge between the worship of Apollo
and that of Dionysus.[4]

We do not mean to infer that there is a natural development in religion from the worship of chthonic deities to
monotheism. We are simply saying that wherever we find
the tendency to worship one Supreme Being, there is usually
a long history of other religious structures prior to this
development. Neither are we implying that monotheism,
or the worship of a single Supreme Being, is the apex of
the history of religions. The worship of a Supreme Being
as the defining characteristic of a religious system is peculiar
to the Semitic religions. While this structure appears in
other religions, it does not constitute their defining characteristic. We shall have more to say on this topic when we
discuss the Hebrew myth of creation.

Let us make a distinction between the myths which
are presented in this chapter. All of the myths imply the
existence of a single Supreme Being and/or creation from a
void or nothing. In some of the myths, e.g., the Tuamotuan,
the Hebrew, the Zuñi, the Egyptian, the Mayan, the Poly-

nesian, the Maori, and the creation myth from Rig Veda X. 129, equal emphasis is given to the Supreme Being who performs the creative act and the manner in which he formed it. In the Polynesian myth, the Australian myth, and the Theogony of Hesiod, the manner of the creative act is stressed, but little or no prominence is given to a Supreme Being. The classical type of creation-from-nothing myth is illustrated by the former category. The latter category is a variant of the classical type. In the classical type of creation-from-nothing myths, four characteristics may be distinguished. First of all, the Creator deity is all-powerful. He does not share his power with any other deity or structure of reality. Secondly, and a correlate of the first point, the deity exists by himself, alone, in a void, or space. There is no material or reality prior to him in time or power. He creates the cosmos out of the void or nothingness in which he exists. Thirdly, the mode of creation is conscious, ordered, and deliberate; it reveals a definite plan of action. Finally, the Creator is free since he is not bound by the inertia of a prior reality.

Let us examine these characteristics as they occur in the myths.

1) In the Tuamotuan myth we read, "Then Kiho mused of all (potential) things whatever; and he caused his thought to be evoked, and thereupon he spoke to his Actuating self, saying, 'May I be eloquent of my indwelling occult knowledge, may I be expressive of my outpouring eloquence, in order that all assembled beings shall give ear.' "[5]

The Creator deity is all-powerful because he is wise; he knows the potentiality of all forms, but he has at the same time the power to create, to make these forms actual and concrete. In the Hebrew and Egyptian myths the very style of the language expresses the power of the deity. "And God said, 'Let there be light;' and there was light."[6] In the

Egyptian myth, Khepri's language carries the same power, "Then I spewed with my mouth; I spat out what was Shu, and I sputtered out what was Tefnut."[7] It is not only in the creation of specific forms that the power of the deity is manifest, but insofar as the mode of creation is expressive of his nature, his very essence is revealed as a plenitude of power.

Eldson Best provides us with a list of the names and titles of the Polynesian supreme being, Io.

Io. He is the core of all gods; none excel him.

Io-nui. He is greater than all gods.

Io-matua. He is the *matua* (parent) of the heavens and of their different realms; of the worlds, of clouds, of insects, of birds, of rats, of fish, of moons, of stars, of lightning, of winds, of waters, of trees, of all plant-life, of land, sea, and streams, as also all other things. There is no single thing that does not come under the control of Io-matua; he is the parent of all things—of man, and of all lesser gods under him; he is truly parent of all.

Io-matua-te-kora (Io the Parentless). This name of his denotes he has no parents, no mother, no elder or younger brothers, or sisters; he is nothing but himself.

Io-taketake. This name of his denotes the permanence of himself and all his acts, his thoughts, and his governments; all are enduring, all are firm, all are complete, all are immovable. . .

Io-te-wananga. That is to say, he is assuredly the source of all knowledge, whether pertaining to life, or to death, or to evil, or to good, or to dissensions or lack of such, or to peace-making or to failure to make peace; naught is there outside his influence.

Io-te-toi-o-nga-rangi (Io the Crown of the Heavens). This name shows that he is the god of the uppermost of all the heavens; there is no heaven beyond that one which is known as the Toi-o-nga-rangi. That is the first of the heavens, from which descent is made to the eleven heavens below the Toi-o-nga-rangi (or uppermost of the heavens). . . .

Io-mataaho. His appearance as he moves abroad is as that of radiant light only; he is not clearly seen by any being of the heavens, of the worlds, or divisions abroad.

Io-te-whiwhi. This name denotes that nothing can possess anything of its own volition; by his intention only can it possess aught, or not so possess, no matter who or what it be—persons or supernational beings, or realms, or heavens, or divisions of such, or moons, or suns, or stars, or waters, or winds, or rains. . . .[8]

The long list above leaves no doubt concerning the omnipotence of Io. The fact that Io possesses all of the attributes and qualities which are normally assigned to the many departmental deities shows that the appearance of this religious structure comes late in Polynesian religion. The departmental deities represent the discovery of sacredness on various levels of culture. These discoveries were not made simultaneously. Every polytheistic pantheon presupposes a long religious history. In a sense the Supreme Being is that religious structure which recapitulates and revalorizes all aspects of sacredness into a unitary form. Here again, we can see the untenability of Schmidt's theory of an "urmonotheism."

Strehlow illustrates this point in his commentary on the Australian myth. The Great Father is a creator but he did not create all things.

Consider, firstly, the interest taken by native myth-makers in speculations about the origin of life. All human beings, by reason of the prevailing system of totemism, are held to have originated from one or other of these legendary ancestors. How then did the ancestors themselves originate? Various answers are given in different tribes and even in different tribal groups. In the Northern Aranda group, where we come upon a strongly patrilineal order of claiming descent, the answer is given as stated above. Here we find the idea of the Great Father, who was ever from the beginning, and from whose body both the animals and the men of a certain totem have originated. It must be stressed, too, that no mention is made of women in this myth: from the original Great Father only sons have descended.[9]

An aspect of monotheism is the worship of a single

Supreme Being, but this is only one dimension of its meaning. This Supreme Being's power must be related to the concrete forms of cultural life. The early sky deities are understood by Schmidt to represent an "urmonotheism" and have little or no relationship to the concrete structures of cultural life. It is precisely this aspect of monotheism which forces all monotheistic religious structures into the theological problem of the one and the many. In the Polynesian system this problem is dealt with by assigning different names and attributes to Io. In Christianity the doctrine of the Trinity serves a similar purpose. In Judaism the Word of God is the Law and the prophets. Within the Muslim community, the Koran is the concrete pole of the monotheistic structure. In the classical formulations of monotheism, the attempt is always made to maintain the distinction between the sovereignty and transcendence of the deity and his concrete embodiment. Though Hinduism and Buddhism are not monotheistic religions, a similar problem can be seen in some of their theological formulations. Insofar as ultimate reality cannot be identified with any of its concrete manifestations (saṃsāra) some attempt is made to reconcile the ultimate which is nonbeing and the multiplicity of beings in the universe.

We have already said that the worship of a single Supreme Being presupposes a long cultural and religious history. It should be added at this point that a certain monotheistic tendency is present in all genuine religious experience. This arises from the simple fact that a worshiper cannot worship more than one deity at a time. If we accept Joachim Wach's definition of religious experience as the "total response of the total being to what is apprehended as ultimate reality"[10] then the religious response is a total response to particular and concrete manifestations which embodies ultimate reality. This means that even in polytheistic religious structures only one god is venerated at

any particular time. Moreover, this fact explains the transmutations of qualities and attributes from one deity to
another in polytheistic religions. For example, Khepri, the
Egyptian deity who appears under the form of a beetle, is
a manifestation of the solar deity. He is also called "he who
becomes." The Egyptian solar deity appears under a variety
of forms.[11] These forms are dictated by the particular form
of sacredness which the worshiper recognizes in the deity.
The Akhenaten reform must be recognized as an attempt to
stabilize all the qualities of sacredness under one form—
the form of the solar disc, Aten. Such a reform would
mean that the transmutations of the qualities of the solar
deity from one form to another would no longer be possible.

2) The deity exists by himself in space as in a void.

In the case of Khepri, we have a manifestation of the
Egyptian solar deity in his procreative form. As Khepri,
the power of the sun asserts its sovereignty over the chaos
of darkness. As such he asserts that he was the first to come
into being.

> I am he who came into being as Khepri. When I had come into
> being, being (itself) came into being, and all beings came into being
> after I came into being. Many were the beings which came forth from
> my mouth, before heaven came into being, before earth came into
> being, before the ground and creeping things had been created in this
> place, I put together (some) of them in Nun as weary ones, before I
> could find a place in which I might stand.[12]

In this passage Khepri is the Creator of Nun, the primordial
chaos. Not the primordial chaos but Khepri is the source of
all the universe. Through a deliberate act, Khepri brings
all structures of creation into being.

We notice the same conception in the Memphis theology. In the Memphis theology, Ptah is the supreme deity of
creation. In distinction from Khepri, who is a manifestation

of solar symbolism, Ptah is a manifestation of an earth symbolism.

(There) originated in the heart and on the tongue (of Ptah) (something) in the image of Atum.

Great and exalted is Ptah who bequeathed his power to all the gods and their Kas through his heart and on his tongue. . . .

It happened that heart and tongue prevailed over (all other) members, considering that he (Ptah) is (as heart) in every body, (as tongue) in every mouth, of all gods, people, beast, crawling creatures, and whatever else lives, while he thinks (as heart) and commands (as tongue) everything that he wishes. . . .

Every divine word came into being through that which was thought by the heart and commanded by the tongue.

And thus the Kas* were made and the Hemsut** were created that they make all sustenance and all food—by this speech (that was thought by the heart and was spoken by the tongue).

(And so justice is done to him) who does what is liked, (and evil is done to him) who does what is hated.

And so life is given to the peaceful, death to the criminal.

And so are done all labor and all arts, the action of the arms, the going of the legs, the movement of all members according to this command which was thought by the heart and issued from the tongue and which constitutes the significance of things.[13]

In the Memphite theology of Ptah, it is maintained that Ptah is prior to the sun. Ptah creates the primordial chaos and the sun emerges from this chaos. Because he is a supreme Creator deity no reality exists before him. These two versions of Egyptian mythology illustrate this point in the case of ancient Egypt. The Zuñi myth begins with the sentence, "Before the beginning of the new-making, Awonawilone (the Maker and Container of All, the All-father Father) solely and being, there was nothing else whatsoever throughout the great space of the ages save everywhere black dark-

* Frankfort interprets Ka to mean an impersonal vital force which may reside in man or any object.
** Hemsut is the female counterpart of Ka.

ness in it, and everywhere void desolation."[14] This same motif can be seen in the initial statements of the Hebrew, Mayan, Maori, Polynesian, and Tuamotuan myths.

The Creator deity is, by virtue of his aloneness, detached from the world and therefore not subject to the categories which subsequently apply to the cosmos. He is therefore eternal: having no beginnings he likewise has no end. Temporality begins with the creation of specific phenomena. Before this stage of creation there is no time, only eternity or primordial time. Time can be renewed just because there is a reality which does not participate in time; the Creator himself is the source of all time. Everything done by this deity is perfect, and because of their perfection his creative acts become the divine models or archtypes for all temporal forms.

In the Maori myth the relationship between the myth and its role as an archtype is stated explicitly.

> And now my friends, there are three very important applications of those original sayings, as used in our sacred rituals. The first occurs in the ritual for implanting a child within the womb. The next occurs in the ritual for enlightening both the mind and the body. The third and last occurs in the ritual on the solemn subjects of death, and of war, of baptism, of genealogical recitals, and such important subjects, as the priests most particularly concerned themselves in.[15]

3) The method of creation is conscious, deliberate and orderly.

In the Tuamotuan myth, we observe the very orderly manner in which the creative acts of Kiho progressively bring into being the structures of the cosmos. In the Egyptian myth, these words are spoken by Khepri, "I planned in my heart . . . ," and in the Zuñi myth, Awonawilone creates by means of his innate knowledge. In the Maori, Mayan and Hebrew myths the supreme deity creates through his word.

This form of creation is different from all the other methods we have discussed in the previous chapters. In the Emergence myths, creation seems to result from some involuntary activity within the womb of the earth. The cosmos is created through a process of metamorphosis. Contrast this with the statement in the Hebrew myth, "And God said, 'Let there be light;' and there was light." In the World-Parent myths the offspring must overcome the primordial parents before creation can take place. There is usually a fight between a parent and the offspring before this can be accomplished. Nothing of this fight against a previous form of reality is to be found in the creation-from-nothing myths. The same difference exists between the myths here and those myths which emphasize chaos, egg, or earth divers.

A conscious and deliberate effort lies behind the structures of the cosmos, which participate in power and holiness, because they have been created through the will of the deity. We have placed another group of myths in this chapter and have called them a variation of the creation-from-nothing myths. They contain some of the essential characteristics of the creation-from-nothing myths, but not all of them.

The Australian myth of the Great Father attributes creation to a single male deity, but in this myth the conscious and deliberate acts of creation are not present. Though his first creative acts are a result of his thoughts, the bull-roarer and a full-grown man emerge from his body while he is asleep. There is furthermore a flaw in the creation since enough bandicoots have not been created to provide an adequate food supply. The power to rectify this error is not actualized by the Great Father. This flaw in the creation is present in the Mayan myth, one of our classical types, but the rectification of this flaw leads to the total destruction of the world and the creation of a new and perfect one. In other words, that which is created by the Supreme Beings in the classical types of "creation-from-nothing" myths must be perfect.

In the Theogony of Hesiod, Void comes into being first, then Earth and Eros or Desire. From Void comes Darkness and Night, and from Night comes Light and Day. Though we have Void existing in the beginning, there is no Supreme Being present in the Void. The Earth seems to emerge from the Void by a kind of metamorphosis. The coupling of the various creatures of the metamorphosis produces a variety of other creatures. The cosmos is not ordered under the control of any law. The old motifs of World Parents and divine offspring come to the fore, and order is not established until Zeus is invited to take charge of the cosmos and to order it.

> . . . Mother Earth advised them to invite Zeus, with far-sighted kin, to be king and lord over the gods. . . . Zeus' first royal consort was Metis [Wisdom] the wisest of gods and men. . . . Zeus' second consort was Themis [Law], and that radiant lady gave birth to the Hours—Good Order, Justice, and prosperous Peace. . . .[16]

In contrast to these variants, the classical creation-from-nothing myths assert that the cosmos is created as a model of a plan in the mind of the deity. In the Mayan myth, the Forefathers who represent the unity and diversity of attributes of the supreme deity deliberate about the creation; then at a certain moment they shout:

> Thus let it be done! Let emptiness be filled. Let the water recede and make a void, let the earth appear and become solid; let it be done. This they spoke. . . . Then the earth was created by them. So it was, in truth, that they created the earth. Earth! they said, and instantly it was made.[17]

One is equally impressed with the order which is present in the Hebrew myth. Particular forms are created on successive days by the deity.

4) The revelation of purpose and the freedom of the deity.

We spoke above of the very explicit archtypes in the Maori myth. This is an instance of the purposiveness of the supreme deity. The cosmos itself is a result of his reflections; thus each particular form in creation and the cosmos as a whole are instruments of his purposes.

We have referred to some of the myths in this chapter as classical examples of creation-from-nothing myths. We did not mean to imply that all of the religious systems in which these myths appear are to be identified as monotheistic religions. They are, rather, examples of the monotheistic tendency which we find in most religions. True monotheistic religious systems occur where the monotheistic structure becomes the dominant religous attitude of the entire religious system.

Though Ptah and Khepri in Egypt express the monotheistic structures, these patterns in the final analysis are a part of a religious system which is permeated by the dying and rising god in the form of Isis-Osiris-Horus. In other words, the immanence of divine power in the structures of Mother Earth, fecundity, and nature symbolism remain paramount.

Among Maoris, and among the Polynesians generally, the supreme deity in the form of Io or some other deity is limited to a small priestly cult. This conception of deity never superseded the worship of departmental deities who are derivatives from the World Parent mythological type. The meaning of the supreme deity does not lead to a new discovery of sacrality. Its meaning is thus expressed in the Maori myth in the old forms of procreation and purification.

A similar judgment must be made concerning the Mayan myth. In the myth from Rig Veda X. 129, we have a conception of a being who creates, but his uniqueness and detachment from creation are not emphasized. A general skepticism is expressed concerning his nature and essence. Though his power asserts itself in creation, he remains hidden, his plans and purposes are shrouded in secrecy.

> Who knows for certain? Who shall declare it?
> Whence was it born, and whence came this creation?
> The gods were born after this world's creation:
> Then who can know from whence it has arisen?[18]

Of the myths in this chapter, only the Hebrew myth is a part of a monotheistic religious structure. The monotheistic structure is the dominant religous form in Judaism because the Hebrews discovered in this form a new dimension of sacredness. To have one god meant for them to have one world and one time. The Hebrew myth must be seen in relationship to the exodus of the children of Israel from Egypt. We are certain that the myth in Genesis was written much later than the Exodus, probably in the eighth century B.C. The Exodus was the real beginning of the cosmos for the Hebrews. In this event Yahweh showed himself to be a powerful and purposive deity. His power manifested itself in the defeat of the Egyptians and in the creation of a people from a group of slaves who were no people. He gave them a land which was previously not their land. His decisive action took place in the time of man and not in primordial time. In the Hebrew myth, the structures of natural phenomena do not become the essential forms through which Yahweh expresses his power. To be sure, the Hebrews assimilate a great deal from the Canaanites and other Ancient Near Eastern peoples, but the religious structures of these peoples are always in tension with the overwhelming

monotheistic symbolism of Yahweh. Eliade expresses the
meaning of this monotheism as follows:

> But, for the first time, we find affirmed, and increasingly accepted, the
> idea that historical events have a value in themselves, insofar as they
> are determined by the will of God. This God of the Jewish people is
> no longer an Oriental divinity, creator of archetypal gestures, but a
> personality who ceaselessly intervenes in history, who reveals his will
> through events (invasions, sieges, battles, and so on). Historical facts
> thus become "situations" of man in respect to God, and as such acquire
> a religious value that nothing had previously been able to confer on
> them. It may, then, be said with truth that the Hebrews were the first
> to discover the meaning of history as the epiphany of God, and this
> conception, as we should expect, was taken up and amplified by Chris-
> tianity.[19]

In a similar vein, Bruno Bettelheim contrasts circumcision among primitives and Hebrews.[20] In most primitive
societies circumcision takes place at puberty. The male youth
is able after circumcision to participate in sexual intercourse on an adult level, and he is also permitted to marry.
In other words, the newness of his life as an adult is immediately related to the structures of nature through his
greater capacity for participation in sexual activity. Among
the Hebrews, circumcision takes place during infancy. The
child does not know the significance of the act at the time
it takes place. Since the act does not coincide with the discovery of a new structure of reality for the infant he must
be told at a later date the meaning of the act. In the formula
of the ritual, the father tells the son that this act was done
in obedience to the will of God and is a sign of the covenant
between God and the Hebrews. The Hebrews are thus
related to God through faith.[21]

The creation myth in Genesis is the Hebrews' reflection
on the beginnings of the world—a reflection which is an
expression of the dominant monotheistic structure in their
life.

The evaluation of man takes a new turn in Judaism. The definitive act of Yahweh is an act which takes place in history. This action does not conform to the structures of nature but to the will and power of Yahweh, who is detached from nature. Nature becomes historical and history is the story of the relations between Yahweh and his people. This relationship begins at a certain time and will come to an end at a definitive time.

> The God who sustains the world is not a static source, but one who is active from *olam* to *olam*. The source is nothingness; God's act of creation is the only reality. God is not contingent on the world, the world is only and always contingent on God. This is expressed in the *theologoumenon of creatio ex nihilo,* which, though suggested by only one passage in the Bible (II Macc. 7:28) is deeply anchored in the Jewish consciousness. The paradox of a creation from nothingness— not a mere ordering, not even a founding, but a kind of magical evocation, is already inherent in the contrast between the two Biblical terms *bara,* "to create by the word," and *asa,* "to make," "to produce". . . .* [22]

This basic religious structure is taken over into Christianity. The problem of the relationship between creation and nature has been a watershed of philosophical and theological thought in Western culture and remains a central topic of discussion even today.[23]

We might summarize the discussions of Altizer, Brandon, and Eliade by asking the following questions: Is it possible for a linear notion of time to bear the weight of human history? If time is real, then all of the suffering and misfortunes of time must also be real. How is it possible for the human being to bear up under this weight of misery? In addition to these problems, does not the monotheistic structure separate man from nature in the external

---

* The Hebrew term *olam* is from J. Pedersen who discusses it (*Israel,* Vol. I, Geoffrey Cumberlege [Oxford, 1946], p. 491) as follows: "Primeval time absorbs in it the substance of all time, and is therefore the beginning of all time; *olam* is history and thus the world as a compact whole."

sense and from his own human nature, making it impossible for him to live in a cosmos? If one accepts the Jewish-Christian monotheistic structure, how can nature become a religious resource?

It is not the place for us to enter into a discussion of these problems in this book. We mention them to illustrate the importance of a certain mythological problem for our contemporary culture.

AUSTRALIAN MYTH OF THE GREAT FATHER[24]

In the very beginning everything was resting in perpetual darkness: night oppressed all the earth like an inpenetrable thicket. The gurra ancestor—his name was Karora—was lying asleep in everlasting night, at the very bottom of the soak of Ilbalintja; as yet there was no water in it, but all was dry ground. Over him the soil was red with flowers and overgrown with many grasses; and a great tnatantja* was swaying above him. This tnatantja had sprung from the midst of the bed of purple flowers which grew over the soak of Ilbalintja. At its root rested the head of Karora himself: from thence it mounted up towards the sky as though it would strike the very vault of the heavens. It was a living creature, covered with a smooth skin like the skin of a man.

And Karora's head lay at the root of the great tnatantja: he had rested thus ever from the beginning.

And Karora was thinking, and wishes and desires flashed through his mind. Bandicoots began to come out from his navel and from his arm-pits. They burst through the sod above, and sprang into life.

And now dawn was beginning to break. From all quarters men

* Tnatantja is the decorated pole used in the native ceremonies.

saw a new light appearing: the sun itself began to rise at Ilba-lintja, and flooded everything with its light. Then the gurra an-cestor was minded to rise, now that the sun was mounting higher. He burst through the crust that had covered him: and the gaping hold that he left behind became the Ilbalintja Soak, filled with the sweet dark juice of the honeysuckle buds. The gurra ancestor rose, feeling hungry, since magical powers had gone out from his body.

As yet he feels dazed; slowly his eyelids begin to flutter; then he opens them a little. He gropes about in his dazed state; he feels a moving mass of bandicoots all around him. He is now standing more firmly on his feet. He thinks, he desires. In his great hunger he seizes two young bandicoots; he cooks them some little distance away, close to the spot where the sun is stand-ing, in the white-hot soil heated by the sun; the sun's fingers alone provide him with fire and hot ashes.

His hunger satisfied, his thoughts turn towards a helpmate. But now evening is approaching over the earth; the sun hides his face with a veil of hair-string, covers his body with hair-string pen-dants, vanishes from the sight of men. And Karora falls asleep, stretching his arms out on both sides.

While he is asleep, something emerges from underneath his arm-pit in the shape of a bull-roarer.* It takes on human form, and grows in one night to a full-grown young man: this is his first-born son. At night Karora wakes up, because he feels that his arm is being oppressed with the weight of something heavy: he sees his first-born son lying at his side, his head resting on his father's shoulder.

Dawn breaks. Karora rises; he sounds the loud vibrating call known as raiankintja. The son is thereby stirred into life. He

---

* The bull-roarer is a piece of flat wood pointed at both ends. It has a hole drilled into one end and through this a length of hair-string is threaded. Often the end with the drill hole is rounded rather than pointed. Bull-roarers are twirled vigorously in ceremonies where the young men are summoned by their humming or whistling sound.

rises; he dances the ceremonial dance around the father who is sitting adorned with full ceremonial designs worked in blood and feather-down. The son totters and stumbles; he is still only half awake. The father puts his body and chest into a violent quiver; then the son places his hands upon him. The first ceremony has come to an end.

The son is now sent by his father to kill some more of the bandicoots which are playing peacefully about near by in the shade. The son brings them back to his father who cooks them in the sun-glowing soil as before, and shares the cooked meat with his son. Evening has come again, and soon both are asleep. Two more sons are born that night to the father, from out of his arm-pits; these he calls into life on the following morning by the raiankintja call as before.

This process is repeated for many days and nights. The sons do the hunting; and the father brings into life an increasing number of sons each night—as many as fifty on some nights. But the end cannot be delayed overlong; soon father and sons have succeeded in devouring all the bandicoots which had originally sprung from Karora's body. In their hunger the father sends his sons away on a three-days' hunt, to scour the great Ilbalintja Plain as far as Ininta and Ekallakuna. For hours they search patiently amongst the tall white greas, in the half-light of the almost limitless expanse of mulga-trees. But the vast mulga thicket is devoid of bandicoots, and they have to return.

It is the third day.

The sons are returning, hungry and tired, through the great stillness. Suddenly a sound comes to their ears, a sound like that of a whirling bull-roarer. They listen; they proceed to search for the man who may be swinging it. They search and search and search. They stab with their tjurunga sticks into all bandicoot nests and resting places. Suddenly something dark and hairy darts up and is gone. A shout goes up—'There goes a sandhill

wallaby'. They hurl their tjurunga sticks after it and break its leg.
And then they hear the words of a song coming from the injured
animal:

I, Tjenterama, have now grown lame,

Yes, lame; and the purple everlastings are clinging to me. 'I
am a man as you are; I am not a bandicoot.' With these words
the lame Tjenterama limps away.

The astonished gurra brothers continue on their way home to
their father. Soon they see him approaching. He leads them back
to the soak. They sit on its edge in circles, one circle around the
other, ever widening out like ripples in disturbed water. And
then the great pmoara flood of sweet honey from the honeysuckle
buds comes from the east and engulfs them; it swirls them back
into the Ilbalintja Soak.

Here the aged Karora remained; but the sons were carried by
the flood under the ground to a spot in the mulga thicket.* Here
they rejoined the great Tjenterama, whose leg they had un-
wittingly broken with their tjurunga sticks.

Today, at that new ceremonial ground the natives point out
the rocks and stones which represent the undying bodies of the
gurra brothers which lie on top of the round stone which is said
to be the body of Tjenterama; and this Tjenterama whom they
had injured, is now their new chief; and in all the present-day
bandicoot ceremonies Tjenterama is represented as the great
gurra chief of Ilbalintja. Karora, the natives say, remained behind at his original home: he is lying in eternal sleep at the bottom of the Ilbalintja Soak; and men and women who approach
the soak to quench their thirst may do so only if they bear in
their hands bunches of green inuruna boughs which they lay
down on the edge of the soak. For then Karora is pleased with
their coming and smiles in his sleep.

* Three miles further on.

THE THEOGONY OF HESIOD[25]

II, 116-153

First of all, the Void came into being, next broad-bosomed Earth, the solid and eternal home of all, and Eros [Desire], the most beautiful of the immortal gods, who in every man and every god softens the sinews and overpowers the prudent purpose of the mind. Out of Void came Darkness and black Night, and out of Night came Light and Day, her children conceived after union in love with Darkness. Earth first produced starry Sky, equal in size with herself, to cover her on all sides. Next she produced the tall mountains, the pleasant haunts of the gods, and also gave birth to the barren waters, sea with its raging surges—all this without the passion of love. Thereafter she lay with Sky and gave birth to Ocean with its deep current, Coeus and Crius and Hyperion and Iapetus; Thea and Rhea and Themis [Law] and Mnemosyne [Memory]; also golden-crowned Phoebe and lovely Tethys. After these came cunning Cronus, the youngest and boldest of her children; and he grew to hate the father who had begotten him.

Earth also gave birth to the violent Cyclopes—Thunderer, Lightner, and bold Flash—who made and gave to Zeus the thunder and the lightning-bolt. They were like the gods in all respects except that a single eye stood in the middle of their foreheads, and their strength and power and skill were in their hands.

There were also born to Earth and Sky three more children, big, strong, and horrible, Cottus and Briareus and Gyes. This unruly brood had a hundred monstrous hands sprouting from their shoulders, and fifty heads on top of their shoulders growing from their sturdy bodies. They had monstrous strength to match their huge size.

III, 154-210

Of all the children born of Earth and Sky these were the boldest, and their father hated them from the beginning. As each of them was about to be born, Sky would not let them reach the light of day; instead he hid them all away in the bowels of Mother Earth. Sky took pleasure in doing this evil thing. In spite of her enormous size, Earth felt the strain within her and groaned. Finally she thought of an evil and cunning stratagem. She instantly produced a new metal, gray steel, and made a huge sickle. Then she laid the matter before her children; the anguish in her heart made her speak boldly: "My children, you have a savage father; if you will listen to me, we may be able to take vengeance for his evil outrage: he was the one who started using violence."

This was what she said; but all the children were gripped by fear, and not one of them spoke a word. Then great Cronus, the cunning trickster, took courage and answered his good mother with these words: "Mother, I am willing to undertake and carry through your plan. I have no respect for our infamous father, since he was the one who started using violence."

This was what he said, and enormous Earth was very pleased. She hid him in ambush and put in his hands the sickle with jagged teeth, and instructed him fully in her plot. Huge Sky came drawing night behind him and desiring to make love; he lay on top of earth stretched all over her. Then from his ambush his son reached out with his left hand and with his right took the huge sickle with its long jagged teeth and quickly sheared the organs from his own father and threw them away, backward over his shoulder. But that was not the end of them. The drops of blood that spurted from them were all taken in by Mother Earth, and in the course of the revolving years she gave birth to the powerful Erinyes [Spirits of Vengeance] and the huge Giants with shining armor and long spears. As for the organs themselves, for a long time they drifted round the sea just as they were when Cronus cut them off with the steel edge and threw them from the land into the waves of the ocean; then white foam issued from the divine flesh, and in the foam a girl began to grow. First she came near the holy Cythera, then reached Cyprus, the land surrounded by sea. There she stepped out, a goddess, tender and beautiful, and round her slender feet the green grass shot up. She is called Aphrodite by gods and men, because she came near to Cythera, and the Cyprian, because she was born in watery Cyprus. Eros [Desire] and beautiful Passion were her attendants both at her birth and at her first going to join the family of the gods. The rights and privileges assigned to her from the beginning and recognized by men and gods are these: to preside over the whispers and smiles and tricks which girls employ, and the sweet delight and tenderness of love.

Great Father Sky called his children the Titans, because of his feud with them: he said that they blindly had tightened the noose and had done a savage thing for which they would have to pay in time to come.

IV, 211-336

Night gave birth to hateful Destruction and the black Specter and Death; she also bore Sleep and the race of Dreams—all these the dark goddess Night bore without sleeping with any male. Next she gave birth to Blame and painful Grief, and also the Fates and the pitiless Specters of Vengeance: it is these goddesses who keep account of the transgressions of men, then Deceit and Love and accursed Old Age and stubborn Strife.

Hateful Strife gave birth to painful Distress and Distraction and Famine and tearful Sorrow; also Wars and Battles and Murders and Slaughters; also Feuds and Lying Words and Angry Words; also Lawlessness and Madness—two sisters that go together—and the Oath, which, sworn with willful falsehood, brings utter destruction on men.

PLATE 17. *Baga dance mask. Africa.*

PLATE 18. *Bobo dance mask. Africa.*

PLATE 19. *Bambara dance mask. Africa.*

PLATE 20. *Dogon female figure. Africa.*

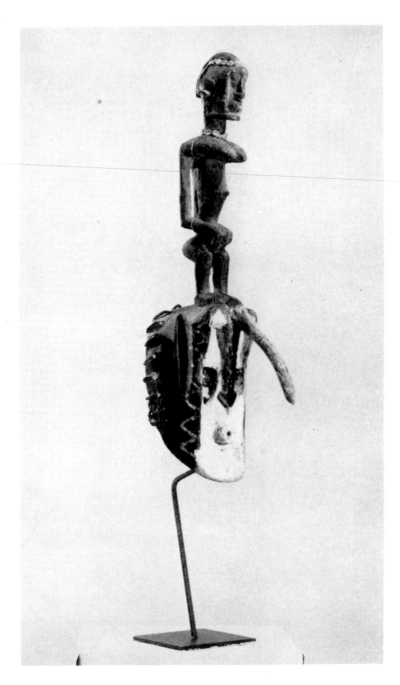

PLATE 21. *Dogon mask with figure. Africa.*

PLATE 22. *Mask. Melanasia.*

PLATE 23. *Ceremonial board. New Guinea.*

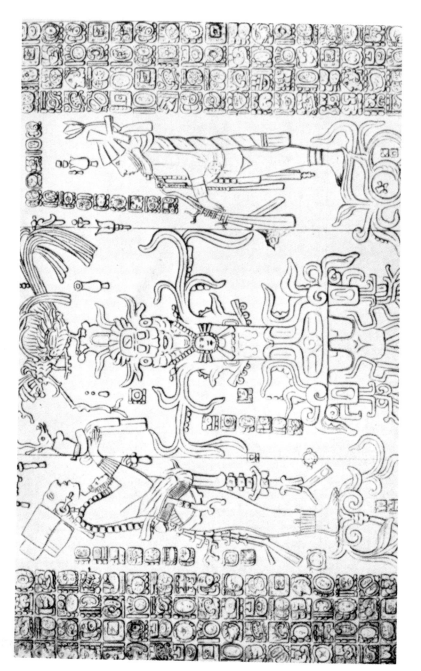

PLATE 24. *Bas relief. Mayan temple.*

HYMN OF CREATION FROM
RIG VEDA X. 129[26]

1. There was then neither non-existence nor existence;
   There was no air, nor sky that is beyond it.
   What was concealed? Wherein? In whose protection?
   And was there deep unfathomable water?

2. Death then existed not nor life immortal;
   Of neither night nor day was any token.
   By its inherent force the One breathed windless:
   No other thing than that beyond existed.

3. Darkness there was at first by darkness hidden;
   Without distinctive marks, this all was water.
   That which, becoming, by void was covered,
   That One by force of heat came into being.

4. Desire entered the One in the beginning;
   It was the earliest seed, of thought the product.
   The sages searching in their hearts with wisdom,
   Found out the bond of existence in non-existence.

5. Their ray extended light across the darkness:
   But was the One above or was it under?
   Creative force was there, and fertile power:
   Below was energy, above was impulse.

6. Who knows for certain? Who shall here declare it?
   Whence was it born, and whence came this creation?
   The gods were born after this world's creation:
   Then who can know from whence it has arisen?

7. None knoweth whence creation has arisen;
   And whether he has or has not produced it:
   He who surveys it in the highest heaven,
   He only knows, or haply he may know not.

ANCIENT MAYA CREATION MYTH
FROM THE POPOL VUH[27]

This is the account of how all was in suspense, all calm, in silence, all motionless, still, and the expanse of the sky was empty.

This is the first account, the first narrative. There was neither man, nor animal, birds, fishes, crabs, trees, stones, caves, ravines, grasses, nor forests: there was only the sky.

There was nothing brought together, nothing which could make a noise, nor anything which might move, or tremble, or could make noise in the sky.

There was nothing standing; only the calm water, the placid sea, alone and tranquil. Nothing existed.

There was only immobility and silence in the darkness, in the night. Only the Creator, the Maker, Tepeu, Gucumatz, the Forefathers, were in the water surrounded with light. They were hidden under green and blue feathers, and were therefore called Gucumatz. By nature they were great sages and great thinkers. In this manner the sky existed and also the Heart of Heaven, which is the name of God and thus He is called.

Then came the word. Tepeu and Gucumatz came together in the darkness, in the night, and Tepeu and Gucumatz talked together. They talked then, discussing and deliberating; they agreed, they united their words and their thoughts.

Then while they meditated, it became clear to them that when dawn would break, man must appear. Then they planned the creation, and the growth of the trees and the thickets and the birth of life and the creation of man. Thus it was arranged in the darkness and in the night by the Heart of Heaven who is called Huracan.

The first is called Caculha Huracan. The second is Chipi-

Caculha. The third is Raxa-Caculha. And these three are the Heart of Heaven.

Then Tepeu and Gucumatz came together; then they conferred about life and light, what they would do so that there would be light and dawn, who it would be who would provide food and sustenance.

Thus let it be done! Let the emptiness be filled! Let the water recede and make a void, let the earth appear and become solid; let it be done. Thus they spoke. Let there be light, let there be dawn in the sky and on the earth! There shall be neither glory nor grandeur in our creation and formation until the human being is made, man is formed. So they spoke.

Then the earth was created by them. So it was, in truth, that they created the earth. Earth! they said, and instantly it was made.

Like the mist, like a cloud, and like a cloud of dust was the creation, when the mountains appeared from the water; and instantly the mountains grew.

Only by a miracle, only by magic art were the mountains and valleys formed; and instantly the groves of cypresses and pines put forth shoots together on the surface of the earth.

And thus Gucumatz was filled with joy, and exclaimed: "Your coming has been fruitful, Heart of Heaven; and you, Huracan, and you, Chipi-Caculha, Raxa-Caculha!"

"Our work, our creation shall be finished," they answered.

First the earth was formed, the mountains and the valleys; the currents of water were divided, the rivulets were running freely between the hills, and the water was separated when the high mountains appeared.

Thus was the earth created, when it was formed by the Heart of Heaven, the Heart of Earth, as they are called who first made it fruitful, when the sky was in suspense, and the earth was submerged in the water.

So it was that they made perfect the work, when they did it after thinking and meditating upon it.

POLYNESIAN CREATION MYTH[28]

He existed, Taaroa was his name.
In the immensity (space)
There was no earth, there was no sky.
There was no sea, there was no man.
Above, Taaroa calls.
Existing alone, he became the universe.
Taaroa is the origin, the rocks
Taaroa is the sands,
It is thus that he is named.
Taaroa is the light;
Taaroa is within;
Taaroa is the germ.
Taaroa is beneath;
Taaroa is firm;
Taaroa is wise.
He created the land of Hawaii,
Hawaii the great and sacred,
As a body or shell for Taaroa . . .

A MAORI COSMOGONY[29]

1. Io dwelt within breathing-space of immensity.
   The Universe was in darkness, with water everywhere.
   There was no glimmer of dawn, no clearness, no light.
   And he began by saying these words,—
   That He might cease remaining inactive:

"Darkness, become a light-possessing darkness."
And at once light appeared.
(He) then repeated those self-same words in this manner,—
That He might cease remaining inactive;
"Light, become a darkness-possessing light."
And again an intense darkness supervened.
Then a third time He spake saying:
"Let there be one darkness above,
Let there be one darkness below (alternate).
Let there be a darkness unto Tupua,
Let there be a darkness unto Tawhito;
It is a darkness overcome and dispelled.
Let there be one light above,
Let there be one light below (alternate).
Let there be a light unto Tupua,
Let there be a light unto Tawhito.
A dominion of light,
A bright light."
And now a great light prevailed.
(Io) then looked to the waters which compassed him about,
and spake a fourth time, saying:
"Ye waters of Tai-kama, be ye separate.
Heaven, be formed." Then the sky became suspended.
"Bring-forth thou Tupua-horo-nuku."
And at once the moving earth lay stretched abroad.

2. Those words (of Io) became impressed on the minds of our
ancestors, and by them were they transmitted down through the
generations. Our priests joyfully referred to them as being:
"The ancient and original sayings.
The ancient and original words.
The ancient and original cosmological wisdom.
Which caused growth from the void,
The limitless space-filling void,
As witness the tidal-waters,

The evolved heaven,
The birth-given evolved earth."

3. And now my friends, there are three very important applications of those original sayings, as used in our sacred rituals. The first occurs in the ritual for implanting a child within the barren womb. The next occurs in the ritual for enlightening both the mind and the body. The third and last occurs in the ritual on the solemn subjects of death, and of war, of baptism, of genealogical recitals, and such like important subjects, as the priests most particularly concerned themselves in.

The words by which Io fashioned the Universe—that is to say, by which it was implanted and caused to produce a world of light—the same words are used in the ritual for implanting a child in a barren womb. The words by which Io caused light to shine in the darkness are used in the rituals for cheering a gloomy and despondent heart, the feeble aged, the decrepit; for shedding light into secret places and matters, for inspiration in song-composing, and in many other affairs, affecting man to despair in times of adverse war. For all such the ritual to enlighten and cheer, includes the words (used by Io) to overcome and dispel darkness. Thirdly, there is the preparatory ritual which treats of successive formations within the universe, and the genealogical history of man himself.

THE TUAMOTUAN STORY OF CREATION[30]

The Dwelling Places of Kiho

It is said that Kiho dwelt in the Void. It was said that Kiho dwelt beneath the foundations of Havaiki (in a place) which was called the Black-gleamless-realm-of-Havaiki.

Dwelling there below Kiho had no parents; he had no friend; he had no mate; there was none but him; he was the root, he was the stability.

It was said that, at that time, Kiho conversed only with his Astral-double (Activating Self).

His musings were within himself; his acts were performed by his Activating-self.

That place wherein Kiho dwelt was said to be the Non-existence-of-the-land; the name of that place was the Black-gleamless-realm-of-Havaiki.

It was there that Kiho dwelt; indeed, in that place he created all things whatsoever.

Hereafter (I give) the names of his dwelling places.

Kiho dwelt in his heaven at the nadir of the Night-realm,
Kiho dwelt in his heaven in the Black-gleamless-realm,
Kiho dwelt in his heaven in the Many-portioned-realm-of-night,
Kiho dwelt in his heaven in the Many-portioned-realm-of-night,
These places were situated within the Night-sphere.
Kiho dwelt below in Foundation-of-waters,
Kiho dwelt below in Foundation-unstable,
Kiho dwelt below in Foundation-thrust-upward.
Kiho dwelt below in Foundation-solidifying,
Kiho dwelt below in Foundation-quaking,
Kiho dwelt below in Foundation-extending,
Kiho dwelt below in Foundation-separated,
Kiho dwelt below in Foundation-(first)-appearing,
Kiho dwelt below in Foundation-tipping,
Kiho dwelt below in Foundation-moving-hither-and-thither,
Kiho dwelt below in Foundation-uprisen.
These rock-formations were situated in the Dark-teeming-waters; they were said to be the places wherein Kiho dwelt.
Kiho dwelt in the Zenith-of-the-heavens,
Kiho dwelt in the Narrow-borderlands-of-the-heavens,
Kiho dwelt in the Upper-regions-of-the-heavens,

Kiho dwelt in the Lower-regions-of-the-heavens,
Kiho dwelt in the Navel-of-the-heavens,
Kiho dwelt in the Planes-of-the-heavens,
Kiho dwelt in the Red-glow-of-the-heavens.
This is indeed that heaven which Kiho gave over to Atea.

(It is clear from the above that Kiho did not dwell solely in his special sphere, the Ragi-po, but rather was viewed as inhabiting, or immanent in, the Ragi-marama, "World-of-daylight," or "Earth-sphere.")

It was also said that the Dark-teeming-waters were the first thing that Kiho evolved.

It was there that he dwelt in the house called Upholding-house-of-the-heavenly-regions.

The Principal Heaven Spheres

There were three principal heaven-spheres (not-Earth-regions) created by Kiho; these were:

1. The Night-sphere-of-darkness of Kiho, or Region-of-the-spirit-world,

2. The Day-sphere-of-light of Atea, or Region-of-the-Earth-world,

3. The Sky-sphere of Tane, or Region-of-the-skies.

Account of the Creation of the Three Principal Spheres of Kiho

Kiho-the-source, of whom I tell, is he who was said to be the god whose deeds are here recounted; and these are the deeds he performed up to the time of Atea.

Whilst Kiho was, the heavens were not;—there was no land, there was no man; there was no thing whatsoever.

Kiho-the-sleeper slumbered immemorially in the Void.
Kiho-the-precursor awoke.

Then Kiho glanced upward into the Black-gleamless-night, that is to say, the first beginning of all things whatsoever.

Thereupon Kiho glanced down at his dwelling-place within the Black-gleamless-night, and thus spake Kiho, "This is indeed the utterly black night of Havaiki."

Then Kiho mused of all (potential) things whatsoever; and he caused his thought to be evoked, and thereupon he spake to his Activating-self, saying, "May I be eloquent of my indwelling occult knowledge; may I be expressive of my outpouring eloquence, in order that all assembled beings shall give ear!"

Began to stir the inner-urge of the Dark-teeming-waters,

Began to stir the inner-urge of the land,

Began to stir the inner-urge of Havaiki.

(The night world lay in deep sleep beneath the Non-existence-of-the-land.)

It was the inner-urge stirring,

It was the inner-urge burgeoning,

It was the inner-urge sheath-wrapped,

It was the inner-urge reaching upward,

It was the inner-urge branching out above,

It was the inner-urge taking root below.

It was the inner-urge that would soon stand erect upon the Earth.

It was the inner-urge that would soon stand erect in Twilight-dark-Havaiki.

Non-existent was the upward urge of the land.

Non-existent was the stratification of the land,

Non-existent was the viscosity of the land,

Non-existent was the rigidity of the land,

Non-existent was the deployment of the land,

Non-existent was the multiplicity of the land,

Non-existent was the . . . of the land,

Non-existent was the divarication of the land,

Non-existent was the overhanging rim of the land,

Non-existent was the . . . of the land.

Foundation-darkness was sleeping beneath the Non-existence-of-the-land,

Foundation-light was sleeping beneath the Non-existence-of-the-land,

Foundation-fissured was sleeping beneath the Non-existence-of-the-land,

Foundation-thundering was sleeping beneath the Non-existence-of-the-land,

Columnar-support-of-land was sleeping beneath the Non-existence-of-the-land,

Sky foundation was sleeping beneath the Non-existence-of-the-land,

. . . was sleeping beneath the Non-existence-of-the-land,

Dark-concave-dome was sleeping beneath the Non-existence-of-the-land,

Gushing-murmur-of-waters was sleeping beneath the Non-existence-of-the-land,

Contiguous-support was sleeping beneath the Non-existence-of-the-land,

Standing-in-small segments was sleeping beneath the Non-existence-of-the-land,

Long-standing-scintillation was sleeping beneath the Non-existence-of-the-land,

Havaiki was sleeping beneath the Non-existence-of-the-land,

Peaha was sleeping beneath the Non-existence-of-the-land.

Fruitfulness was sleeping beneath the Non-existence-of-the-land,

Sky-expanse was sleeping beneath the Non-existence-of-the-land.

Intense-desire-speeding-to-the-night was sleeping beneath the Non-existence-of-the-land,

The-foundation-of-Kuporu was sleeping beneath the Non-existence-of-the-land,

The radiant-realm-of-Tane was sleeping beneath the Non-exis-tence-of-the-land.

Then Kiho created the Primordial-waters through the potency of his outpouring eloquence.

And they commenced to evolve.

And they were evolved.

Now indeed Kiho spake to his Activating-self, saying, "Make thou violently to quake the rock-base of Havaiki that I become cognizant of all things,—that all things whatsoever be set apart in their rightful places!"

And at once Kiho made his eyes to glow with flame—and the darkness became light.

Now indeed his Activating-self caused the Rock-foundation of Havaiki to quake, and Kiho saw the position of all things where they were.

Then Kiho floated up upon the surface of the Primordial-waters,—it was his Activating-self who did so; he lay there floating upon his back.

Then Kiho created Foundation-of-the-night-world; it was a land-realm, it was below.

Then Kiho created Foundation-of-the-light-world; it was a sky-realm, it was above.

(These two realms were situated in the first plane.)

Now Kiho turned over upon his face in that place.

Then Kiho created Foundation-fissured; it was a land-realm, it was below.

Then Kiho created Foundation-thundering; it was a sky-realm, it was above.

(These two realms were situated in the second plane.)

Now Kiho raised himself up on an elbow in that place.

Then Kiho created Colmnar-support-of-the-land; it was a land-realm, it was below.

Then Kiho created Sky-base; it was a sky-realm, it was above.

(These two realms were situated in the third plane.)

Now Kiho raised himself up on his hands and knees in that place.

Then Kiho created Matau-heti; it was a land-realm, it was below.

Then Kiho created Dark-concavity; it was a sky-realm, it was above.

(These two realms were situated in the fourth plane.)

Now Kiho arose to a stooping posture in that place.

Then Kiho created Gushing-murmur-of-waters; it was a land-realm, it was below.

Then Kiho created Contiguous-support; it was a sky-realm, it was above.

(These two realms were situated in the fifth plane.)

Now Kiho arose to a forward-leaning posture in that place.

Then Kiho created Standing-in-small-segments; it was a land-realm, it was below.

Then Kiho created Long-standing-scintillation; it was a sky-realm, it was above.

(These two realms were situated in the sixth plane.)

Now Kiho straightened up to a shortened posture in that place.

Then Kiho created Havaiki; it was a land-realm, it was below.

Then Kiho created Peaha; it was a sky-realm, it was above.

(These two realms were situated in the seventh plane.)

Now Kiho straightened up to a fully extended posture in that place.

Then Kiho created Fructifier-of-the-soil; it was a land-realm, it was below.

Then Kiho created Sky-expanse; it was a sky-realm, it was above.

(These two realms were situated in the eighth plane of the Night-region-of-the-Spirit-world.)

This is what the sages told me concerning these last two realms, that is to say, Atea-ragi (Sky-expanse) and Fakahotu-henua (Fructifier-of-the-soil):

Sky-expanse was above,

Fructifier-of-the-soil was underneath.

Whence sprang the offspring of Sky-expanse!

Now Kiho set apart the sea in its place, and set apart the soil in its place, and set apart the white sand—leaving it in Havaiki; he then set apart the reddish earth for the mountains; he set apart the black sand for Vavau; then he took the foam of the waves and the viscous clay, and cast them down beneath his feet; then he trod upon them, saying, "You are indeed the origin of stratified rock foundations; may you rise, may you thrust upward, may you become firm!"

He then left the white sand along the rocky borders of the bedrock-foundation of Havaiki, and (when) all these deeds had been accomplished, he created the upper-heavens of Atea.

Then Kiho looked upon his Astral-self (Activating-self) who was lying stretched out below (him); then he took the red sand (earth) and shaped it together; next he exhaled upon it his vitalizing breath, and the sand became imbued with life, thereupon his Astral-self entered wholly into that red sand and immediately became transformed into a sentient being; this living creature was sleeping; then it awoke.

Now Kiho spake, saying, "Thou are Atea of the legion-of-the-gods to become as a firm foundation for Havaiki-the-above, as a sanctuary for the spirit-legions."

Atea then saw that the god was lying upon his face.

Then Kiho again spake thus to Atea:

"Thou art he who shall become far-famed through me,

Thou art he whom I shall inform with all esoteric arts and lore,

Thou shalt be the Expounder,

Thou art he whom I shall cause to beget progeny,

Thou art he whom I shall imbue with fertility that Havaiki teem with life.

Thou art he whom I shall avenge,

Thou art he whom I shall extol,

Thou art he whom I shall install in the Domed-firmament of
Atea,
Thou shalt embark upon wars of reprisal,—
Thou shalt demean the prestige of my Prince,
Thou shalt impale my Prince upon thy spear;
Thou shalt be the instigator of disaster,
Thou shalt be the progenitor of fatherlands,
Thou shalt become the forefront of the Legion-of-the-gods that
thou create the new Sky spheres;
Thou shalt evoke thy Activating-self,
Thou shalt make level the Sacred-heaven-of-Atea that my
Prince may dwell therein, that he stand upright in his Sky-sphere;
Multitudes shall invoke him,—
See to it that thou troublest him not, and let the Spirit-legions
be created;
Thou shalt rise upward,
Thou shalt soar upward,
Thou shalt inform infinite space,
Thou shalt become established in thy Heaven-sphere;
Thou art the Pillar of the Skies,
Thou art the Tie beam—
Verily thou art the Wall-plate of thy Heaven.
Thou art the First,
Thou art the Last,
Thou art the Above,
Thou art the Below—
Thou art the Completer!"
Then Kiho undid his girdle and gave it to Atea. The name of
the girdle was "The-crimson-girdle-of-Atea."
It was said that Kiho knew not death; he turned his back upon
Atea and disappeared (going) to the Black-gleamless-realm-of-
Havaiki.

THE EGYPTIAN MYTH OF THE REPULSING OF THE DRAGON AND THE CREATION[31]

THE BOOK OF KNOWING THE CREATIONS OF RE AND OF OVERTHOWING APOPHIS. THE WORDS TO BE SPOKEN.

The All-Lord said, after he had come into being:

I am he who came into being as Khepri. When I had come into being, being (itself) came into being, and all beings came into being after I came into being. Many were the beings which came forth from my mouth, before heaven came into being, before earth came into being, before the ground and creeping things had been created in this place, I put together (some) of them in Nun as weary ones, before I could find a place in which I might stand. It (seemed) advantageous to me in my heart; I planned with my face; and I made (in concept) every form when I was alone, before I had spat out what was Shu, before I had sputtered out what was Tefnut, and before (any) other had come into being who could act with me.

I planned in my own heart, and there came into being a multitude of forms of beings, the forms of children and the forms of their children. I was the one who copulated with my fist, I masturbated with my hand. Then I spewed with my own mouth; I spat out what was Shu, and I sputtered out what was Tefnut. It was my father Nun who brought them up, and my Eye followed after them since the ages when they were distant from me.

After I had come into being as the sole god, there were three gods beside me. I came into being in this land, whereas Shu and Tefnut rejoiced in Nun, in which they were. They brought to me my Eye with them. After I had joined together my members, I wept over them. That is how men came into being from the tears which came forth from my Eye. It was angry with me, after it returned and found that I had made another in its place, having replaced it with the Glorious Eye, which I had made. Then I advanced its place on my head, and after it had ruled this entire land, *its rage fell away to its roots,* for I had replaced what had been taken away from it. I came forth from the roots, and I created all creeping things and whatever lives among them. Then Shu and Tefnut brought forth Geb and Nut. Then Geb and Nut brought forth Osiris, Horus Khenti-en-irti, Seth, Isis, and Nephthys from the body, one of them after another; and they brought forth their multitudes in this land.

THE HEBREW MYTH OF CREATION[32]

Vss. 1 and 2 In the beginning God created the heavens and the earth. The earth was without form and void, and darkness was upon the face of the deep; and the Spirit of God was moving over the face of the waters.

Vss. 3 and 4 And God said, "Let there be light"; and there was light. And God saw that the light was good; and God separated the light from the darkness.

Vs. 5 God called the light Day, and the darkness he called Night. And there was evening and there was morning, one day.

Vss. 6 to 8 And God said, "Let there be a firmament in the midst of the waters, and let it separate the waters from the waters." And God made the firmament and separated the waters which were under the firmament from the waters which were above the firmament. And it was so. And God called the firmament Heaven. And there was evening and there was morning, a second day.

Vss. 9 to 13   And God said, "Let the waters under the heavens be gathered together into one place, and let the dry land appear." And it was so. God called the dry land Earth, and the waters that were gathered together he called Seas. And God saw that it was good. And God said, "Let the earth put forth vegetation, plants yielding seed, and fruit trees bearing fruit in which is their seed, each according to its kind, upon the earth." And it was so. The earth brought forth vegetation, plants yielding seed according to their own kinds, and trees bearing fruit in which is their seed, each according to its kind. And God saw that it was good. And there was evening and there was morning, a third day.

Vss. 14 to 19   And God said, "Let there be lights in the firmament of the heavens to separate the day from the night; and let them be for signs and for seasons and for days and years, and let them be lights in the firmament of the heavens to give light upon the earth." And it was so. And God made the two great lights, the greater light to rule the day, and the lesser light to rule the night; he made the stars also. And God set them in the firmament of the heavens to give light upon the earth, to rule over the day and over the night, and to separate the light from the darkness. And God saw that it was good. And there was evening and there was morning, a fourth day.

Vss. 20 to 22   And God said, "Let the waters bring forth swarms of living creatures, and let birds fly above the earth across the firmament of the heavens." So God created the great sea monsters and every living creature that moves, with which the waters swarm, according to their kinds, and every winged bird according to its kind. And God saw that it was good. And God blessed them, saying, "Be fruitful and multiply and fill the waters in the seas, and let birds multiply on the earth."

Vs. 23   And there was evening, and there was morning, a fifth day.

Vss. 24 and 25 And God said, "Let the earth bring forth living creatures according to their kinds; cattle and creeping things and beasts of the earth according to their kinds and the cattle according to their kinds, and everything that creeps upon the ground according to its kind." And God saw that it was good.

Vs. 26 Then God said, "Let us make man in our image, after our likeness; and let them have dominion over the fish of the sea, and over the birds of the air, and over the cattle, and over all the earth, and over every creeping thing that creeps upon the earth."

Vss. 27 to 29 So God created man in his own image, in the image of God he created him; male and female he created them. And God blessed them, and God said to them, "Be fruitful and multiply, and fill the earth and subdue it; and have dominion over the fish of the sea and over the birds of the air and over every living thing that moves upon the earth." And God said, "Behold, I have given you every plant yielding seed which is upon the face of all the earth, and every tree with seed in its fruit; you shall have them for food.

Vss. 30 and 31 And to every beast of the earth, and to every bird of the air, and to everything that creeps on the earth, everything that has the breath of life, I have given every green plant for food." And it was so. And God saw everything that he had made, and behold, it was very good. And there was evening and there was morning, a sixth day.

Chap. 2 Vss. 1 to 3 Thus the heavens and the earth were finished, and all the host of them. And on the seventh day God finished his work which he had done, and he rested on the seventh day from all his work which he had done. So God blessed the seventh day and hallowed it, because on it God rested from all his work which he had done in creation.

ZUÑI MYTH OF THE GENESIS OF THE WORLDS, OR THE BEGINNING OF NEWNESS[33]

Before the beginning of the new-making, Awonawilone (the Maker and Container of All, the All-father Father), solely had being. There was nothing else whatsoever throughout the great space of the ages save everywhere black darkness in it, and everywhere void desolation.

In the beginning of the new-made Awonawilone conceived within himself and thought outward in space, whereby mists of increase, steams potent of growth, were evolved and uplifted. Thus, by means of his innate knowledge, the All-container made himself in person and form of the Sun whom we hold to be our father and who thus came to exist and appear. With his appearance came the brightening of the spaces with light, and with the brightening of the spaces the great mist-clouds were thickened together and fell, whereby was evolved water in water; yea, and the worldholding sea.

With his substance of flesh (yepnane) outdrawn from the surface of his person, the Sun-father formed the seed-stuff of twain worlds, impregnating therewith the great waters, and lo! in the heat of his light these waters of the sea grew green and scums (k'yanashotsiyallawe) rose upon them, waxing wide and weighty until, behold! they became Awitelin Tsita, the "Four-fold Containing Mother-earth," and Apoyan Ta'chu, the "All-covering Father sky."

CHAPTER FIVE

EARTH-DIVER MYTHS

THE EARTH-DIVER SYMBOLISM refers to the creation motif in which a divine being (usually an animal) dives into water to bring up the first particles of earth. The particles of earth are the germs from which the entire universe grows. We shall isolate three elements in these myths: First, the symbolism of water; secondly, the symbolism of the descent into the water; and thirdly, the antagonism between the divine beings.

1) The Water Symbolism

It is clear in these myths that water is the unformed, unstable and pregnant reality out of which the universe comes. It is the symbol of the uncreated, chaos. In these myths, however, the water is not inhabited by monstrous and demonic beings. A certain passivity is present in this symbolism of water. Even when water animals are mentioned, as in the Huron myth, they are "animals of the kind that live in and upon water."[1] They are not the grotesque animals referred to in the version of the Babylonian myth reported by Berossus.

In the Dogon myth reported by Griaule (Chapter Three),

we recognize in Ogotemmêli's account the importance of water. Behind all of the manifestations of the cosmos and the gods is the symbol of water. It is the reality from which all life emerges. A cosmos without water is impure. We find no explicit statements in the earth-diver myths concerning the relationship between the primordial waters and the subsequent creation, but it is clear from the myths that the life of the world inheres in the water which lies underneath its depths. If the earth represents the stable reality of the cosmos, the bountiful source of this reality is water.

The water symbolism is furthermore a sign of destruction. The story of the flood which is found in many cultures is a story of the destruction of an old world and the beginning of a new one. Destruction is thus purification and renewal. The earth-diver myths from North America reflect the tensions between a hunting-fishing cultural complex and the birth of an agricultural society. The relationship between the animals in the myths may be interpreted as an attempted resolution between differing religious structures. In the Huron myth reported by Hale, the bad brother creates serpents, panthers, wolves, and bears. The good brother creates innocent and useful animals, i.e., domesticated animals.

In the myth from the Vishnu Purana, the water symbolism is subordinated to a supreme being, Narayana. Narayana is intimately related to the water; his very name means "he whose place of moving was the waters," but creation does not emerge unaided from the waters. The earth is brought up from the water because Narayana was desirous to raise it. If Coomaraswamy's theory that the water symbolism in India is a product of the pre-Aryan agricultural societies of Mohenjo-daro and Harappa, the water symbolism in this myth does not express the tension between hunting-fishing and agricultural religious structures, but between monotheistic and agricultural structures. In typically Indian fashion the monotheistic structure is blended into the older water symbolism. The earth which lies in the depths of the water acknowledges Narayana as the supreme lord and offers a hymn of praise to him. The symbolism of water as the creator, preserver, and destroyer of all things is taken over by the supreme being in his manifestations in the forms of Brahma, Vishnu, and Rudra, respectively.

In this connection, we are reminded of the flood account in the Bible. In the creation myth given in the first chapter of Genesis, God has already subordinated the waters. He later used the waters to destroy the earth, but he promises Noah that the earth will never be destroyed by water again. The rainbow is a sign of this promise. The God of Genesis does not take on the symbolism of water but remains superior to it. The earth is stabilized by his power and will not continually go through the cycles of creation, preservation and destruction.

2) *The Descent into the Water*

The descent into the water is analogous to a descent into the underworld or a return to the womb. The purpose of such descents into the unformed and chaotic is renewal and stability. The symbolism of baptism is derived from this element in the water symbolism. By plunging into the water the old is washed away and the new creation emerges. Maui, the cultural hero of the Polynesians, enters into the vagina of a female giant. He hopes to gain immortality (eternal stability) for man by passing through the body of the giant from her vagina to her mouth.[2] Unfortunately, he is unable to accomplish this task. To establish a new dimension of human existence is not an easy task. In the Huron myth, several animals descend into the water before the tortoise finally brings up a little earth in his mouth. The turtle in the Maidu myth is in the water for six years before bringing up a little earth, and in the Rumanian myth Satan brings up earth after diving four times. A similar story is related in the Trohohi Yokuts myth. A great manifestation of power is necessary before a new creation can be accomplished.

The inertia of the primary "stuff" of creation must be overcome. This is true whether the primary "stuff" is represented by the symbolism of water or of World Parents. In the monotheistic mythological structures the power of the supreme being commands or wills creation from the waters. With the exception of the Indian myth from the Vishnu Purana, no such being is found in the earth-diver myths in this chapter. Those who attempt to make a new world are lesser beings, lacking the grandeur and power of a supreme deity. Their creation is the result of a trial-and-error method. Also lacking is the plenitude of creation as it is expressed in the monotheistic structure. The earth divers scarcely bring up the necessary amount of earth—a little under the fingernails, a little in the mouth.

3) *Antagonism Between the Divine Beings*

Earl W. Count, in attempting to explain the dualistic notions in the Eurasian earth-diver myths, relates them to the dualistic conceptions stemming from the religions of the Near East.

> Briefly, there is hardly room for doubt that the dualistic dress stems from the Middle Ages, when the various Gnostic and Irano-Chaldean religious systems for the allegiance of the inner-Asiatic falls—Finno-Ugric, Turko-Mongul, eastern Slavic. The systems which have left their most striking impress have been: Maydaism, Zervonism, Manicheism, Bogomilism, Nestorian, Buddhism, eastern Christian Orthodoxy —all *selon le cas*. Repeatedly it is possible to recognize, even in the very names of the *dramatis personae* (Satanail, Shaitan, Burkhon, Shulumya, Anromori, Khurmuzta, Zarvon, Mai-tere) more than one of the influences in one and the same story.[3]

The influence of the "high religions" of the Near East can be seen in the myths from Central Asia, Rumania and Siberia. Does this mean that the dualistic notion has its origins in Ancient Near Eastern religions? We think not. Dualism seems to be a generic feature of all religious life. To the extent that religion expresses a qualification of life, dualisms appear. On a simple level a dualism may develop if the right hand is regarded as more powerful than the left. On a more profound level the dualism resulting from the discovery of sexuality has a profound effect upon religious life. We have associated the dualism in the earth-diver myths with the tension between hunting-fishing and agricultural orientations. The clearest example of this tension is found in the Huron myth. A woman, a divine person, falls from the sky. She is pregnant with twins, one of whom is disposed toward the good; the other has a predilection for evil. The evil twin refuses to be born in the usual manner and breaks through the side of the mother, killing her. From her body spring the products of agriculture—vegetables, maize, beans, etc. This myth is very much like the Mande African myth in Chapter Three.

The mother (earth) is on the side of the good twin. The evil twin whose name means flinty represents the old culture of the hunter. Flint refers to the material used to make weapons. Even though the evil brother seems to possess greater physical power, he cannot finally defeat the good twin. The power of the mother to revive and resuscitate is greater than the physical power of the evil twin.

In the Maidu myth, the coyote represents the opposition, but in a milder form. He does not possess the great power of the evil twin in the Huron myth. He is clever, however, and attempts to imitate the creative act of Earth Initiate. He fails because at a crucial point he laughs instead of remaining silent. The power of Earth Initiate is dramatized by his renewal of Ku'ksū.

In the Siberian, Rumanian, and Central Asiatic myths the dualism is expressed by Jewish-Christian and Buddhist symbols. In these myths, the agricultural and hunting-fishing tensions are in the background or have been totally lost. The ethical character of the struggle is emphasized.

THE MAKING OF THE WORLD (HURON)[4]

In the beginning there was nothing but water, a wide sea, which was peopled by various animals of the kind that live in and upon the water. It happened then that a woman fell down from the upper world. It is supposed that she was, by some mischance, pushed down by her husband through a rift in the sky. Though styled a woman, she was a divine personage. Two loons, which were flying over the water, happened to look up and see her falling. To save her from drowning they hastened to place themselves beneath her, joining their bodies together so as to form a cushion for her to rest on. In this way they held her up, while they cried with a loud voice to summon the other animals to their aid. The cry of the loon can be heard to a great distance, and the other creatures of the sea heard it, and assembled to learn the cause of the summons. Then came the tortoise (or "snapping turtle," as Clarke called it), a mighty animal, which consented to relieve the loons of their burden. They placed the woman on the back of the tortoise, charging him to take care of her. The tortoise then called the other animals to a grand council, to determine what should be done to preserve the life of the woman. They decided that she must have earth to live on. The tortoise directed them all to dive to the bottom of the sea and endeavor to bring up some earth. Many attempted it—the beaver, the muskrat, the diver, and others—but without success.

Some remained so long below that when they rose they were dead. The tortoise searched their mouths but could find no trace of earth. At last the toad went down, and after remaining a long time rose, exhausted and nearly dead. On searching his mouth the tortoise found in it some earth, which he gave to the woman. She took it and placed it carefully around the edge of the tortoise's shell. When thus placed, it became the beginning of dry land. The land grew and extended on every side, forming at last a great country, fit for vegetation. All was sustained by the tortoise, which still supports the earth.

When the woman fell she was pregnant with twins. When these came forth they evinced opposite dispositions, the one good, the other evil. Even before they were born the same characters were manifested. They struggled together, and their mother heard them disputing. The one declared his willingness to be born in the usual manner, while the other malignantly refused, and, breaking through his mother's side, killed her. She was buried, and from her body sprang the various vegetable productions which the new earth required to fit it for the habitation of man. From her head grew the pumpkin-vine; from her breasts the maize; from her limbs the bean and the other useful esculents. Meanwhile the twins grew up, showing in all they did their opposing inclinations. The name of the good one was Tijuskeha, which means, Clarke said, something like saviour, or good man. The evil brother was named Tawiskarong, meaning flinty, or flint-like, in allusion probably to his hard and cruel nature. They were not men, but supernatural beings, who were to prepare the world to be the abode of men. Finding that they could not live together, they separated, each taking his own portion of the earth. Their first act was to create animals of various kinds. The bad brother made fierce and monstrous creatures, proper to terrify and destroy mankind—serpents, panthers, wolves, bears, all of enormous size, and huge mosquitoes, "as large as turkeys." Among other things he made an immense toad, which drank up all the fresh water that was on the earth. In the meantime the good brother, in his province, was creating the innocent and useful animals. Among the rest he made the partridge. To his surprise, the bird rose in the air and flew toward the territory of Tawiskarong. Tijuskeha asked him whither he was going. The bird replied that he was going to look for water, as there was none left in that land, and he heard there was some in the dominion of Tawiskarong. Tijuskeha then began to suspect mischief. He followed the course which the partridge had taken and presently reached the land of his evil brother. Here he encountered the snakes, ferocious brutes, and enormous insects which his brother had made, and overcame them. Finally he came to the monstrous toad, which he cut open, letting the water flow forth. He did not destroy the evil animals—perhaps had not the power to do so—but he reduced them in size, so that men would be able to master them.

The spirit of his mother warned him in a dream to beware of his evil brother, who would endeavour to destroy him by treachery. Finally they encountered, and as it was evident that they could not live together on the earth, they determined to decide by a formal combat (a duel, as Clarke styled it) which of them should remain master of the world. It was further agreed that each should make known to the other the only weapon by which he could be overcome. This extraordinary article of their agreement was probably made necessary by the fact that without such a disclosure the contest would have lasted forever. The good brother declared that he could be destroyed only by being beaten to death with a bag full of corn, beans, or some other product of the bread kind. The evil brother rejoined that he could be killed only by the horn of a deer or of some other wild animal. (In these weapons it seems evident that there is some reference to the different characters or attributes of the brothers.) They set off a fighting-group, or "list," within which the combat was to take place. Tawiskarong had the first turn, or, as duellists would say, the first fire. He set upon his brother with a bag of corn or beans, chased him about the ground, and pounded him until he was nearly lifeless and lay as if dead. He revived, however (perhaps through the aid of his mother's spirit), and, recovering his strength, pursued in turn his evil brother, beating him with a deer's horn until he killed him. But the slain combatant was not utterly destroyed. He reappeared after death to his brother, and told him that he had gone to the far west, and that thenceforth all the races of men after death would go to the west, like him. "And," said Clarke, "It is the belief of all the pagan Indians that after death their spirits will go to the far west, and dwell there."

The old chief, Joseph White, on another occasion, supplied a curious addition to the foregoing narrative, in exemplification of the opposite character of the two brothers. This story was in substance as follows:

"When the brothers were preparing the land for the Indians to live in, the manner of their work was that as often as the good brother made or designed anything for the benefit of mankind, the bad brother objected, and devised something to counteract the good intention, so far as he could. Thus, when the good brother made rivers for the Indians to journey on, it was his design that each river should have a twofold current (or rather, perhaps, a double channel), in which the streams should flow in opposite directions. Thus the Indians would be able always to float easily downstream. This convenient arrangement did not please the bad brother. He maintained that it would be too good for the people. 'Let them at least,' he said, 'have to work one way up stream.' He was not content merely to defeat his brother's design of the return current, but he created at the same time rapids and cataracts for the further delay and danger of voyagers."

CREATION MYTH FROM VISHNU PURANA (HINDU)[5]

Maitreya.—Tell me, mighty sage, how, in the commencement of the (present) Kalpa, Náráyaná, who is named Brahmá, created all existent things.

Paráśara.—In what manner the divine Brahmá, who is one with Nárayáná, created progeny, and is thence named the lord of progeny (Prajápati), the lord god, you shall hear.

At the close of the past (of Pádma) Kalpa, the divine Brahmá, endowed with the quality of goodness, awoke from his night of sleep, and beheld the universe void. He, the supreme Náráyaná the incomprehensible, the sovereign of all creatures, invested with the form of Brahmá, the god without beginning, the creator of all things; of whom, with respect to his name Náráyaná, the god who has the form of Brahmá, the imperishable origin of the world, this verse is repeated: "The waters are called Nárá, because they were the offspring of Nárá (the supreme spirit); and, as, in them, his first (Ayana) progress (in the character of Brahmá) took place, he is thence named Náráyaná (he whose place of moving was the waters)." He, the lord, concluding that within the waters lay the earth, and being desirous to raise it up, created another form for that purpose; and, as, in preceding Kalpas, he has assumed the shape of a fish or a tortoise, so, in this, he took the figure of a boar. Having adopted a form composed of the sacrifices of the Vedas, for the preservation of the whole earth, the eternal, supreme, and universal soul, the great progenitor of created beings, eulogized by Sanaka and the other saints who dwell in the sphere of holy men (Janaloka); he, the supporter of spiritual and material being, plunged into the ocean. The goddess Earth, beholding him thus descending to the subterranean regions, bowed in devout adoration, and thus glorified the god:—

Príthiví (Earth).—Hail to thee, who art all creatures; to thee, the holder of the mace and shell: elevate me now from this place, as thou hast upraised me in days of old. From thee have I proceeded; of thee do I consist; as do the skies and all other existing things. Hail to thee, spirit of the supreme spirit; to thee, soul of soul; to thee, who art discrete and indiscrete matter; who art one with the elements and with time. Thou art the creator of all things, their preserver, and their destroyer, in the forms, O lord, of Brahmá, Vishńu, and Rudra, at the seasons of creation, duration, and dissolution. When thou hast devoured all things, thou reposest on the ocean that sweeps over the world, meditated upon, O Govinda, by the wise. No one knoweth thy true nature; and the gods adore thee only in the forms it hath pleased thee to assume. They who are desirous of final liberation worship thee as the supreme Brahma; and who that adores not Vasudeva shall obtain emancipation? Whatever may be apprehended by the mind, whatever may be perceived by the senses, whatever may be discerned by the intellect, all is but a form of thee. I am of thee, upheld by thee; thou art my creator, and to thee I fly for refuge: hence, in this universe, Mádhaví (the bride of Mádhavá or Vishńu) is my designation. Triumph to the essence of all wisdom, to the unchangeable, the imperishable: triumph to the eternal; to the indiscrete, to the essence of discrete things: to him who is both cause and effect; who is the universe; the sinless lord of sacrifice; triumph. Thou art sacrifice; thou art the oblation; thou art the mystic Omkara; thou art the sacrificial fires; thou art the Vedas, and their dependent sciences; thou art, Hari, the object of all worship. The sun, the stars, the planets, the whole world; all that is formless, or that has form; all that is visible, or invisible; all. Purushottama, that I have said, or left unsaid; all this, Supreme, thou art. Hail to thee, again and again! hail! all hail!

Parásara.—The auspicious supporter of the world, being thus hymned by the earth, emitted a low murmuring sound, like the chanting of the Sama Veda; and the mighty boar, whose eyes were like the lotus, and whose body, vast as the Níla mountain, was of the dark colour of the lotus-leaves, uplifted upon his ample tusks the earth from the lowest regions. As he reared his head, the waters shed from his brow purified the great sages, Sanandana and others, residing in the sphere of the saints. Through the indentations made by his hoofs, the waters rushed into the lower worlds with a thundering noise. Before his breath the pious denizens of Janaloka were scattered; and the Munis sought for shelter amongst the bristles upon the scriptural body of the boar, trembling as he rose up, supporting the earth, and dripping with moisture. Then the great sages, Sanandana and the rest, residing continually in the sphere of saints, were inspired with delight; and, blowing lowly, they praised the stern-eyed upholder of the earth.

The Yogins.—Triumph, lord of lords supreme; Keśava, sovereign of the earth, the wielder of the mace, the shell, the discus, and the sword: cause of production, destruction, and existence. THOU ART, O god: there is no other supreme condition but thou. Thou, lord, art the person of sacrifice: for thy feet are the Vedas, thy tusks are the stake to which the victim is bound; in thy teeth are the offerings; thy mouth is the altar; thy tongue is the fire; and the hairs of thy body are the sacrificial grass. Thine eyes, O omnipotent, are day and night; thy head is the seat of all, the place of Brahma; thy name is all the hymns of the Vedas; thy nostrils are all oblations: O thou, whose snout is the ladle of oblation; whose deep voice is the chanting of the Sama Veda; whose body is the hall of sacrifice; whose joints are the different ceremonies; and whose ears have the properties of both voluntary and obligatory rites; do thou, who art eternal, who art in size a mountain be propitious. We acknowledge thee, who hast traversed the world, O universal form, to be the beginning, the continuance, and the destruction of all things: thou art the supreme god. Have pity on us, O lord of conscious and unconscious beings. The orb of the earth is seen seated on the tip of thy tusks, as if thou hadst been sporting amidst a lake where the lotus floats, and hadst borne away the leaves covered with soil. The space between heaven and earth is occupied by thy body, O thou of unequalled glory, resplendent with the power of pervading the universe, O lord, for the benefit of all. Thou art the aim of all: there is none other than thee, sovereign of the world: this is thy might, by which all things, fixed or movable, are pervaded. This form, which is now beheld, is thy form, as one essentially with wisdom. Those who have practised devotion conceive erroneously of the nature of the world. The ignorant, who do not perceive that this universe is of the nature of wisdom, and judge of it as an object of perception only, are lost in the ocean of spiritual ignorance. But they who know true wisdom, and whose minds are pure, behold this whole world as one with divine knowledge, as one with thee, O god. Be favourable, O universal spirit: raise up this earth, for the habitation of created beings. Inscrutable deity, whose eyes are like lotuses, give us felicity. O lord, thou art endowed with the quality of goodness: raise up, Govinda, this earth, for the general good. Grant us happiness, O lotus-eyed. May this, thy activity in creation, be beneficial to the earth. Salutation to thee. Grant us happiness, O lotus-eyed.

Parásara.—The supreme being thus eulogized, upholding the earth, raised it quickly, and placed it on the summit of the ocean, where it floats like a mighty vessel, and, from its expansive surface, does not sing beneath the waters. Then, having levelled the earth, the great eternal deity divided it into portions, by mountains. He who never wills in vain created, by his irresistible power, those mountains again upon the earth, which had been consumed at the destruction of the world. Having then divided the earth into seven great portions or continents, as it was before, he con-

PLATE 25. *God of Rain. Mayan façade.*

PLATE 26. *Slab from Sarcophagus. Mayan temple.*

PLATE 27. *Pregnant woman. Australia.*

PLATE 28a. *Dutchman* WURAMU *figure.*
Arnhem Land, Australia.

PLATE 28b. *Son of the Great Ancestor.*
Arnhem Land, Australia.

PLATE 29. *Hopi mural.*

PLATE 30. *Sculpture. Indian shrine.*

PLATE 31. *Sculpture. Indian shrine.*

PLATE 32. *"Bear Mother." Haida Indian.*

structed, in like manner, the four (lower) spheres, earth, sky, heaven, and the sphere of the sages (Maharloka). Thus Heri, the four-faced god, invested with the quality of activity, and taking the form of Brahmá, accomplished the creation. But he (Brahmá) is only the instrumental cause of things to be created; the things that are capable of being created arise from nature as a common material cause. With exception of one instrumental cause alone, there is no need of any other cause; for (imperceptible) substance becomes perceptible substance according to the powers with which it is originally imbued.

MAIDU CREATION MYTH[6]

In the beginning there was no sun, no moon, no stars. All was dark, and everywhere there was only water. A raft came floating on the water. It came from the north, and in it were two persons, —Turtle (A'nŏshma) and Father-of-the-Secret-Society (Pehē'ipe). The stream flowed very rapidly. Then from the sky a rope of feathers, called Pŏ'kelma, was let down, and down it came Earth-Initiate. When he reached the end of the rope, he tied it to the bow of the raft, and stepped in. His face was covered and was never seen, but his body shone like the sun. He sat down, and for a long time said nothing. At last Turtle said, "Where do you come from?" and Earth-Initiate answered, "I come from above." Then Turtle said, "Brother, can you not make for me some good dry land, so that I may sometimes come up out of the water?" Then he asked another time, "Are there going to be any people in the world?" Earth-Initiate thought awhile, then said, "Yes." Turtle asked, "How long before you are going to make people?" Earth-Initiate replied, "I don't know. You want to have some dry land: well, how am I going to get any earth to make it of?" Turtle answered, "If you will tie a rock about my left arm, I'll dive for some." Earth-Initiate did as Turtle asked, and then, reaching around, took the end of a rope from somewhere, and tied it to Turtle. When Earth-Initiate came to the raft, there was no rope there: he just reached out and found one. Turtle said, "If the rope is not long enough, I'll jerk it once, and you must haul me up; if it is long enough, I'll give two jerks, and then you must pull me up quickly, as I shall have all the earth that I can carry." Just as Turtle went over the side of the boat, Father-of-the-Secret-Society began to shout loudly.

Turtle was gone a long time. He was gone six years; and when he came up, he was covered with green slime, he had been down so long. When he reached the top of the water, the only earth he had was a very little under his nails; the rest had all washed away. Earth-Initiate took with his right hand a stone knife from under his left armpit, and carefully scraped the earth out from under Turtle's nails. He put the earth in the palm of his hand, and rolled it about till it was round; it was as large as a small pebble. He laid it on the stern of the raft. By and by he went to look at it: it had not grown at all. The third time he went to look at it, it had grown so that it could be spanned by the arms. The fourth time he looked, it was as big as the world, the raft was aground, and all around were mountains as far as he could see. The raft came ashore at Tadoikö, and the place can be seen today.

When the raft had come to land, Turtle said, "I can't stay in the dark all the time. Can't you make a light, so that I can see?" Earth-Initiate replied, "Let us get out of the raft, and then we will see what we can do." So all three got out. Then, Earth-Initiate said, "Look that way, to the east! I am going to tell my sister to come up." Then it began to grow light, and day began to break; then Father-of-the-Secret-Society began to shout loudly, and the sun came up. Turtle said, "Which way is the sun going to travel?" Earth-Initiate answered, "I'll tell her to go this way, and go down there." After the sun went down, Father-of-the-

Secret-Society began to cry and shout again, and it grew very dark. Earth-Initiate asked Turtle and Father-of-the-Secret-Society, "How do you like it?" and they both answered, "It is very good." Then Turtle asked, "Is that all you are going to do for us?" and Earth-Initiate answered, "No, I am going to do more yet." Then he called the stars each by its name, and they came out. When this was done, Turtle asked, "Now what shall we do?" Earth-Initiate replied, "Wait, and I'll show you." Then he made a tree grow at Ta'doikö,—the tree called Hu'kĭmtsa; and Earth-Initiate and Turtle and Father-of-the-Secret-Society sat in its shade for two days. The tree was very large, and had twelve different kinds of acorns growing on it.

After they had sat for two days under the tree, they all went off to see the world that Earth-Initiate had made. They started at sunrise, and were back by sunset. Earth-Initiate travelled so fast that all they could see was a ball of fire flashing about under the ground and the water. While they were gone, Coyote (Olä'li) and his dog Rattlesnake (Kaudi or So'la) came out of the ground. It is said that Coyote could see Earth-Initiate's face. When Earth-Initiate and the others came back, they found Coyote at Ta'doikö, but no one could go inside of Earth-Initiate's house. Soon after the travellers came back, Earth-Initiate called the birds from the air, and made the trees and then the animals. He then took some mud, and of this made first a deer; and after that, he made all the other animals. Some-times Turtle would say, "That does not look well: can't you make it some other way?"

Some time after this, Earth-Initiate and Coyote were at Marysville Buttes (E'stobüsin Yā'mani). Earth-Initiate said, "I am going to make people." In the middle of the afternoon he began, for he had returned to Ta'doikö. He took dark red earth, mixed it with water, and made two figures,—one a man, and one a woman. He laid the man on his right side, and the woman on his left, inside his house. Then he lay down himself, flat on his back, with his arms stretched out. He lay thus and sweated all the afternoon and night. Early in the morning the woman began to tickle him in the side. He kept very still, did not laugh. By and by he got up, thrust a piece of pitch-wood into the ground and fire burst out. The two people were very white. No one to-day is as white as they were. Their eyes were pink, their hair was black, their teeth shone brightly, and they were very handsome. It is said that Earth-Initiate did not finish the hands of the people, as he did not know how it would be best to do it. Coyote saw the people, and suggested that they ought to have hands like his. Earth-Initiate said, "No, their hands shall be like mine." Then he finished them. When Coyote asked why their hands were to be like that, Earth-Initiate answered, "So that, if they are chased by bears, they can climb trees." This first man was called Ku'ksu; and the woman Morning-Star Woman (La'idamlülüm kü'le).

When Coyote had seen the two people, he asked Earth-Initiate how he had made them. When he was told, he thought, "That is not difficult. I'll do it myself." He did just as Earth-Initiate had told him, but could not help laughing, when, early in the morning, the woman poked him in the ribs. As a result of his failing to keep still, the people were glass-eyed. Earth-Initiate said, "I told you not to laugh," but Coyote declared he had not. This was the first lie.

By and by there came to be a good many people. Earth-Initiate had wanted to have everything comfortable and easy for people, so that none of them should have to work. All fruits were easy to obtain, no one was ever to get sick and die. As the people grew numerous, Earth-Initiate did not come as often as formerly; he only came to see Ku'ksu in the night. One night he said to him, "Tomorrow morning you must go to the little lake near here. Take all the people with you. I'll make you a very old man before you get to the lake." By the time he had reached it, he was a very old man. He fell into the lake, and sank down out of sight. Pretty soon the ground began to shake, the waves overflowed the shore, and there was a great roaring under the water, like thunder. By and by Ku'ksū came up out of the water, but young again, just like a young man. Then Earth-Initiate came and spoke to the people, and said, "If you do as I tell you, everything will be well. When any of you grow old, so old that you cannot walk, come to this lake, or get someone to bring you here. You must then go down into the water as you have seen Ku'ksū do, and you will come out young again." When he had said this, he went away. He left in the night, and went up above.

CENTRAL ASIATIC MYTH[7]

In a Central Asian Earth-Diver myth, the central figures are the creator, Otshirvani (the Bodhisattva Vairapani), and his assistant Chagan-Shukuty.

When these mighty beings descended from heaven they saw a frog (= turtle) diving in the water. Otshirvani's companion raised it from the depths and placed it on its back on the water. "I shall sit on the stomach of the frog," said Otshirvani, "dive thou to the bottom and bring up what thy hand finds." Chagan-Shukuty dived twice, and the second time he succeeded in bringing up some earth. Then Otshirvani told him to sprinkle it on the stomach of the frog (turtle), on which they sat. The frog itself sank out of sight and only the earth remained visible above the surface of the water. Resting there, the gods fell asleep and while they were sleeping, Shulmus, the devil, arrived and saw the two friends lying on the earth which they had just created and which was yet so small that there was scarcely room for a third on it. The devil decided to make use of his chance and drown these beings together with their earth. But when he attempted to seize hold of the edge of the earth, he no longer saw the ocean. He took the sleeping friends under his arm and began to run toward the shore with them. But while he ran the earth grew. When he saw that his attempt was vain he dropped his burden and barely succeeded in escaping when Otshirvani awoke. The latter then explained to his companion how the devil had meant to destroy them but how the earth had saved them.

A RUMANIAN CREATION MYTH[8]

Before the creation of the earth God and Satan were alone over the waters. When God had decided to make the earth he sent Satan to the bottom of the ocean. Satan was to bring back particles of earth in his (God's) name. Satan dived into the waters three times but did not succeed in bringing back any particles to the surface because he was attempting to take the earth in his own name. Finally, he dived a fourth time in his and in God's name. This time he at least brought some of it up, as much that is, as could remain under his fingernails (or claws). Out of this God finished a sort of cake (a clod) and sat upon it in order to rest himself. Satan thought; "God is sleeping." He thus desired to take the earth particles of the clod and throw them into the ocean. In this way he thought he would become Lord. But everytime he touched the clod it grew larger, until it had become an immense earthen ball. Because of this the waters were displaced, and as God awoke he saw that there was not enough room for the waters. Since he knew no remedy, he sent the bee to the hedgehog, the wisest of all animals, which he had created in the meantime. The hedgehog did not want to give any remedy since, indeed, God was all knowing. The bee however, hid itself and listened to the hedgehog speaking to himself. He was overheard saying; "Evidently God does not know that he must make valleys and mountains in order to make room for the waters." The bee returned to God with the news she had overheard from the wise hedgehog. The hedgehog nevertheless, cursed the bee because it had eavesdropped. Hence forth she should eat nothing but dung. God however, rewarded the bee and declared that her dung should not be dirty or despised, but should be good to eat—and this is honey.

SIBERIAN–ALTAIC MYTH[9]

In the beginning when there was nothing but water, God and the "First Man" moved about in the shape of two black geese over the waters of the primordial ocean. The devil, however, could not hide his nature, but endeavoured ever to rise higher, until he finally sank down into the depths. Nearly suffocating, he was forced to call to God for help, and God raised him again into the air with the power of his word. God then spoke: "Let a stone rise from the bottom of the ocean!" When the stone appeared, "Man" seated himself upon it, but God asked him to dive under the water and bring land. Man brought earth in his hand and God scattered it on the surface of the water saying: "Let the world take shape!" Once more God asked Man to fetch earth. But Man then decided to take some for himself and brought a morsel in each hand. One handful he gave to God but the other he hid in his mouth, intending to create a world of his own. God threw the earth which the devil had brought him beside the rest on the water, and the world at once began to expand and grow harder, but with the growing of the world the piece of earth in Man's mouth also swelled until he was about to suffocate so that he was again compelled to seek God's help. God inquired: "What was thy intention? Didst thou think thou couldst hide earth from me in thy mouth?" Man now told his secret intentions and at God's request spat the earth out of his mouth. Thus were formed the boggy places upon the earth.

POHONICHI MIWOK MYTH OF THE BEGINNING OF THE WORLD[10]

Before there were people there was only water everywhere. Coyote looked among the ducks and sent a certain species (Chukehansi: yimeit) to dive. At first it said it was unable to. Then it went down. It reached the bottom, bit the earth, and came up again. Coyote took the earth from it and sent it for chanit (Yokuts name) seeds. When the duck brought these he mixed them with the earth and water. Then the mixture swelled until the water had disappeared. The earth was there.

TRUHOHI YOKUTS MYTH[11]

Far in the south was a mountain. It was the only land. Everything else was water. The eagle was the chief. The people had nothing to eat. They were eating the earth and it was nearly gone. Then Coyote said: "Can we not obtain earth? Can we not make mountains?" The eagle said: "I do not know how." Coyote said: "There is a man that we will ask." Then they got the magpie. The eagle said: "Can we obtain earth?" The magpie said: "Yes." "Where?" "Right below us." Then all the ducks dived and tried to bring up the earth. Some were gone half a day. They could not reach the bottom and died and floated up. The eagle said: "When you reach the ground take hold of it and bite it, and fill your nose and ears." For six days they dived and found nothing. There was only one more to go down, the mudhen. Then the eagle said, "Now you go. Let us see if you can find the earth." The mudhen said: "Good." Then he dived. It was gone for a day and a night.

In the morning it came up. It was dead. They looked it over. It had earth in its nails, its ears, and its nose. Then they made the earth from this ground. They mixed it with chiyu seeds and from this they made the earth. After six days the eagle said to the wolf: "Now go around." Then the wolf went where the Sierra Nevada now is and around to the west and came back along where the Coast Range is. The eagle said: "Do not touch it for six days. Let it dry first." All the people said: "Very well, we will let it become dry." But soon Coyote said: "I will try it. It is getting hard now." He traveled along where the Sierras are. That is why these are rough and broken now. It is from his running over the soft earth. Then he turned west and went back along the Coast Range. That is why there are mountains there also. Coyote made it so. Now the eagle sent out the prairie falcon and the raven (Khotoi). He told them: "Go around the world and see if the earth is hard yet." Then the prairie falcon went north along the Sierra Nevada and Khotoi went north along the Coast Range. Each came back the way he had gone. Now at first the Sierra Nevada was not so high as the Coast Range. When the two returned the eagle said: "How is the earth? Is it hard?" "Yes" they said. Then the prairie falcon said: "Look at my mountains. They are the highest," but Khotoi said: "No, mine are higher." The prairie falcon said: "No, yours do not amount to anything. They are low." Then the eagle and Coyote sent the people to different places. They said: "You go to that place with your people. You go to that spring." So they sent them off, and the people went to the different places where they are now. They were still animals, but they became people. For a little while after they had all gone the eagle and Coyote stayed there. Then Coyote said: "Where will you go?" The eagle said: "I am thinking about it. I think I will go up." Coyote said: "Where shall I live?" The eagle said: "Here." But Coyote said: "No, I will go with you." The eagle told him: "No, you must stay here. You will have to look after this place here." So they talked for six days. Then

the eagle took all his things. "Goodby," he said, "I am going."
Then he went. Coyote looked up. He said, "I am going too."
"You have no wings. You cannot," said the eagle. "I will go." said
Coyote, and he went. Now they are together in the sky above.

THE CREATION OF THE WORLD, THE ORIGIN OF THE NEGRITOS[12]

In the beginning was a great water. Out of this Tahobn, the
dung-beetle, brought forth the earth in a small pack. This pack
grew higher and higher. Everything would have become mountains
if the bear (Kawab) had not come and trampled down the hills.
Thus the flat lands were made. Kaei sat above and saw how the
earth had come into being. He climbed down to it and created the
Rankel and then ascended to heaven again.

The Kensieu told Schebesta that at first only Pedn and Manoid
his wife existed. The sun was already there, but not the earth.
Then Tahobn, the dung-beetle, made the earth by pulling it out
of the mud. The sun dried it and made it firm. When Pedn and
Manoid saw the earth they descended to it. When the earth came
into being trees grew out of it, but there were no animals or birds.
Pedn and Manoid got two children in the following way. Manoid
dreamt of a child and begged Pedn for one. Pedn went out to get
some fruit and spread out a cloth for the fruit to fall on it, and,
when the fruit fell, it became a child which began to scream. It
was a boy. Manoid dreamt again, this time about a female child
and begged her husband for it, so Pedn did as before and the
fruit which fell into the cloth became a girl. The boy was Capai
(identified in a story that Schebesta gives as the *kakuh*-bird) and
the girl was called Pa'ig (identified in the same story with *baul*,
the tortoise.) Both were *Cenoi-halek*. As there were no people,
they married each other and had children. Two of these were

Encogen and Kadjegn, both "grandchildren" of Ta Pedn. When Encogen came to a rock he heard the rushing of water. He shot an arrow into the rock so that water gushed forth. He became famous through this deed.

CREATION MYTH OF THE GAROS[13]

In the beginning, what is now the Earth was a vast watery plain. There was no land, and darkness was over everything.

Tatara-Rabuga determined to create the Earth, so he sent a lesser spirit, Nostu-Nōpantu, in the shape of a woman, to carry out his will. There was no dry place for her to set foot on, so she took up her abode in a spider's web which was stretched over the water. Tatara-Rabuga gave her for material a handful of sand, but when she set about her task she found that she could not make the particles stick together. So she sent the big crab down under the water to fetch some clay, but it was too deep, and he was obliged to return with his errand unfulfilled. Nostu then sent Chipongnokma-Balponggitel, the small crab, to do her behest, but he was afraid, and returned without having performed his errand. Last of all, Nostu chose Chiching-Barching, a beetle, and sent him down, and he returned with a lump of clay, with the aid of which Nostu-Nōpantu fashioned the Earth.

She created the Earth, which was called Mané-Pilté, and the big rocks Mojar, and the little rocks Dinjar, but all was still wet and unfit to walk upon. So Nostu prayed Tatara-Rabuga to help her, and he placed the sun in the sky, and the moon, and sent wind, and the three between them dried up and hardened the surface of the Earth.

Then Tatara gave the earth a *riking* or petticoat (the Earth is spoken of as a woman) and a *pagri* made of clouds, and caused hair to grow on her in the shape of the *prap tree (Ficus Rumphi)*, the *bolong*, the *sawé* (sago palm), the *rejok* and *re* (kinds of cane), and the *ampang* (thatching grass).

Of the animals which Tatara created, the first was the hulock ape, and his mission on earth was to utter loud cries and of productiveness. After the hulock, the hanuman and the common brown monkey were created, and then all other beasts.

In the water, the first animal created was the frog, for he was appointed to proclaim the advent of rain to all living things by his loud croak. After the frog, the many fishes of the deep were created.

Under the Earth there was much water, but on the surface there was none. Seeing this, the creator made rivers to flow and sent Noréchiré-Kimrébokré, or the rain, to water the Earth, and he sent a voice (thunder) before the rain to announce its coming.

Man had not yet been created, so Tatara called around him the lesser spirits, and declared his intention of placing man on earth. He chose a goddess named Susimé, and sent her down to prepare it for its new inhabitants.

The first abode of man was Amitong-Asiljong (somewhere in the east), and the first man and woman were Sani and Muni, whose children, Gancheng and Dujong, were the parents of Nōrō and Mandé, who were the progenitors of the Garo race.

The first inhabitants of the Earth had no rice to eat, so they had to satisfy their hunger with roots and fruit which they found in the forest.

The first human beings to cultivate the soil were two dwarfs, Bōnéjasku and his wife Jané-Gandō. They cleared the forest as is done at the present day, and Tatara-Rabuga, to whom they made an offering of pumpkins, rewarded their industry by causing rice to grow.

GASHOWU YOKUTS MYTH[14]

The prairie falcon and the raven made the earth at a time when everything was water. The beaver, the otter, the mud-hen, the mallard duck, and a duck called potikh dived and tried to reach bottom, but could not do so. Then k'uik'ui, a small duck, dived, reached the bottom, and grasped the sand there. As he rose up, it washed out of his hands, his mouth, and his ears. Only a little was left under his finger-nail. When he came to the surface, he gave this to the prairie falcon. The prairie falcon had tobacco. This he mixed with the sand. Then he divided it, and gave half to the raven, whom he called his friend. They went far to the north. There they separated. The prairie falcon sent the raven to go southward on the west. He himself came southward along the east where these mountains are now. As they went they dropped the sand from between the thumb and finger. As the sand fell into the water it began to boil and the world grew from underneath. Then the raven surpassed the prairie falcon. These large mountains which are now here were then in the west. When the prairie falcon arrived he saw that the raven's mountains were the larger. Then he changed them about. He put one in the place of the other without the raven's knowledge.

So if it had not been for k'uik'ui and the prairie falcon the world would not have been made. But it was the prairie falcon who first wanted the world.

WUKCHAMNI YOKUTS MYTH[15]

Everything was water except a very small piece of ground. On this were the eagle and Coyote. Then the turtle swam to them.

They sent it to dive for the earth at the bottom of the water. The turtle barely succeeded in reaching the bottom and touching it with its foot. When it came up again, all the earth seemed washed out. Coyote looked clearly at its nails. At last he found a grain of earth. Then he and the eagle took this and laid it down. From it they made the earth as large as it is. From the earth they also made six men and six women. They sent these out in pairs in different directions and the people separated. After a time the eagle sent the Coyote to see what the people were doing. Coyote came back and said: "They are doing something bad. They are eating the earth. One side is already gone." The eagle said: "That is bad. Let us make something for them to eat. Let us send the dove to find something." The dove went out. It found a single grain of meal. The eagle and Coyote put this down on the ground. Then the earth became covered with seeds and fruit. Now they told the people to eat these. When the seeds were dry and ripe the people gathered them. Then the people increased and spread all over. But the water is still under the world.

YAUELMANI YOKUTS MYTH[16]

At first there was water everywhere. A piece of wood (wicket, stick, wood, tree) grew up out of the water to the sky. On the tree there was a nest. Those who were inside did not see any earth. There was only water to be seen. The eagle was the chief of them. With him were the wolf, Coyote, the panther, the prairie falcon, the hawk called po'yon, and the condor. The eagle wanted to make the earth. He thought: "We will have to have land." Then he called k'uik'ui, a small duck. He said to it: "Dive down and bring up earth." The duck dived, but did not reach the bottom. It died. The eagle called another kind of duck. He told it to dive. This duck went far down. It finally reached the bottom. Just as it touched the mud there it died. Then it came up again. Then the eagle and the other six saw a little dirt under its finger nail. When the eagle saw this he took the dirt from its nail. He mixed it with telis and pele seeds and ground them up. This was in the morning. Then he set it in the water and it swelled and spread everywhere, going out from the middle. (These seeds were ground and mixed with water swell.) In the evening the eagle told his companions: "Take some earth." They went down and took a little earth up in the tree with them. Early in the morning, when the morning star came, the eagle said to the wolf: "Shout." The wolf shouted and the earth disappeared, and all was water again. The eagle said: "We will make it again," for it was for this purpose that they had taken some earth with them into the nest. Then they took telis and pele seeds again, and ground them with the earth, and put the mixture into the water, and it swelled out again. Then early next morning, when the morning star appeared, the eagle told the wolf again: "Shout!" and he shouted three times. The earth was shaken by an earthquake, but it stood. Then Coyote said: "I must shout, too." He shouted and the earth shook a very little. Now it was good. Then they came out of the tree on the ground. Close to where this tree stood there was a lake. The eagle said: "We will live here." Then they had a house there and lived there.

Now every evening when the sun went down tokho (sokhon, tobacco) came there and went to the water in the lake. (Coyote wanted to catch it.) The eagle asked him: "How will you do it?" Coyote said: "Well, I will do it." He went off into the brush, rolled string on his thigh, and made it into a snare, which he put into the water. Tokho came, entered the water, and was caught. Coyote tried to take hold of it, but it was too hot. He could not touch it. It was like fire. Only after the sun came up was he able to take hold of it. Now, after he had held it all night, the tokho said to him: "Take me to the house." Coyote asked: "What does Tokho mean?" It said: "I am tobacco (sokhon). Give me to the

prairie falcon." Coyote brought it to the house and said: "Who
wants this?" The eagle did not want it. None of the seven wanted
it except the prairie falcon. He said: "I will take it." Coyote asked
it: "What are you good for?" The tobacco said: "I am good for
many things. If there is anything you want to have, use me, and
then whatever it is that you wish will be so." The prairie falcon
said: "I will try it." At night he took a little of the tobacco in his
mouth and blew out: "Pu! I want it to rain." Then it began to
rain. It rained all night.

Then Coyote said: "We will make a woman of a deer." Then
they killed a deer. They put it under a blanket of tules. It was
entirely covered. When the morning star came it got up. It was a
person (yokots) now. It was a woman. Coyote said: "I will sleep
with her." That night he slept with her. In the morning he was
dead. The woman was not hurt. The prairie falcon took a sharp
water kress (kapi). He said: "Stick it in his anus and he will get
up." One of them put it in. Coyote got up hurriedly. "Ah, I was
sleepy," he said. He said: "That is not good. It is not sweet. All
men will die. We shall have to do it differently." Then he killed
her. He left her under the blanket over night. Then he said:
"To-night I will try it again." Then he slept with her. In the
morning he got up early. "This is all right," he said. "This is
good. We will let it be like that." This is how people came to be:
deer was the mother. They made her by means of tobacco, blowing (spitting) it out while they said what they wished. But the
prairie falcon ate nothing but tobacco. He lived on that. Thus the
earth was made.

CHAPTER SIX

CONCLUSION

IN THIS BOOK we have attempted to give an historical-phenomenological interpretation to the religious structures found in various types of myths. These structures represent the manner in which the world has been confronted in some of the cultures of mankind and how this confrontation has produced specific ideas and conceptions of the world. We have also shown that new apprehensions of the sacred produce new mythological forms, the older forms becoming irrelevant. Several of the mythological forms discussed are closely related to the discovery of new dimensions of culture, e.g., flint tools, agriculture, sexuality. This fact has not led us to interpret the meaning of mythological forms as simply an aspect of early tool-making or economic activity. The discovery of new dimensions of culture is identical with man's discovery of new dimensions of his being and in turn this discovery reveals new aspects of sacrality and holiness. It is man's ability to respond and to discover new dimensions of his being which lies behind the notion of revelation.

The myths which we have discussed are related to primitive and pre-modern societies. Something remains to be said about the relevance of myth for modern man. We shall discuss this problem in two parts; first, the use of myth as a tool of historical research and, second, the possibility of myth as a mode of orientation in the modern period.

1) Myth as a Tool of Historical Research

The study of history in the West has progressively moved from a provincial concern with the Western tradition and its roots in the ancient Near East to a study of the civilization of India, China, Japan. These historical studies may be encompassed within the framework of a history of civilization. Civilization is used in this context to denote a precise stage of cultural development. If the study of a civilization is carried out along historical lines of inquiry, in such an interpretation the relationship of religion to the other aspects of civilization becomes an important part of the study. This is especially true in those non-Western civilizations which are still influenced to a large degree by traditional orientations. Traditional forms as expressed in myth continue to influence the conduct and behavior of many people in these civilizations. Any adequate historical interpretation must pay attention to the mythological symbols within a particular civilization.

If the historical interpretation of civilization is subordinated to a contemporary study, the interpretation of mythical-symbolic forms may still prove to be a valuable tool. Every form within a contemporary civilization has a history and often the history of that form may shed as much light on its meaning as its function at any particular time. The use of anthropological methods in the study of the roots of classical Greek culture is a case in point.

But even if one concentrates on the present status of a civilization, the symbolic interpretation is useful. Contemporary anthropological theory defines cultures as "wholes." These "wholes" represent the complex manner in which economic activity, kinship systems, philosophy, religion, use and manufacture of artifacts, etc., cohere and interrelate within a community of people. One could almost say that every civilization is founded on a mythic apprehension of reality. It may well be that the religious symbol provides us with a key for the understanding of that particular response to reality which we call culture.

Rudolf Otto in his *Idea of the Holy* attempted to work out this problem within the framework of a Kantian philosophy. In his theory of schematization he related the basic religious apprehension to the various dimensions of culture. The discipline of cultural anthropology was not available to him and thus his understanding of this problem was inadequate. The relationship of man's religious experience to his historical cultural situation remains a fruitful area of historical research.

2) *Myth and the Modern Situation*

We are now living through a crisis situation. This crisis is related to the transitional character of our age. A part of this situation has to do with the integration of the communities of man, popularly referred to by the phrase, "one world." Though the ideal of "one world" has a long history, the possibility of its realization is present only in our time. Profound changes in the cultures of mankind have taken place and will continue to take place in the future. A new human "situation" is almost upon us.

Teilhard de Chardin reports that the archaeologist Henri Breuil said to him, "We have only cast off the last moorings which held us to the Neolithic-age."[1] If this statement is true we can understand the magnitude of the change through which we are going. The Neolithic age began about six thousand years ago. The discovery of agriculture and the domestication of animals provided the basic structural characteristics of this period. The expressions of man's world in terms of these structures lies behind all of the religions of the great civilizations. It is difficult to imagine otherwise. If we are seeing the end of the Neolithic age, what new structures will inform the future period? The attack upon mythological structures as adequate forms for the expression of modern man's life is in fact an attack upon the formalized mythological categories of the classical religions of the great world cultures. The formalized mythological categories which are products of a Neolithic age seem irrelevant to the structures of reality defined in terms of the new science and technology.

Changes of this kind have occurred before in the history of religion and culture. Specific mythological structures give way to new revelations. But we know that the structure of the myth cannot be reduced to its historical-materialistic dimensions. Involved in every myth is the expression of the uniquely human element. It is this intention of the myth which is timeless. If a new age is emerging, it must be understood in mythic terms for it is in these terms that the new is ordered and humanized. The study and understanding of the mythological forms of the past may sensitize us to this level of human awareness. By understanding the appearances of the gods in the past we may see and know the gods who will establish the new heavens and the new earth.

APPENDICES

APPENDIX I

CREATION AND SACRIFICE

IN THE INTRODUCTORY COMMENTARY
to the emergence myths, we emphasized the symbolism of earth as mother. In the emergence myths the earth brings forth man and his world as a mother brings forth a child. The world in these myths goes through definite stages of development until it is brought forth as a completed whole.

From the perfect symbol of the mother, ordered and harmonious life emerges. This rather logical development within the womb of the mother is in sharp contrast to myths which emphasize the sacrificial motif as the basis for the cosmos. In the Mesopotamian myth, Enuma Elish, Marduk, after defeating Tiamat, cuts her body into two parts; one part becomes the heavens, the other, the earth. In the Mande myth from West Africa, Faro, the twin, must be sacrificed before the earth becomes habitable. In Hesiod's Theogony Mother Earth persuades one of her offspring, Cronus, to cut off his father's sexual organs. The father, who is the sky, would not allow his offspring to see the light of day. They remain shut up in the body of the mother. The castration of the father is an attempt on the part of the offspring and mother to break the rule of the father over them so that the offspring may have light, i.e., see the light of day.

In the Prose Edda, we read that the cosmos is made up of the dismembered body of the primordial giant Ymir and in Rig Veda X. 90, the cosmos is the result of the sacrifice of man.

A. E. Jensen reports a myth from Ceram which tells of the dismemberment of a young maiden, Hainuwele, who had grown from a coconut palm.

In each case, the sacrificial victim is a residue of great power. Tiamat in Enuma Elish is the great mother possessing all the potencies of life; Faro in West Africa is the bisexual twin, a symbol of power and perfection; the sky father in Hesiod's Theogony is the powerful agent of creation and fertility, holding absolute sway over earth mother and her offspring. Ymir, the primordial giant, possesses the great power inherited from a race of primordial beings. Hainuwele's power is shown in her magical ability to produce valuable goods. Even her excrement contained articles of great value.

The killing or sacrifice of these powerful beings effects a redistribution of power. Instead of the power residing in one being, it now flows into every part of the universe. It is made accessible to all beings. The parts of the sacrificed beings become the stable and life-giving sources of the cosmos. But sacrifice is also the coming of death. Life and death thus inhere in the same act. Without the redistribution of sacred power no cultural life is possible, but the generalizing of the power is accomplished only in death.

MYTH FROM CERAM[2]

Nine families of mankind came forth in the beginning from Mount Nunusaku, where the people had emerged from clusters of bananas. And these families stopped in West Ceram, at a place known as the "Nine Dance Grounds," which is the jungle between Ahiolo and Varoloin.

But there was a man among them whose name was Ameta, meaning "Dark," "Black," or "Night," and neither was he married nor had he children. He went off, one day, hunting with his dog. And after a little, the dog smelt a wild pig, which it traced to a pond into which the animal took flight; but the dog remained on the shore. And the pig, swimming, grew tired and drowned, but the man, who had arrived meanwhile, retrieved it. And he found a coconut on its tusk, though at that time there were no cocopalms in the world.

Returning to his hut, Ameta placed the nut on a stand and covered it with a cloth bearing a snake design, then lay down to sleep. And in the night there appeared to him the figure of a man who said: "The coconut that you placed upon the stand and covered with a cloth you must plant in the earth; otherwise it won't grow." So Ameta planted the coconut the next morning, and in three days the palm was tall. Again three days and it was bearing blossoms. He climbed the tree to cut the blossoms, from which he wished to prepare himself a drink, but as he cut he slashed his finger and the blood fell on a leaf. He returned home to bandage his finger and in three days came back to the palm to find that where the blood on the leaf had mingled with the sap of the cut blossom the face of someone had appeared. Three days later, the trunk of the person was there, and when he returned again in three days he found that a little girl had developed from his drop of blood. That night the same figure of a man appeared to him in a dream. "Take your cloth and snake design," he said, "wrap the girl of the cocopalm in the cloth carefully and carry her home."

So the next morning Ameta went with his cloth to the cocopalm, climbed the tree, and carefully wrapped up the little girl. He descended cautiously, took her home, and named her

Hainuwele. She grew quickly and in three days was a nubile maiden. But she was not like an ordinary person; for when she would answer the call of nature her excrement consisted of all sorts of valuable articles, such as Chinese dishes and gongs, so that her father became rich.

And about that time there was to be celebrated in the place of the Nine Dance Grounds a great Maro Dance, which was to last nine full nights, and the nine families of mankind were to participate. Now when the people dance the Maro, the women sit in the center and from there reach betel nut to the men, who form, in dancing, a large ninefold spiral. Hainuwele stood in the center at this Maro festival, passing out betel nut to the men. And at dawn, when the performance ended, all went home to sleep.

The second night, the nine families of mankind assembled on the second ground; for when the Maro is celebrated it must be performed each night in a different place. And once again, it was Hainuwele who was placed in the center to reach betel nut to the dancers; but when they asked for it she gave them coral instead, which they found very nice. The dancers and the others, too, then began pressing in to ask for betel nut and she gave them coral. And so the performance continued until dawn, when they all went home to sleep.

The next night the dance was resumed on a third ground, with Hianuwele again in the center; but this time she gave beautiful porcelain dishes, and everyone present received such a dish. The fourth night she gave bigger porcelain dishes and the fifth great bush knives; the sixth, beautifully worked betel boxes of copper; the seventh, golden earrings; and the eighth, glorious gongs. The value of the articles increased, that way, from night to night, and the people thought this thing mysterious. They came together and discussed the matter.

They were extremely jealous that Hainuwele could distribute such wealth and decided to kill her. The ninth night, therefore, when the girl was again placed in the center of the dance ground, to pass out betel nut, the men dug a deep hole in the area. In the innermost circle of the great ninefold spiral the men of the Lesiela family were dancing, and in the course of the slowly cycling movement of their spiral they pressed the maiden Hainuwele toward the hole and threw her in. A loud, three-voiced Maro Song drowned out her cries. They covered her quickly with earth, and the dancers trampled this down firmly with their steps. They danced on till dawn, when the festival ended and the people returned to their huts.

But when the Maro festival ended and Hainuwele failed to return, her father knew that she had been killed. He took nine branches of a certain bushlike plant whose wood is used in the casting of oracles and with these reconstructed in his home the nine circles of the Maro Dancers. Then he knew that Hainuwele had been killed in the Dancing Ground. He took nine fibres of the cocopalm leaf and went with these to the dance place, stuck them one after the other into the earth, and with the ninth came to what had been the innermost circle. When he stuck the ninth fiber into the earth and drew it forth, on it were some of the hairs and blood of Hainuwele. He dug up the corpse and cut it into many pieces, which he buried in the whole area about the Dancing Ground—except for the two arms, which he carried to the maiden Satene: the second of the supreme Demi-virgins of West Ceram. At the time of the coming into being of mankind Satene had emerged from an unripe banana, whereas the rest had come from ripe bananas; and she now was the ruler of them all. But the buried portions of Hainuwele, meanwhile, were already turning into things that up to that time had never existed anywhere on earth—above all, certain tuberous plants that have been the principal food of the people ever since.

Ameta cursed mankind and the maiden Satene was furious at the people for having killed. So she built on one of the dance grounds a great gate, consisting of a ninefold spiral, like the one formed by the men in the dance; and she stood on a great log inside this gate, holding in her two hands the two arms of Hainuwele. Then, summoning the people, she said to them: "Because you have killed, I refuse to live here any more; today I shall leave. And so now you must all try to come to me through this gate. Those who succeed will remain people, but to those who fail something else will happen."

They tried to come through the spiral gate, but not all succeeded, and everyone who failed was turned into either an animal or a spirit. That is how it came about that pigs, deer, birds, fish, and many spirits inhabit the earth. Before that time there had been only people. Those, however, who came through walked to Satene; some to the right of the log on which she was standing, others to the left; and as each passed she struck him with one of Hainuwele's arms. Those going left had to jump across five sticks of bamboo, those to the right, across nine, and from these two groups, respectively, were derived the tribes known as the Fivers and the Niners. Satene said to them: "I am departing today and you will see me no more on earth. Only when you die will you again see me. Yet even then you shall have to accomplish a very difficult journey before you attain me."

And with that, she disappeared from the earth. She now dwells on the mountain of the dead, in the southern part of West Ceram, and whoever desires to go to her must die. But the way of her mountain leads over eight other mountains. And ever since that day there have been not only men but spirits and animals on earth, while the tribes of men have been divided into the Fivers and the Niners.

A related myth tells of the remaining divine maiden, Rabia, who was desired in marriage by the sun-man Tuwale. But when her parents placed a dead pig in her place in the bridal bed, Tuwale claimed his bride in a strangely violent manner, causing her to sink into the earth among the roots of a tree. The efforts of the people to save her were in vain: they could not prevent her from sinking even deeper. And when she had gone down as far as to the neck, she called her mother: "It is Tuwale, the sun-man, who has come to claim me. Slaughter a pig and celebrate a feast; for I am dying. But in three days, when evening comes, look up at the sky, where I shall be shining upon you as a light." That was how the moon-maiden Rabia instituted the death feast. And when her relatives had killed the pig and celebrated the death feast for three days, they saw for the first time the moon, rising in the east.

MYTH FROM RIG VEDA X. 90[3]

"When the gods made a sacrifice
  with the Man as their victim,
Spring was the melted butter, Summer the fuel,
  and Autumn the oblation.

"From that all-embracing sacrifice
  the clotted butter was collected.
From it he made the animals
  of air and wood and village.

"From that all-embracing sacrifice
  were born the hymns and chants,
from that the metres were born,
  from that the sacrificial spells were born.

"Thence were born horses,
  and all beings with two rows of teeth.
Thence were born cattle,
  and thence goats and sheep.

"When they divided the Man,
   into how many parts did they divide him?
What was his mouth, what were his arms,
   what were his thighs and his feet called?

"The brāhman was his mouth,
   of his arms was made the warrior,
his thighs became the vaiśya,
   of his feet the śūdra was born."

"The moon arose from his mind,
   from his eye was born the sun,
from his mouth Indra and Agni,
   from his breath the wind was born.

"From his navel came the air,
   from his head there came the sky,
from his feet the earth, the four quarters from his ear,
   thus they fashioned the worlds.

With Sacrifice the gods sacrificed to Sacrifice—
   these were the first of the sacred laws.
These mighty beings reached the sky,
   where are the eternal spirits, the gods."

THE BEGUILING OF GYLFI[4]

Then said Gangleri: "How did the races grow thence, or after what fashion was it brought to pass that more men came into being? Or do ye hold him God, of whom ye but now spake?" And Jafnhárr answered: "By no means do we acknowledge him God; he was evil and all his kindred; we call them Rime-Giants. Now it is said that when he slept, a sweat came upon him, and there grew under his left hand a man and a woman, and one of his feet begat a son with the other; and thus the races are come;

these are the Rime-Giants. The old Rime-Giant, him we call Ymir."

Then said Gangleri: "Where dwelt Ymir, or wherein did he find sustenance?" Hárr answered: "Straightway after the rime dripped, there sprang from it the cow called Audumla; four streams of milk ran from her udders, and she nourished Ymir." Then asked Gangleri: "Wherewithal was the cow nourished?" And Hárr made answer: "She licked the ice-blocks, which were salty; and the first day that she licked the blocks, there came forth from the blocks in the evening a man's hair; the second day, a man's head; the third day the whole man was there. He is named Búri: he was fair of feature, great and mighty. He begat a son called Borr, who wedded the woman named Bestla, daughter of Bölthorn the giant; and they had three sons: one was Odin, the second Vili, the third Vé. And this is my belief, that he, Odin, with his brothers, must be ruler of heaven and earth; we hold that he must be so called; so is that man called whom we know to be mightiest and most worthy of honor, and ye do well to let him be so called."

Then said Gangleri: "What covenant was between thee, or which was the stronger?" And Hárr answered: "The sons of Borr slew Ymir the giant; lo, where he fell there gushed forth so much blood out of his wounds that with it they drowned all the race of the Rime-Giants, save that one, whom giants call Bergelmir, escaped with his household; he went upon his ship, and his wife with him, and they were safe there. And from them are come the races of the Rime-Giants, as is said here:

> Untold ages ere earth was shapen,
> Then was Bergelmir born;
> That first I recall, how the famous wise giant
> On the deck of the ship was laid down."

Then said Gangleri: "What was done then by Börr's sons, if thou believe that they be gods?" Hárr replied: "In this matter there is no little to be said. They took Ymir and bore him into the middle of the Yawning Void, and made of him the earth: of his blood the sea and the waters; the land was made of his flesh, and the crags of his bones; gravel and stones they fashioned from his teeth and his grinders and from those bones that were broken." And Jafnhárr said: "Of the blood, which ran and welled forth freely out of his wounds, they made the sea, when they had formed and made firm the earth together, and laid the sea in a ring round about her; and it may well seem a hard thing to most men to cross over it." Then said Thridi: "They took his skull also, and made of it the heaven, and set it up over the earth with four corners; and under each corner they set a dwarf: the names of these are East, West, North, and South. Then they took the glowing embers and sparks that burst forth and had been cast out of Muspellheim, and set them in the midst of the Yawning Void, in the heaven, both above and below, to illumine heaven and earth. They assigned places to all fires: to some in heaven; some wandered free under the heavens; nevertheless, to these also they gave a place, and shaped their courses. It is said in old songs, that from these the days were reckoned, and the tale of years told, as is said in Völuspar.

APPENDIX II

THE ANCESTORS AS CREATORS

IN THE CHAPTER on World-Parent myths we interpreted the offspring as the agents of creation. In myths which do not present us with the World-Parent structure, the ancestors of man assume the creative roles. In the Djanggawul myth from Australia we see a good example of this type of myth.

The Djanggawul came from an eternal land. They seem to have a purpose in coming to Arnhem Land. The emphasis given to their sexual relations and the size of their sexual organs makes them bearers of creative power. From the description of the organs, the Djanggawul seems at one point to resemble hermaphroditic characters. "The penis of Djanggawul . . . had a long foreskin, suggesting that it had not been circumcised, at various intervals along the penis were notches, or penis "rings" or ridges. . . . The elder Sister's clitoris . . . was the longer, while the younger Sister's was almost snakelike in appearance."

Djanggawul and his sisters travel over the country.

Wherever they stop, they have sexual intercourse and leave people and "Dreamings." The "Dreamings" are totemic symbols which regulate the social life and food supply of the Australian Aborigines. Their wanderings over the land make the land sacred and a fit habitation for man.

In this manner, the moieties, the food supply and the entire cosmos is revealed to the Australians of Arnhem Land.

THE DJANGGAWUL MYTH (AUSTRALIA)[5]

In the beginning there were land and sky, animals and birds, foliage and trees. There was sea, too, in the waters of which were fish and other creatures; and upon the land were beings of totemic origin. All these things were there, as they had always been; but man, as we know him to-day, was not among them.

Far out to sea, out of sight of the Arnhem Land mainland, was an island known as Bralgu (Bu'ralgu), the land of the Eternal Beings, which later became the home of the *dua* moiety dead. It lay to the south-east of Port Bradshaw, somewhere beyond Groote Eylandt.

It was here, at Bralgu, that the Djanggawul were living. They are said to have come from a big ceremony or meeting, in an unknown land far beyond the isle of Bralgu. On their arrival there they held another large ceremony, much larger than the contemporary *dua nara,* and used all their sacred objects. At that time they possessed a great many emblems, but only a few of these could be brought in the bark canoe to the Australian mainland.

They did not, however, spend very long at Bralgu, for it was only a "half-way" resting place on the journey they were attempting.

There were three of them: Djanggawul himself, his elder Sister, Bildjiwuraroiju, and his younger Sister, Miralaidj. With them, too, was another man, named Bralbral. The Two Sisters and their Brother, however, were nearly always known as the Djanggawul. Djanggawul himself had an elongated penis, and each of the Two Sisters had a long clitoris; these were so long that they dragged upon the ground as they walked. The penis of Djanggawul, *gurlga* or *dulparu* (ordinary name for penis) had a long foreskin (*dabin*), suggesting that it had not been circumcised; at various intervals along the penis were notches, or penis "rings" or "ridges," as on an ordinary penis towards the apex. These rings were called *bugalil*, a term also applied to the sacred invocations at present used among the north-eastern Arnhem Land peoples (*dua* moiety, *bugali*, or *jiritja* moiety, *bugalili*). The elder Sister's clitoris (the ordinary term being *gadin*, and the "inside" term *ngeribngerib*) was the longer, while the younger Sister's was almost snakelike in appearance.

At Bralgu, as they walked around with these, they left grooves in the ground from their dragging. And when the Djanggawul Brother had coitus with his Sisters, he lifted aside their clitorises, entering them in the usual way. He was able to have incestuous relations with his Sisters, because at that time there were no marriage rules, no moities and no prohibition. Djanggawul had been having coitus with Bildjiwuraroiju for a long time; her breasts had grown large and "fallen down" with milk, and she had produced many children. Miralaidj, though, was quite young, having just passed puberty, and her breasts were rounded and firm.

They lived at Bralgu for some little time, putting people there, and leaving "Dreamings" in the form of totemic origins, sacred emblems and body paintings. They also instituted their rituals and ceremonies. The Brother's penis and the Sisters' clitorises were sacred emblems, like *rangga* poles.

At last they made ready their bark canoe, and loaded it with "Dreamings," sacred drawings and emblems; the latter were kept in a conically-shaped *ngainmara* mat. When all this was ready

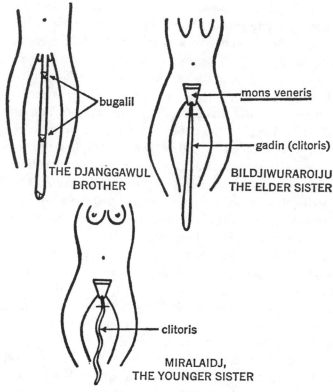

FIG. 6—The Djanggawul (from rough drawings by native informants.

they themselves, with their companion Bralbral, climbed into the canoe. Then they paddled out to sea, leaving the island of Bralgu far behind. For days and days they paddled, until they sighted the Arnhem Land mainland. At last they came to it, landing near Rose River. But they soon left this part of the country, and continued paddling along the coast until they reached Jelangbars, Port Bradshaw.

Near Gangudol Island, while still in their canoe, the Ancestral Beings saw some trees, in the branches of which were perched two *lindaridj* parakeets, drying themselves in the first rays of the sun. As they passed this island, the *djigai* morning pigeon was crying. "Maybe that bird is crying out on the land," said the Djanggawul, and so they sang about it. They saw, too, trepang on Bauwuling (or Bauwljans) Islands, and there were many *lindaridj* on Gagubam. A black cockatoo, immediately it caught sight of them, flew over to what are now the sacred sandhills near Ngadibaulwi (or Ngadibalji) rocks.

As the Djanggawul were nearing Port Bradshaw, and while they were still paddling, they could see the white foam from waves breaking around the sacred rock of Gulbinbol, just outside the entrance to the bay. As they looked they saw, too, myriads of small *lindaridj* parakeets flying over the mainland, the sun's rays catching the redness of their breast feathers. There was a constant roar of waves pounding on the beach. They paddled farther into the bay, coming to the Garingan rock, and saw the wide curving beach of Jelangbara. They sang with joy, and allowed the surf to take their canoe into the shallow water.

Then they dragged their canoe on to the beach and unloaded it, making this a sacred place. Jelangbara is the largest Djanggawul centre in north-eastern Arnhem Land and, today, the most important.

Here the Djanggawul Brother wished to shorten his Sisters' clitorises. But the elder Sister said, "No, wait till we reach Arnhem Bay. We can have a good rest, and put Dreamings there." So they walked around, still dragging the clitorises and elongated penis, leaving marks on the ground which may be seen to-day.

Leaving their canoe, the Djanggawul walked along the coast until they came to Ngadibalji, where they saw the *djawuldjanwul* mangrove bird. Here too the Djanggawul Brother left his hairbelt, but retained the parakeet-feathered waist-band and armbands he was wearing. The hairbelt is now a sandhill. On the sandhill, were track marks of the *damwmindjari* (*damburindari* or *waburunggu*) wild duck; these birds were eating the *murnji*, or wild peanut roots. On the opposite side was a large barren sandhill, on the surface of which were tracks of the *djanda* goanna, as well as of many birds. A *gamaru* tree with non-edible "apple"-like nuts was growing there, too. This tree is sacred; it is a *jirijiri* bullroarer tree, and to-day only those who are very old may look upon it. Here the Djanggawul paused and heard again the cry of the *ngadili* (*dangadilji* or *rirambung*) black cockatoo. Here too is the sacred waterhole, *milngur,* which the Djanggawul made by inserting the *mauwulan rangga* pole: a spring flows from it down to the beach. It is said that the four Beings entered this hole, and made their camp within.

Later, they walked farther along, and saw two *djanda* goanna resting on the peak of a sandhill. "Ah," said the Brother, "I am very surprised to see this goanna. I had better put it Dreaming (*wongar*) for this country." Bangguli is the goannas' "inside" sacred name. The goanna crawled up the smooth surface of the sandhill, dislodging the sand. It attempted to climb on to the sacred *djuda* pole (that is, tree) the Djanggawul had placed there, but could not do so, because the Djanngawul was still there. To-day the *djuda* ironwood (or "black" bark) tree is still there, at Mauwulanggalngu, where it grew from the sacred *rangga*.

After leaving the sandhills the Djanggawul continued walking along. Near the beach at Gumararanggu (named from the *gamaru* tree there), still on the Port Bradshaw peninsula, they heard the noise made by the black *malgu* flying fox, and saw more sandhills and goannas, as well as *gunjan* beach worms.

Coming to Wabilinga Island, which was later to become a large Macassan settlement, they saw the Baijini folk who were working there. They were cooking trepang, where the tamarind trees stand to-day. The Djanggawul were much perturbed and said to the Baijini, "Baijini, you had better move from here to your own place; for this place must belong to us, and we are going to establish a sacred site." So some of the Baijini moved to the other side of the island, and some went to Dagu (vagina or vulva) on the mainland. But they left behind them on the island ashes from their fires, the criss-cross elongated bars on which their trepang was left to dry, some huts, and a *djiru* trepang-stirring "spoon" or ladle. Djanggawul picked this up and looked at it. "Ah," he said, "this is a good colour. I shall have it for myself." The *djiru* was black, a colour that the Djanggawul now used for the first time, together with blackness from the charcoal in the ashes of the Baijini fires. In this way, the locality became partly *dua*, from the Djanggawul, and partly *jiritja*, from the Baijini.

Another *jiritja* moiety Ancestral Being, named Laintjung, was also present at this site. He exchanged gifts with the Djanggawul, and in return for some red parakeet feathered string gave them some black clan patterns, and opossum fur string. That is why, today, each moiety has something belonging to the other: the *jiritja* took from the *dua*, and vice versa. Laintjung was also given a red parakeet feathered *jiridbald* waist-band and some *judumiri* arm-bands. He possessed, too, a piece of cloth which he had obtained from the Baijini, but the Djanggawul refused to take any of this. The Djanggawul had apparently come prepared for this meeting with people of the *jiritja* moiety. They had half expected trouble from them when they requested the Baijini to move, and carried in readiness *gundmara* ("inside" name) fighting dilly bags.

Leaving Wabilinga Island behind them, the Djanggawul moved to Gagubam, where they heard the *djawuldjawul* mangrove bird calling out in the early morning. After this they heard "people and children" crying; and here spirit footprints of children may be seen on the rocks. These are the spirits who are as yet unborn, and remain in the uterus of the elder Sister, Bildjiwuraroiju. After leaving Gagubam the Djanggawul passed Bauwuling (or Bauwijara) where they saw *bauwaldja* catfish swimming after small fish and *bunabi* trepang slugs. And above Bauwuling, in the fresh water well on dry land, surrounded by mangroves and salt water, was *biabia* refuse from the trepang.

After spending some time in the Port Bradshaw country, establishing sacred sites, they decided to walk down the beach towards Caledon Bay; but there were so many totemic folk in those parts that they again got into their canoe and paddled down to Gambuga(wi) at Caldeon Bay, in territory of the Karlpu linguistic group. There they are said to have made a sacred place, and put special *djuda*. These were *rangga* emblems which, with others, they had carried from Bralgu in the *ngainmara* mat, and trees sprang up as they were pushed into the ground.

When they had done this they looked up, and saw a big dry weather cloud mirage, called *wulma*. It was coming from Buguwolumiri, in the country of the Djapu linguistic group, towards the "bottom" (or southern part) of Blue Mud Bay; so they travelled towards that place, and put more dreamings there. Their clitorises and penis were still dragging on the ground.

Then they saw another *wulma* towards the "top" of Blue Mud Bay, at Bugaliji, in Djarlwak linguistic group territory. They paddled around the coast to that place and left dreamings there. Then, abandoning their canoe, they went on foot through the bush until they came to Balimauwi; this is also in Djarlwak country, on the northern side of Rose River. They made a big camp, building a number of different "shades" of huts, which to-day are paperback trees; and there they also placed many dreamings.

Thus through the greater part of the country about Port Bradshaw, below Jelangbara almost to Rose River, all along the coast and even a little way inland, the Djanggawul left special drawings symbolically related to themselves and to totemic beings. They left, too, sacred *rangga* emblems, such as the *djuda*, the *djanda* (goanna) and *mauvulan* (associated with water springs), as well as sacred baskets. At all those places, moreover, they established their cult, with the singing of songs and the ritual of the *dua* moiety *nara* ceremonies.

While at Balimauwi, they looked up into the north western sky and saw a great *wulma* hanging over Ngaluwi ("inside" name

Waguralgu) at Arnhem Bay, in the territory of the Ngeimil and Dadawi linguistic groups. The Djanggawul eventually reached this place and made a camp, putting many dreamings there. They made a fish trap and caught many fish to eat. They also put the wild banana palm, and Djanggawul with his *mauwulan rangga* poked holes in the ground from which water flowed.

After a time they left Ngaluwi, walking along until they reached Gulugboi(wi), where they made a big "shade." They pushed their *djuda* into the ground, and trees sprang forth; and they put the *banggada* plants there.

At Daramur (or Darar'woi), inland from Arnhem Bay, the Djanggawul saw a *djanda* goanna in a fresh-water swamp that was covered with wild banana *dara* leaves; this was in Ngeimil territory.

Farther on a Mingu well, also in Ngeimil country, a *djanda* emerged from an open well which contained partially submerged banana foliage: new shoots had come up, completely covering the surface of the water.

Passing on to Djaddjananggu (also Ngeimil), they found a swamp where they saw *waragai* or *marabinj* fish; here too they saw lily roots and foliage, with flowers, and many ducks. Close by was the Maijulwi billabong where the *dadam* lily, with its round edible bulbs, was growing in great profusion. The Djanggawul Brother himself declared part of Maijulwi sacred, so that to-day only two tracks, one at each side, lead down to its banks; women may go down one of these only to get water, and must always return by the same road.

Continuing on, the Djanggawul reached Nganmaruwi, where they erected another large "shade." During all the time they had been on the Australian mainland, there is no mention of the Brother's having coitus with his Sisters: but while they were living here, he said to Bildjiwuraroiju, "I want to copulate with you, Sister."

But the elder Sister was shy. "Why?" she asked him.

"I want to put a few people in this place," the Brother replied.
So he lifted her clitoris and inserted his long penis. He did the
same with Miralaidj. So they continued living there, and he copulated as a husband does with his wives.

After some time, Bildjiwuraroiju became pregnant, and her
brother said to her, "Sister, may I have a look at you?"

"What for?" she asked.

"Because I want to put some people in this place."

"All right," she replied. She opened her legs a little, resting
her clitoris on her left leg. The Brother sat before his Sister and
placed his index finger into her vagina, up to the first joint. Then
he pulled it away, and at the same time a baby boy came out.
Bildjiwuraroiju was careful to open her legs only a little; if she
had spread them out, children would have flowed from her, for
she kept many people stored away in her uterus. These people
(or children) in her uterus were like *rangga* emblems kept in the
conical-shaped *ngainmara* mat, for the latter is a uterus symbol.

As the baby boy came out, the Brother stood listening to hear
the sound of his cry. As soon as he heard this, he took hold of
the child and put him on to the grass near by. Then he returned
to his Sister, and saw a baby girl coming out. After she had cried,
he lifted her gently and placed her under the *ngainmara* mat,
which served to shelter her from the sun. The crying of a male
child is *akai'dugung*, a forceful "heavy" sound; while that of a
girl is *akai njumulgunin*, a "small sound."

Then another male child issued from the elder Sister, and was
put into the grass by the Brother. She continued giving birth to
children of both sexes; when she had finished she closed her legs,
and the Djanggawul Brother said to her:

"Sister, these little boys we will put in the grass, so that later,
when they grow up, they will have whiskers; those whiskers are
from the grass. We will always do that when we remove male
children. And these little girls we have put under the *ngainmara*
mat, hiding them there. That is because they must be smooth and

soft and have no body hair, and because girls are really sacred. They must be kept under the *ngainmara,* just as the *rangga* emblems are kept. We will always do that when we remove female children."

The Djanggawul then left this place. The children they had produced grew up and married, and were the progenitors of the present Aborigines of those parts. From this time, too, the Two Sisters remained always pregnant, from having coitus with their Brother.

NOTES ON THE PLATES

BIBLIOGRAPHY

REFERENCES

INDEX

NOTES ON THE PLATES

17. "Nimba" dance mask, Baga tribe, Guinea, Africa.
18. Bobo dance mask, Mali Federation, Africa.
19. Bambara dance mask, Mali Federation, Africa.
20. Dogon female figure. Mali Federation, Africa.
21. Dogon mask with figure. Mali Federation, Africa.
22. Mask, New Hebrides, Ambrym Islands, Melanesia.
23. Ceremonial Board. Papuan Gulf, New Guinea.
24. Bas Relief from Temple of the Cross, Palenque.

Plates 17–24 follow page 168.

25. Façade of the K'odzp'op with stylizations of the Mayan God of Rain, Chac.
26. Slab from Secret Sarcophagus of the Temple of Inscription. Man is depicted resting on mask of the god of death staring upward at a symbolic representation of a two-headed serpent which is a representation of life.
27. Drawing of a pregnant woman from West Arnhem Land, Australia.
28a. A Dutchman *wuramu* figure. The *wuramu* is always an "outsider." While originally meaning a wild pillaging native, it has also the connotation of a "crook," collector or stealing man who is often identified with the Dutch customs official. This is an example of the manner in which artistic and mythic motifs are used to interpret the contemporary experience of primitive peoples.
28b. Banaitja, the son of Laintjung, the Great Ancestor. This figure is used in the ritual surrounding the myth of the coming of the Great Ancestor.
29. Mural from a Hopi Kiva, Awatovi, Arizona.
30. Sculptures from the wall of the main shrine, Konarak, India.
31. Loving Couples, Konarak, India.
32. "The Bear Mother." Carving in argillite by Skaows-Ke'ay, Haida. Skidegate, British Columbia.

Plates 25–32 follow page 200.

BIBLIOGRAPHY

We have included in this bibliography only those works which deal with the general problem of myth interpretation. Some specific historical studies are mentioned because of their contribution to general theory.

Hartley B. Alexander, *The World's Rim*, (Lincoln, Nebraska: The University of Nebraska Press, 1953)

Hermann Baumann, *Das Doppelte Geschlecht*, (Berlin, Dietrich Reimer, 1955)

Eldson Best, *Maori Religion and Mythology*, Bulletin No. 10, (Wellington: Dominion Museum, 1924)

Bruno Bettelheim, *Symbolic Wounds*, (Glencoe: the Free Press, 1954)

S. F. G. Brandon, *Time and Mankind*, (London: Hutchinson & Co., 1951)

Norman O. Brown, tr. *Hesiod's Theogony*, (New York: The Liberal Arts Press, 1953)

Joseph Campbell, *The Masks of God: Primitive Mythology*, (New York: The Viking Press, Inc. 1959)

——, *The Hero with a Thousand Faces*, (New York: Pantheon Books, 1949)

Ananda Coomaraswamy, "Spiritual Paternity and the Puppet Complex," *Psychiatry: Journal of the Biology and Pathology of Interpersonal Relations,* Vol. 8, No. 3, (Washington: William Alanson White Foundation, 1945) pp. 287-97

————, "Yaksas," *Smithsonian Institution Miscellaneous Collection,* Vol. 80, No. 6, (Washington: Smithsonian Institution, 1928-1931)

Eric Dardel, "The Mythic," *Diogenes,* No. 7, (Chicago: University of Chicago Press, Summer, 1954) p. 49ff.

Mircea Eliade, *The Myth of the Eternal Return,* trans. by Willard R. Trask, (London: Routledge & Kegan Paul, 1955)

————, *Patterns in Comparative Religion,* trans. by Rosemary Sheed, (New York: Sheed and Ward, Inc., 1958)

————, "The Prestige of the Cosmogonic Myth," *Diogenes,* No. 23, (Chicago: Univ. of Chicago Press, Fall, 1954) pp. 1-13

————, and J. M. Kitagawa, *The History of Religions, Essays in Methodology,* (Chicago: University of Chicago Press, 1959)

————, *The Sacred and the Profane,* trans. by Willard R. Trask, (New York: Harcourt Brace, 1959)

————, *Myths, Dreams, and Mysteries,* trans. by Philip Mairet, (London: Harvill Press, 1960)

————, *Images and Symbols,* trans. by Philip Mairet, (New York: Sheed and Ward, Inc., 1961)

A. P. Elkin and Catherine and Ronald Berndt, *Art in Arnhem Land,* (Chicago: University of Chicago Press, 1950)

Papers from Eranos Yearbooks, ed. by Joseph Campbell, (New York: Pantheon Books, Inc.)

   I. *Spirit and Nature* (1954)

   II. *The Mysteries* (1955)

   III. *Man and Time* (1957)

   IV. *Spiritual Disciplines* (1960)

H. Frankfort, *Kingship and the Gods,* (Chicago: University of Chicago Press, 1948)

H. and H. A. Frankfort, John A. Wilson and Thorkild Jacobsen, *Before Philosophy, The Intellectual Adventure of Ancient Man,* (Harmondsworth, Middlesex: Penguin Books, 1951)

Sir James G. Frazer, *The Golden Bough,* Imperial one-volume abridged edition, (New York: The Macmillan Co., 1958)

———, *The New Golden Bough, A New Abridgment* by Theodor Gaster, (New York: Criterion Books, 1959)

Theodor Gaster, *Thespis: Ritual, Myth and Drama in the Ancient Near East,* (Garden City: Anchor Books, New and Revised ed., 1961)

W. K. C. Guthrie, *Orpheus and Greek Religion,* (London: Methuen & Co., Ltd., 1935)

Berard Haile, *Emergence Myth According to the Hanelthnayhe or Upward-Reaching Rite,* rewritten by Mary C. Wheelwright, Navajo Religion Series, Vol. III, (Sante Fe: Museum of Navajo Ceremonial Art, 1949)

C. G. Jung and Carl Kerenyi, *Essays on a Science of Mythology,* (New York: Pantheon Books, Inc., 1950)

Alexander Krappe, *La genese des mythes,* (Paris: Payot, 1938)

———, *Mythologie Universelle,* (Paris: Payot, 1930)

Maurice Leenhardt, *Folk Art of Oceania,* (New York, Tudor Publishing Co., 1950)

G. van der Leeuw, *Religion in Essence and Manifestation,* trans. by J. E. Turner, (London: Allen & Unwin Ltd., 1938)

Gertrude Levy, *The Gate of Horn,* (London: Faber and Faber, 1958)

Bronislaw Malinowski, *Magic, Science and Religion,* (Glencoe; The Free Press, 1948)

Johannes Maringer, *The Gods of Prehistoric Man,* (London: Weidenfeld and Nicolson, 1960)

Max Müller, *Contributions to a Science of Mythology,* (London, New York: Longmans, Green & Co., 1897)

Henry A. Murray, ed., *Myth and Mythmaking,* (New York: George Braziller, Inc., 1960)

Erich Neumann, *The Great Mother,* trans. by Ralph Manheim, (New York: Pantheon Books, Inc., 1955.)

———, *The Origins and History of Consciousness,* trans. by R. F. C. Hull, (New York: Pantheon Books, Inc., 1954)

K. Numazawa, "Background of Myths on the Separation of Sky and Earth from the Point of View of Cultural History," *Scientia,* Vol. 88, (Milan: 1953)

Rudolf Otto, *The Idea of the Holy,* 1st edition, trans. by John Harvey (London: Oxford University Press, 1925)

Raffaele Pettazzoni, *Essays on the History of Religions,* trans. by H. J. Rose, (Leiden, E. J. Brill, 1954)

———, *The All-Knowing God,* trans. by H. J. Rose, (London, Methuen Co., 1956)

James B. Pritchard, ed., *Ancient Near Eastern Texts Relating to the Old Testament,* (Princeton: Princeton University Press, 1950)

Gladys Reichard, *Navaho Religion, A Study in Symbolism,* 2 vols., (New York: Pantheon Books, Inc., 1950)

Joachim Wach, *The Comparative Study of Religions,* ed. by J. M. Kitagawa, (New York: Columbia University Press, 1958)

———, *Types of Religious Experience, Christian and non-Christian,* (Chicago: University of Chicago Press, 1951)

Heinrich Zimmer, *Myths and Symbols in Indian Art and Civilization,* ed. by Joseph Campbell, (New York: Pantheon Books, 1946)

REFERENCES

INTRODUCTION

1. Sir James Frazer, *The Golden Bough*, Imperial one-volume abridged edition (New York: The Macmillan Company, 1958), dust jacket. The twelve-volume edition was published between 1910 and 1920. Several one-volume abridgments followed. The most valuable is Theodor Gaster, ed., *The New Golden Bough, A New Abridgment of Sir James Frazer's Classic Work* (New York: Criterion Books, 1959).
2. See Edward B. Tylor, *Primitive Culture*, Vols. I and II (London: J. Murray, 1873). The title of Vol. II is *Religion in Primitive Culture*, and it is in this volume that Tylor develops his theory of animism. These volumes have recently been reprinted in paperback.
3. See Max Müller's *Contributions to a Science of Mythology* (London & New York: Longmans, Green & Co., 1897).
4. See the following works by Herbert A. Hodges for an introduction to Dilthey's thought: *Wilhelm Dilthey, An Introduction* (London: Routledge & Kegan Paul, 1944); and *The Philosophy of Wilhelm Dilthey* (London: Routledge & Kegan Paul, 1952).
5. Meyer Schapiro, "Style" in *Anthropology Today*, ed. by A. L. Kroeber (Chicago: University of Chicago Press, 1953), pp. 290-91.
6. Joachim Wach's methodological works in English are *Sociology of Religion* (Chicago: University of Chicago Press, 1944); *Types of Religious Experience* (Chicago: University of Chicago Press, 1951); and *The Comparative Study of Religions*, ed. by J. M. Kitagawa (New York: Columbia University Press, 1958).
7. Robert Redfield, *The Primitive World and Its Transformations* (Ithaca: Cornell University Press, 1953), Chap. IV.
8. Mircea Eliade, "Methodological Remarks on the Study of Religious Sym-

bolism," *The History of Religions: Essays in Methodology* (Chicago: University of Chicago Press, 1959), p. 98.

9. G. van der Leeuw, *Religion in Essence and Manifestation*, trans. by J. E. Turner (London: Allen & Unwin Ltd., 1938), p. 206.

10. Raffaele Pettazzoni, "Myths of Beginning and Creation Myths" in *Essays on the History of Religions* (Leiden: E. J. Brill, 1954), p. 31.

11. Rudolf Otto, *The Idea of the Holy* (London: Oxford University Press, 1925), p. 5.

12. van der Leeuw, *op. cit.*, p. 1.

13. Mircea Eliade, *Patterns in Comparative Religion* (New York: Sheed & Ward, Inc., 1958), p. 1.

14. R. R. Marett, *Sacraments of Simple Folks* (London: Oxford University Press, 1933), Chap. I.

15. Ananda Coomaraswamy, *Hinduism and Buddhism* (New York: The Philosophic Library, Inc., 1943).

16. See Eric Dardel, "The Mythic," *Diogenes*, No. 7 (Chicago: University of Chicago Press, Summer, 1954), p. 49.

17. Bronislaw Malinowski, *Magic, Science, and Religion* (Glencoe, Ill.: The Free Press, 1948).

18. Pettazzoni, *op. cit.*, p. 29.

19. See Hermann Baumann's *Das Doppelte Geschlecht* (Berlin: Verlag von Dietrich Reimer, 1955), and *Schöpfung und Urzeit der Menschen im Mythos der africanischer Völker* (Berlin: Verlag von Dietrich Reimer/ Andrews and Steiner, 1936); A. Jensen, *Das religiöse Weltbild einer frühen Kultur* (Stuttgart: A. Schroder, 1948); and the works of the French school of ethnology under the leadership of Marcel Griaule. Griaule's publications include *Masques Dogon* (Paris: Institut d'ethnologie, 1938) and *Dieu d'eau* (Paris: Les Editions du Chêne, 1948). Among his colleagues' publications are G. Dieterlin's *Les Ames des Dogons* (Paris: Institut d'ethnologie, 1941) and *Essai sur la religion bambara* (Paris: Presses Universitaires de France, 1951); S. de Ganay, "Aspect de mythologie et de symbolique bambara," *Journal de psychologie normale et pathologique*, June, 1949, pp. 181-201, publ. by F. Alcan.

20. Wach, *op. cit.*, pp. 32-33.

21. Paul Tillich, *Systematic Theology*, Vol. I (Chicago: University of Chicago Press, 1951), pp. 12-13.

22. Pettazzoni, *op. cit.*, p. 26.

23. van der Leeuw, *op. cit.*, pp. 15-18.

24. Eliade, *Patterns in Comparative Religion, op. cit.*, pp. v-viii.

25. Bruno Bettelheim, *Symbolic Wounds* (Glencoe, Ill.: The Free Press, 1954).

26. C. G. Jung and C. Kerenyi, *Essays on a Science of Mythology* trans. by R. F. C. Hull (New York: Pantheon Books, Inc., 1950); C. G. Jung, *Collected Works*, Vols. I-XVII (New York: Pantheon Books, Inc.,

1953———) ; Erich Neumann, *The Origins and History of Consciousness* (New York: Pantheon Books, Inc., 1954), and *The Great Mother* (New York: Pantheon Books, Inc., 1955).

27. Theodor Gaster, *Thespis: Ritual, Myth and Drama in the Ancient Near East* (new and revised ed.; Garden City: Anchor Books, 1961), p. 23.

28. *Ibid*, p. 24.

29. *Ibid.*, pp. 4-5.

30. Mircea Eliade, *The Myth of the Eternal Return* (New York: Pantheon Books, Inc., 1954).

31. *Ibid*, Chap. I.

32. Claude Levi Strauss, "Le Symbolisme Cosmique dans la Structure Sociale et l'Organisation Cérémonielle de Plusiers Populations Nord et Sud Americaines," in *Le Symbolisme Cosmique des Monuments Religieux* (Rome: Istituto Italiano Per Il Medio Ed Estremo Oriente, 1957).

33. Marcel Griaule and Germaine Dieterlen, "The Dogon" in *African Worlds*, ed. by Daryll Forde (London & New York: Oxford University Press, 1954), pp. 84 ff.

34. H. Frankfort, *Kingship and the Gods* (Chicago: University of Chicago Press, 1948).

35. Baldwin Spencer and F. J. Gillen, *Native Tribes of Central Australia* (London: Macmillan and Co., Ltd., 1899).

36. Mircea Eliade, *Yoga: Immortality and Freedom* trans. by Willard R. Trask (New York: Pantheon Books, Inc., 1950).

37. Maurice Leenhardt, *Folk Art of Oceania* (New York: Tudor Publishing Co., 1950), p. 137.

38. A. P. Elkin and Catherine and Ronald Berndt, *Art in Arnhem Land* (Chicago: University of Chicago Press, 1950), pp. 3-4.

39. Eliade, *Patterns in Comparative Religion*, Chap. II.

40. Mircea Eliade, "Structure and Changes in the History of Religion," trans. by Kathryn Atwater in *City Invincible* ed. by Carl Kraeling (Chicago: University of Chicago Press, 1960), pp. 356-57.

CHAPTER I *Emergence Myths*

1. Verrier Elwin, *Myths of the North East Frontier of India* (Calcutta: Sree Saraswaty Press, Ltd., 1958), p. 8.

2. James Teit, No. 29, "The Old-One and the Earth, Sun, and People" from *Mythology of the Thompson Indians* in the Jessup North Pacific Expedition, Memoir of the American Museum of Natural History, Vol. VIII, Part II (New York: Museum of Natural History, 1912), pp. 321-22.

3. Leo Frobenius, *Der Kopf als Schicksal* (Munich: K. Wolff, 1924), p. 88, quoted by Kerenyi in *Essays on a Science of Mythology*, pp. 141-42.

4. Frank Hamilton Cushing, "Outlines of Zuñi Creation Myths" in *Thirteenth Annual Report of the U.S. Bureau of American Ethnology* (Washington: Smithsonian Institution, 1891–1892), p. 381.

5. Hartley B. Alexander reported in *The World's Rim* (Lincoln, Nebraska: University of Nebraska Press, 1953), pp. 14-15.

6. Gladys A. Reichard, *Navaho Religion: A Study in Symbolism*, Vol. I (New York: Pantheon Books, Inc., 1950), p. 5.

7. Laura Thompson, "Logico-Aesthetic Integration in Hopi Culture," *American Anthropologist, n.s.*, Vol. 47 (1945), pp. 540-53.

8. Washington Matthews, "Myths of Gestation and Parturition," *American Anthropologist*, Vol. 4 (1902), pp. 737-42.

9. Neumann, *Origins and History of Consciousness*, p. 10 and *The Great Mother*, pp. 18 ff.

10. Washington Matthews, tr. *Navaho Legends* (Boston: Houghton Mifflin Co., 1897), pp. 63-70.

11. Berard Haile, *Emergence Myth According to the Hanelthnayhe or Upward-Reaching Rite*, rewritten by Mary C. Wheelwright, Navajo Religion Series, Vol. III (Santa Fe: Museum of Navajo Ceremonial Art, 1949), pp. 1-5.

12. Elsie Clews Parsons, *Pueblo Indian Religion*, Vol. I (Chicago: University of Chicago Press, 1939), pp. 211-12.

13. William Wyatt Gill, *Myths and Songs from the South Pacific* (London: Henry S. King & Co., 1876), pp. 1-8.

CHAPTER II *World-Parent Myths*

1. Eldson Best, *Maori Religion and Mythology*, Bulletin No. 10 (Wellington: Dominion Museum, 1924), p. 33.

2. *Ibid.*, p. 37.

3. Alexander Heidel, *The Babylonian Genesis* (Chicago: University of Chicago Press, 1942), p. 75.

4. K. Numazawa, "Background of Myths on the Separation of Sky and Earth from the Point of View of Cultural History," *Scientia*, Vol. 88 (1953), pp. 28-35.

5. *Ibid.*, p. 33.

6. Alexander M. Stephen, "Hopi Tales," *Journal of American Folklore*, Vol. XLII, No. 162 (Jan.—March, 1929), pp. 10-11.

7. Quoted by M. Mansinha in his article, "Reflections on the Wonder and Enigma of Konarak," *Marg*, Vol. XII, No. 1 (Dec. 1958), p. 29.

8. James B. Pritchard, ed., *Ancient Near Eastern Texts Relating to the Old Testament* (Princeton: Princeton University Press, 1950), p. 60.

9. Sir George Grey, "The Children of Heaven and Earth" in *Polynesian Mythology and Ancient Traditional History* (Auckland: H. Brett, 1885), p. 1.

10. Neumann, *Origin and Birth of Consciousness*, p. 112.

11. Bettelheim, *op. cit.*, Chap. V, "Towards a New Theory."

12. Elwin, *op. cit.*, p. 48.

13. Grey, *op. cit.*, pp. 1-8.

14. Best, *op. cit.*, p. 53.
15. Adolph Erman, *Die Religion der Ägypter* (Berlin: Walter De Gruyter & Co., 1934), pp. 62-63.
16. Cushing, *op. cit.*, pp. 379-82.
17. Erman, *op. cit.*, p. 62.
18. Grey, *op. cit.*, p. 1.
19. Frankfort, *op. cit.*, p. 118.
20. After Al. Scharff, *"Ägyptische Sonnenlieder,* pp. 56-57; revised by J. A. Wilson after British Museum, *Hieroglyphic Texts from Egyptian Stelae, etc.,* part viii, Pl. XXI and p. 24; quoted by Frankfort, *op. cit.*, pp. 158-59.
21. See Raffaele Pettazzoni, *The All-Knowing God,* trans. by H. J. Rose (London: Methuen & Co., 1956), Chap. 2.
22. Ananda Coomaraswamy, "Spiritual Paternity and the Puppet Complex," *Psychiatry: Journal of the Biology and Pathology of Interpersonal Relations,* Vol. 8, No. 3 (Aug., 1945), pp. 287-97.
23. *Ibid.*, p. 291.
24. Cushing, *op. cit.*, p. 381.
25. *Ibid.*
26. Alexander, *op. cit.*, pp. 14-15.
27. Frankfort, *op. cit.*, p. 156.
28. Pritchard, *op. cit.*, pp. 60-72, quoted in Isaac Mendelsohn, ed., *Religions of the Ancient Near East* (New York: Liberal Arts Press, 1955), pp. 19-46.
29. Grey, *op cit.*, pp. 1-8.
30. Erman, *op. cit.*, pp. 62-63, cf. also, E. A. Wallis Budge, *The Gods of the Egyptians,* Vol. II (London: Oxford University Press, 1904), pp. 97-98.
31. Erman, *op. cit.*, pp. 63-65.
32. *Ibid.*, cf. also Chapts. on Myths of Creation from Nothing and from Chaos where Neber-djer represents Re the creator in the Egyptian myth.
33. Budge, *op., cit.*, pp. 94.
34. Cushing, *op. cit.*, pp. 381-82.
35. *Ibid.*, pp. 379-380.
36. Elwin, *op. cit.*, pp. 13-14.
37. *Ibid.*, pp. 48-50.

CHAPTER III *Creation from Chaos and from the Cosmic Egg*

1. H. and H. A. Frankfort, John A. Wilson, and Thorkild Jacobsen, *The Intellectual Adventure of Ancient Man* (Chicago: University of Chicago Press, 1946). Also, see Penguin ed. *Before Philosophy* (Harmondsworth, Middlesex, Penguin Books, 1951), p. 61.
2. Alfred Schoene, *Eusebi chronicorum libri duo,* Vol. I (Berlin: Apud Weidmannos, 1875), Vols. 14-18, as quoted by Heidel, *op cit.*, p. 66.
3. Griaule, *Dieu d'eau,* pp. 24-26.
4. G. Buhler, tr. *The Laws of Manu,* p. 5, in *Sacred Books of the East,* Vol. XXV (Oxford: The Clarendon Press, 1886).

5. Mircea Eliade, *Images and Symbols*, trans. by Philip Mairet (New York: Sheed & Ward, Inc., 1961), pp. 128ff.

6. Cf. Jane Harrison, *Prolegomena to the Study of Greek Religion* (New York: Meridian Books Reprint, Noonday Press, 1955), pp. 625-26, and W. K. C. Guthrie, *Orpheus and Greek Religion* (London: Methuen & Co., Ltd., 1935), p. 84.

7. Baumann, *op. cit.*, p. 377.

8. For Africa, see Baumann, *op. cit.*, pp. 250-342; for Greece, see Guthrie, *op. cit.*, pp. 39-53, and Harrison, *op. cit.*, pp. 454-599; and for India, see Ananda Coomaraswamy, "Yaksas," *Smithsonian Institution Miscellaneous Collection*, Vol. 80, No. 6 (Washington: Smithsonian Institution, 1928-1931).

9. Norman O. Brown, tr. *Hesiod's Theogony* (New York: The Liberal Arts Press, 1953), p. 17.

10. *Supra*, pp. 29-30.

11. Bühler, *op. cit.*, p. 5.

12. Guthrie, *op. cit.*, p. 140, translation of fragment no. 167 from O. Kern's *Orphicorum Fragmenta* (Berlin, 1922).

13. Walter Wili's translation of fragments 21, 21a, 168 from Kern, *op. cit.*, for his article "The Orphic Mysteries and the Greek Spirit," *The Mysteries*, Vol. 2 of *Papers from the Eranos Yearbooks*, ed. by Joseph Campbell (New York: Pantheon Books, Inc., 1955), p. 73.

14. *Ibid.*, p. 74.

15. Harrison, *op. cit.*, p. 628.

16. Guthrie, *op. cit.*, p. 106.

17. Gill, *op cit.*, p. 69.

18. Eliade, *Yoga: Immortality and Freedom*, p. 92.

19. Eliade, *Images and Symbols*, p. 78.

20. *Ibid.*, p. 78.

21. Wili's translation of fragments 54, 68, 70, 75, 85, 89, and 108 from Kern, *op. cit.*, and Thomas Taylor's translation of fragment 87 in *The Mystical Hymns of Orpheus* (London: B. Dobell, 1896) as quoted in Wili, *op. cit.*, pp. 71-72.

22. Bühler, *op. cit.*, p. 5.

23. Schoene, *op. cit.*, as quoted by Heidel, *op. cit.*, pp. 66-67.

24. Claus W. Krieg, *Chinesische Mythen Und Legenden*, (Zurich: Fritz & Wasmuth, 1946), pp. 7-8.

25. Teuira Henry, "Tahitian Folk-Lore" in *Journal of the Polynesian Society*, Vol. X, No. 37 (Wellington: Polynesian Society, Inc., March, 1901), pp. 51-52.

26. Julius Eggeling, tr. Satapatha-Brahmana XI, 1.6, *Sacred Books of the East*, Vol. XLIV (Oxford: Clarendon Press, 1900), pp. 12 ff.

27. W. F. Kirby, tr. *Kalevala: The Land of Heroes*, Vol. I (London: J. M. Dent & Co., 1907), pp. 5-7.

28. Swami Nikhilananda, tr. *The Upanishads,* Vol. IV (New York: Harper & Bros., 1959), pp. 218-19.
29. Germaine Dieterlen, *Africa: Journal of the International African Institute,* Vol. XXVII (London: Oxford University Press, 1957), pp. 126-35.
30. Teuira Henry, *Ancient Tahiti,* Bernice P. Bishop Museum, Bulletin 48 (Honolulu: Bishop Museum Press, 1928), pp. 339-40.
31. W. G. Aston, *Shinto (The Way of the Gods),* (London: Longmans, Green & Co., 1905), pp. 34, 85-86, 89f., 91 f., 93-94.

CHAPTER IV *Creation from Nothing*

1. See A. J. Wensinck, *The Ocean in the Literature of the Western Semites* (Amsterdam: Johannes Muller, 1918).
2. Coomaraswamy, "Yaksas."
3. Frankfort, *op. cit.,* p. 80.
4. Guthrie, *op. cit.,* Chapt. III.
5. Frank J. Stimson, *Tuamotuan Religion,* Bernice P. Bishop Museum, Bulletin 103 (Honolulu: Bishop Museum Press, 1933), p. 14.
6. *The Holy Bible,* Revised Standard Version (New York: Thomas Nelson & Sons, 1946 and 1952), p. 1.
7. Pritchard, *op. cit.,* p. 6.
8. Best, *op. cit.,* pp. 88-90.
9. T. G. H. Strehlow, *Aranda Traditions* (Melbourne: Melbourne University Press, 1947), pp. 7-10.
10. Wach, *Types of Religious Experience,* p. 32.
11. *Supra,* p. 80.
12. Pritchard, *op. cit.,* p. 6.
13. Frankfort, *op. cit.,* p. 29.
14. Cushing, *op. cit.,* p. 379.
15. Hare Hongi, tr. "A Maori Cosmogony," *The Journal of the Polynesian Society,* Vol. XVI, No. 63 (Wellington: Polynesian Society, Inc., Sept., 1907), p. 114.
16. Brown, *op. cit.,* p. 78.
17. Adrian Recinos, *Popol Vuh: The Sacred Book of the Ancient Quiché Maya,* trans. by Delia Goetz and Sylvanus G. Morley (Norman: University of Oklahoma Press, 1950), p. 84.
18. S. Radhakrishnan and C. A. Moore, eds., *A Source Book in Indian Philosophy* (Princeton: Princeton University Press, 1957), p. 24.
19. Eliade, *Myth of Eternal Return,* p. 104.
20. Bettelheim, *op. cit.,* pp. 128 ff.
21. See Eliade's discussion of faith in *Myth of Eternal Return,* pp. 109-11.
22. G. van der Leeuw, "Primordial Time and Final Time," *Man and Time,* Vol. 3 of *Papers from the Eranos Yearbooks, op. cit.,* p. 346.
23. We have already mentioned Eliade's *Myth of Eternal Return,* esp. Chapt.

IV; see also S. F. G. Brandon, *Time and Mankind* (London: Hutchinson & Co., 1951), Chapt. 9; and, Thomas J. J. Altizer, *Oriental Mysticism and Biblical Eschatology* (Philadelphia: Westminster Press, 1961), Chapt. 5.

24. Strehlow, *op. cit.*
25. Brown, *op. cit.*, pp. 56-59.
26. Radhakrishnan and Moore, *op. cit.*, pp. 23-24 (tr. revised).
27. Recinos, *op. cit.*, pp. 81-84.
28. E. S. Craighill Handy, *Polynesian Religion*, Bernice P. Bishop Museum, Bulletin 34 (Honolulu: Bishop Museum Press, 1927), p. 11.
29. Hongi, *op. cit.*, pp. 113 ff.
30. Stimson, *op. cit.*, pp. 12-19.
31. John A. Wilson, tr. "Egyptian Myths, Tales and Mortuary Texts," in Pritchard, *op. cit.*, pp. 6-7.
32. *The Holy Bible*, *op. cit.*, pp. 1-2.
33. Cushing, *op. cit.*, pp. 379-81.

CHAPTER V *Earth-Diver Myths*

1. H. Hale, "Huron Folk-Lore," *Journal of American Folk Lore*, Vol. I (New York: G. E. Stechert & Co., 1888), p. 181.
2. Grey, *op. cit.*, pp. 34-35.
3. Earl W. Count, "The Earth-Diver and the Rival Twins: A Clue to Time Correlation in North Eurasiatic and North American Mythology," in *Indian Tribes of Aboriginal America*, ed. by Sol Tax (Chicago: University of Chicago Press, 1951), p. 61.
4. Hale, *op. cit.*, pp. 181-83.
5. H. H. Wilson, *The Vishnu Purana*, Vol. I (London: Kegan Paul, Trench, Trubner & Co., 1864), pp. 55-57.
6. Roland B. Dixon, "Maidu Myths" Part II in *Bulletin of the American Museum of Natural History*, Vol. XVII (1902–1907), pp. 39-45.
7. Uno Holmberg, *Finno-Ugric, Siberian Mythology*, Vol. IV of *The Mythology of All Races* (Archaeological Institute of America, Boston: 1917), pp. 319-20.
8. Oskar Dahnhardt, *Natursagen*, Vol. I (Berlin and Leipzig: B. G. Trubner, 1907), pp. 42-43. Insectele Marianv, 122.
9. Holmberg, *op. cit.*, pp. 317-18.
10. A. L. Kroeber "Indian Myths in South Central California," *University of California Publications in American Archaeology and Ethnology*, Vol. 4, No. 4, Frederick Ward Putnam, ed. (Berkeley: The University Press, 1906–1907), p. 202.
11. *Ibid.*, pp. 209-11.
12. Ivor H. N. Evans, *The Negritos of Malaya* (London: Cambridge University Press, 1937), pp. 159-60.
13. Archibald Playfair, *The Garos* (London: D. Nutt, 1909), pp. 82-84.

14. Kroeber, *op. cit.*, pp. 204-205.
15. *Ibid.*, pp. 218-219.
16. *Ibid.*, pp. 229-31.

Conclusion and Appendices

1. Teilhard de Chardin, *The Phenomenon of Man* (New York: Harper & Bros., Harper Torchbook, 1961), p. 213.
2. A. E. Jensen, *Das religiöse Weltbild einer frühen Kultur* (Stuttgart: August Schroder Verlag, 1949), pp. 34-38. Trans. and quoted by Joseph Campbell, *The Masks of God: Primitive Mythology* (New York: The Viking Press, 1959), pp. 173-76.
3. A. L. Basham, tr. *Rigveda X. 90* in *The Wonder That Was India* (New York: Grove Press, 1954), pp. 240-41.
4. Snorri Sturluson, *The Prose Edda*, trans. from Icelandic by Arthur Gilchrist Brodeur (New York: American Scandinavian Foundation, 1916), pp. 18-20.
5. Ronald M. Berndt, *Djanggawul: An Aboriginal Religious Cult of North Eastern Arnhem Land* (New York: The Philosophical Library, Inc., 1953), pp. 24-48.

INDEX